Software designed to get every area of your business working together.

LAWSON™

Introducing a Lawson retail software solution that boosts your net profitability by seamlessly connecting your front office and back office. It gets your entire organisation on the same page, including vendors and partners. What's more, it allows you to see and manage how each area of your business affects the other. Having meaningful information like that on hand gives you the power to make faster, smarter business decisions. Learn more at www.lawson.com/successretailuk/, call 01344 360273, or e-mail information@lawson.com.

Who's Who
in
Retailing
2004

Who's Who
in
Retailing
2004

> **There is no charge for inclusion in this directory.** If you would like to be included, or to amend your existing details, please complete and return the form at the back of this directory.

Publisher's note

Every possible effort has been made to ensure that the information contained in this book is accurate at the time of going to press, and the publishers and authors cannot accept responsibility for any errors or omissions, however caused. No responsibility for loss or damage occasioned to any person acting, or refraining from action, as a result of the material in this publication can be accepted by the editor, the publisher or any of the authors.

First published in Great Britain in 2004

Kogan Page Limited
120 Pentonville Road
London N1 9JN
United Kingdom
www.kogan-page.co.uk

British Library Cataloguing in Publication Data

A CIP record for this book is available from the British Library.

ISBN 0 7494 4153 4

Typeset by Egan-Reid Ltd (www.egan-reid.com)
Printed and bound in Great Britain by Selwood Printing Limited

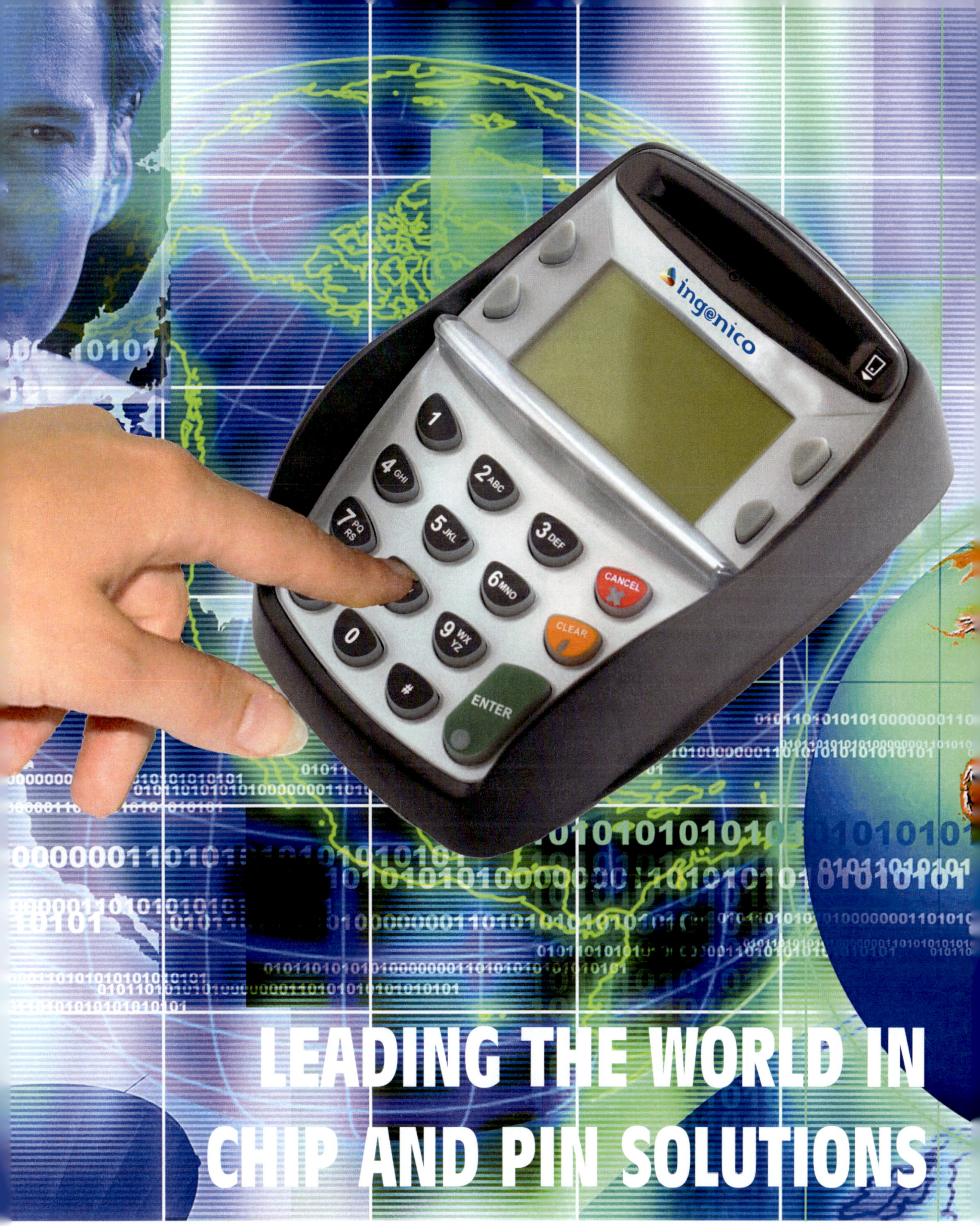

LEADING THE WORLD IN CHIP AND PIN SOLUTIONS

Ingenico is the first company to have deployed its Chip & PIN solution in the United Kingdom. With over 10 years experience of providing Chip & PIN solutions in other countries such as France – where it has been the leading supplier to the retail industry, Ingenico has consistently demonstrated specialized expertise in adapting its solutions to the particular characteristics of each country. As a result, today Ingenico has some 6 million terminals installed in over 70 countries.

We're number one. Why talk to anyone else?

Telephone: +44 (0)131 459 8800   Fax: +44 (0)131 479 8321
www.ingenico.co.uk

Contents

Total solutions for retail

PoS Solutions for Hospitality and Retail

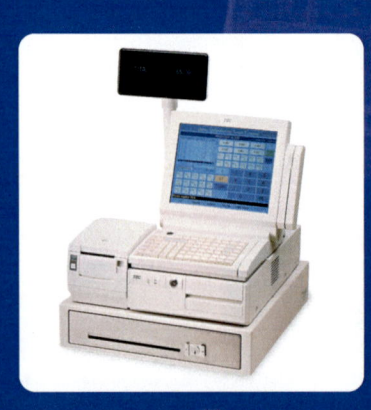

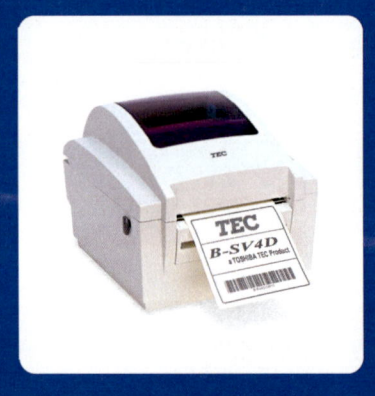
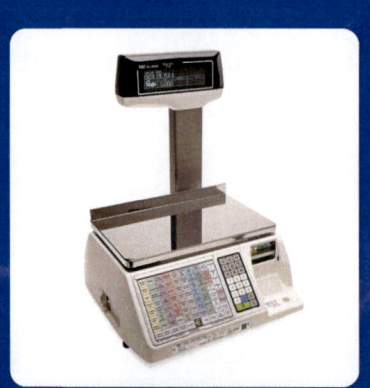

TOSHIBA TEC EUROPE
Retail Information Systems

TOSHIBA TEC Retail Solution Provider

The changes being introduced in January 2005, with the **EMV** global standard, will necessitate all retailers to review current EFT systems. This will include looking at current PoS hardware and software to ensure compatibility with new **EMV** solutions.

At TOSHIBA TEC we are able to provide a complete PoS Solution, tailored to your individual needs. With quality TOSHIBA TEC hardware, in-house software developers and an award winning **EMV** partner, you can be assured that we will take responsibility from project inception, through installation to after-sales support and training. Our knowledge of the portfolio of **EMV** products recommended by our partner, Retail Logic, will ensure that we will specify a complete EFT solution that will integrate seamlessly into your PoS system.

We chose Retail Logic, as our **EMV** partner, due to their status as an internationally recognised supplier of EFT products. They have a reputation for matching products to specific customer needs and are known to many of the major high street players. Their systems work with all major debit and credit card issuers and are approved by all major

banks. In addition, they have recently won two awards for their **EMV** Solution – 'Best Software Sesames Award', at the prestigious Cartes exhibition and conference in Paris and 'Most innovative Product of the Year' at the Advanced Card Awards for Smart-Solution™.

The recent experience TOSHIBA TEC has gained from the development work for the Northampton town trials[*], has given us a unique insight into the intricacies of chip and pin, and we therefore feel that we have the expertise to develop a system specifically for your requirements.

It is clear that **EMV** will happen, and the deadline of January 2005 will not change, time is running out, particularly for those retailers who have not evaluated their solutions for chip and pin. No business will be able to

fund the expected growth in fraud, so it is important to act now and benefit from the increased security **EMV** will bring. Additional benefits are numerous:

- Offline pin reduced fraud
- Faster than signature
- Fewer charge backs
- Indisputable card holder verifications
- Reduced till roll storage (easier dispute resolution)
- Increased floor limits, providing more offline transactions and lower costs

The message is clear, **EMV** is a necessity, so take advantage now of TOSHIBA TEC's wealth of knowledge and experience to evaluate your current EFT system and propose a suitable **EMV** PoS solution.

Toshiba TEC Europe has earned a reputation as a leading manufacturer of retail and industrial information systems through innovative technology and product development that aims to anticipate and uncover potential customer needs. This has resulted in products that provide the functionality, reliability and miniaturisation, which is so important to both the retail and hospitality industries.

About Retail Logic – Founded in 1992, Retail Logic Provides Electronic Funds Transfer (EFT) software for processing credit and debit card payment transactions. Retail Logic is the leading provider of card processing systems. It has the top five UK supermarkets and eight out of the top ten UK retailers as customers.

*N.B. – The Northampton town trials aim to evaluate the impact of chip and pin from a non-technical sense. The success of the trials will be based upon the analysis of, transaction times, fraud statistics, card holders' management of pin codes and satisfactory retailer perceptions. TOSHIBA TEC are continuing to work with a major retailer and acquirer in the development through to implementation phases of these trials.

For further information please contact:
Becky Viccars – 01923 233 688
Email – bviccars@toshibatec-eu.co.uk

TOSHIBA TEC EUROPE
Retail Information Systems

Retail Management at the School of Management, University of Surrey

The retail industry is a competitive one and anyone looking to start a career in retail has a distinct advantage if they hold a relevant qualification. The BSc (Hons) Retail Management programme offered at Surrey provides a first class business education and specialist knowledge of the retail industry to give its graduates an excellent head start. This is reflected in Surrey's graduate recruitment record, 98% of its graduates are employed within six months of graduating.

The BSc (Hons) Professional Development in Retail Management provides excellent opportunities for both retail employers and employees. With staff retention a priority in a competitive marketplace the ability to provide professional development training is an attractive proposition. Employers also benefit from a qualified workforce, without major disruption to everyday business. Employees benefit from a greater depth of industry knowledge, which they can apply 'on the job' as they learn.

The School of Management at the University of Surrey is able to offer these, and further postgraduate retail study and research programmes, with over 30 years experience of providing vocational management degrees and excellent links with the retail industry. Full details can be found at www.som.surrey.ac.uk

Foreword

The next few years promise to be the most challenging in modern times for a retail industry that has reached maturity. Managements are faced with consumers who are increasingly demanding. Simultaneously, they are having to cope with a squeeze on margins. How do you give more out of less?

With selling price inflation in retail now more or less a thing of the past, it has become increasingly difficult to pass on rising operating costs to customers. The need to drive volumes and gain market share has never been greater. Obviously, one needs to ensure that costs are controlled tightly, but trimming can never be enough of an answer.

For much of the post-war period we have seen the progressive switch of the balance of power from manufacturers to retailers. More recently, this development has continued and real power is increasingly moving away from retailers and into the hands of the customer. Although the population has never been more affluent, it is also increasingly demanding. Our multi-faceted lifestyles mean that today's retail industry has never known so much competition for consumer spending in a multitude of directions from mobile phones and health clubs to private education, healthcare and second homes abroad.

As the balance of retail demand moves from being needs-led to being wants-driven, managements need to get much closer to their customers. Product relevance has never been more important in order to stimulate wants-driven demand. Despite this unprecedented competition the opportunities in retail are enormous. Change and market dynamics create potential, and it is not always the biggest that do best, a fact well illustrated by recent history. By the end of 2004 total retail expenditure in the UK will have reached almost £260 billion, a massive marketplace with lots of room for many winners.

The key determinant of who succeeds and who fails among the thousands of businesses fighting to maximize their share of this spend is people. Quality of management is everything. The ability to recognize the challenges discussed above and to develop strategies that effectively deal with them will mark out the real winners.

Richard Hyman
Chairman, Verdict Research Limited

Should you be in this directory? See the form at the back for new entries and amendments

15

Sector Overview

Verdict produces over 40 research reports each year which cover all aspects of retailing and are designed for all involved in the industry.

The company has a team of full-time in-house analysts who use their experience, knowledge and industry contacts to identify, assess and predict the implications of the strategic issues facing each retail sector and location today and tomorrow.

Research is available for the following sectors:

- DIY*
- Electricals*
- Furniture*
- Grocery*
- Homewares
- Health & Beauty
- Clothing
  - Womenswear
  - Footwear
  - Childrenswear
  - Menswear
- Department Stores
- Mail Order
- High Street
- Out-of-Town
- Electronic Shopping*
- Neighbourhood

Further information on a selection of sectors and locations marked (*) follows below.

For more detailed information on any sector, location or the retailers operating within them please call Verdict on 020 7255 6400 or email sales@verdict.co.uk.

Should you be in this directory? See the form at the back for new entries and amendments

17

DIY

In 2002 consumer expenditure on DIY and gardening rose by 7.8 per cent to £14.0 billion. This represents another strong performance, maintaining the sector's position as the best-performing major UK retail market. Of this total, DIY spend was ahead by 8.2 per cent at £10.8 billion, while gardening expenditure grew more slowly – up by 6.6 per cent to £3.3 billion, partly due to unfavourable weather during peak gardening periods.

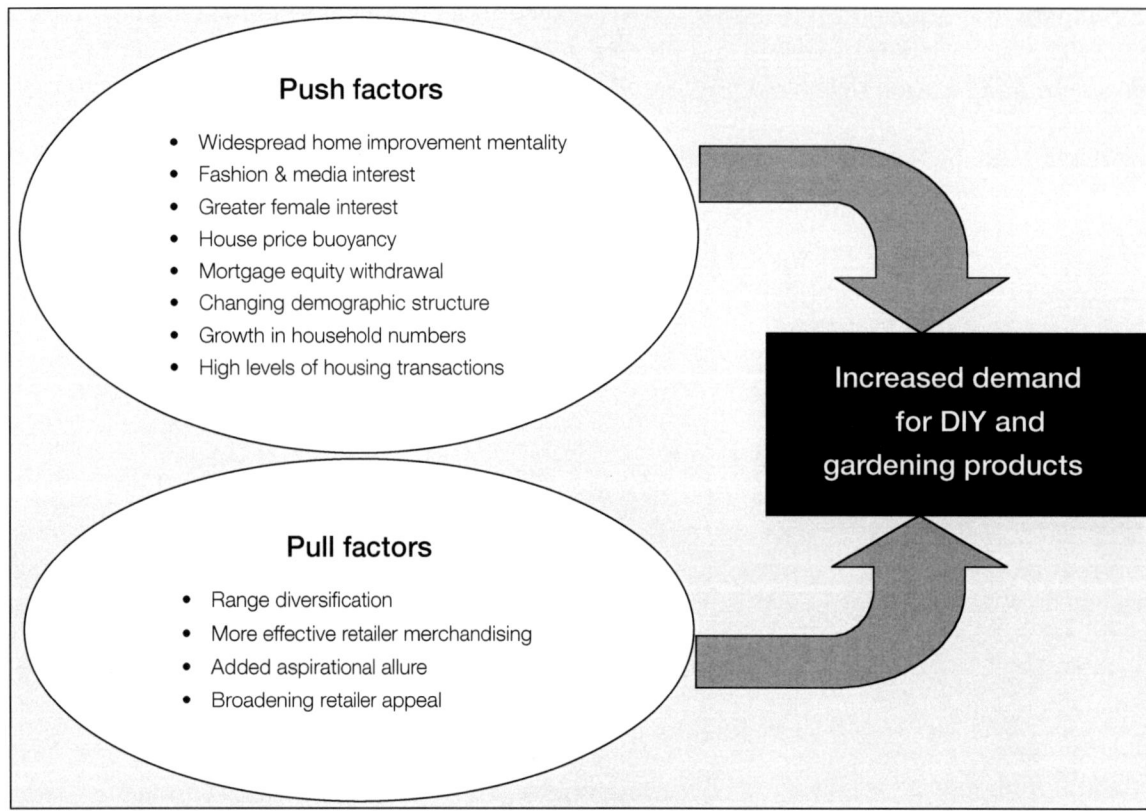

Figure 1 Key drivers of the DIY and gardening market
Source: Verdict Analysis

The DIY and gardening market covers an increasingly diverse range of product categories. Verdict calculates market size by using a number of categories from the Office for National Statistics (ONS), and defines the market so as to reflect the main product categories in which the major retailers are active.

DIY and gardening has been a significant growth market over the past five years. Key reasons for this strong performance have been the positive impact of the extensive media focus on DIY and gardening over this period, as well as healthy levels of housing transactions, strong house price growth, low interest rates and sustained levels of consumer confidence.

DIY retailers benefit from a relatively secure core market – non-specialists would struggle to replicate the breadth of the offer and develop the necessary specialist trading competencies. Yet DIY retailers can take advantage of clear linkages with other home-related categories. DIY retailers are using this as a springboard from which to expand, as they target new categories such as homewares, floorcoverings and furniture.

Should you be in this directory? See the form at the back for new entries and amendments

18

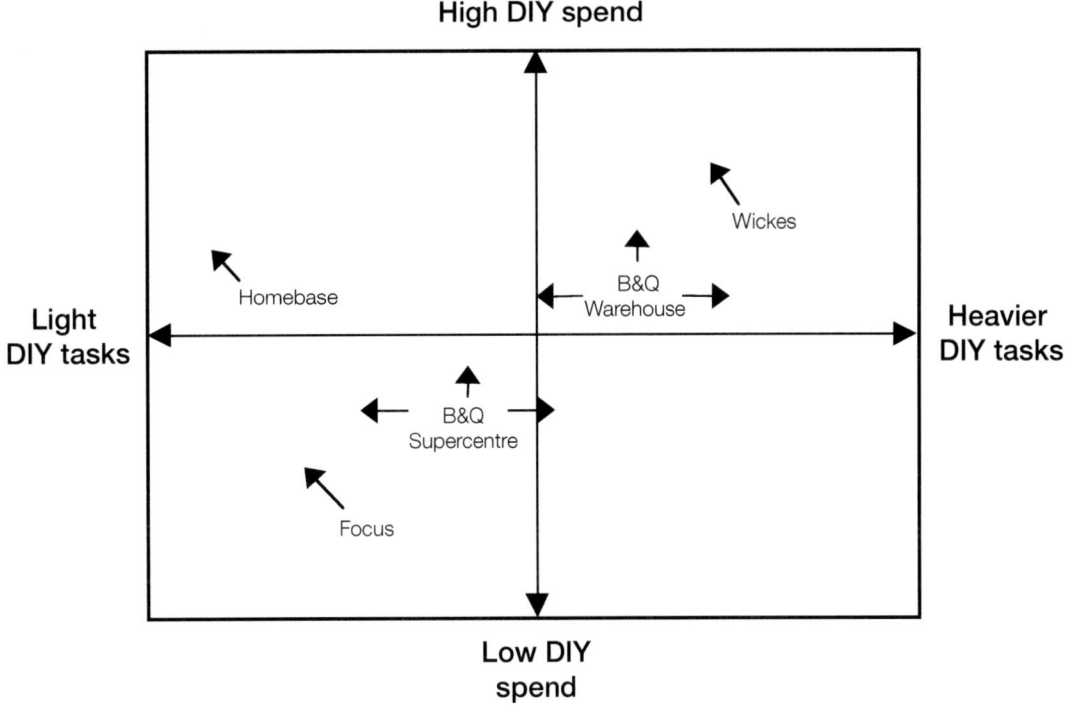

Figure 2 DIY retail brand positioning 2002
Source: Verdict Analysis

A key advantage of DIY stores is the high footfall levels from which they benefit, above all compared with furniture and floorcoverings retailers. Yet with new product ranges comes the need for a different set of trading competencies compared with those required for selling core DIY and gardening lines. Beyond developing the new product ranges, this also creates the need for new selling skills, product knowledge and customer services.

DIY retailers are evolving as the battle moves to a larger arena based around competing for consumers' share of spend on a broader array of products for the home. Indeed, with an increasingly diversified product mix, DIY is becoming a less valid definition of the business of these operators, with home enhancement becoming a more appropriate description.

Those retailers that best rise to these new challenges and have a good understanding of their customers' assorted needs and wants across different store locations will be best placed to succeed. This includes retailers trading from larger store formats that allow greater flexibility in space allocation and the easier conveyance of product category credibility.

MORE INFORMATION ON THIS MARKET AND ITS RETAILERS CAN BE FOUND IN 'DIY AND GARDENING RETAILERS 2003' AND IN 'FORECAST DIY AND GARDENING TO 2008'.

Should you be in this directory? See the form at the back for new entries and amendments

19

ELECTRICALS

The electricals market grew by 5.2 per cent to reach a value of £20.8 billion in 2002. This marked a slowdown from 2001, which was a much stronger year for retail in general. Made up of a diverse collection of sub-categories, it is impacted by new technology and product life cycles at different stages of maturity. As such it is among the most volatile in UK retailing, and this is compounded by the relative ease with which purchases can be deferred in times of economic difficulty.

The market for electrical products is more technology driven than any other. Though some products are only replaced once performance deteriorates, these are becoming fewer, with new technological developments driving the evolution of the sector. The key to selling many new products lies in creating wants-driven demand, and convincing consumers that the purchase of these products will enhance their lives. The product life cycle-driven nature of the sector instils a high level of price deflation, as newer technologies rapidly render older products obsolete. We define the electricals market based on Office of National Statistics (ONS) consumer trends data, industry sources and Verdict analysis.

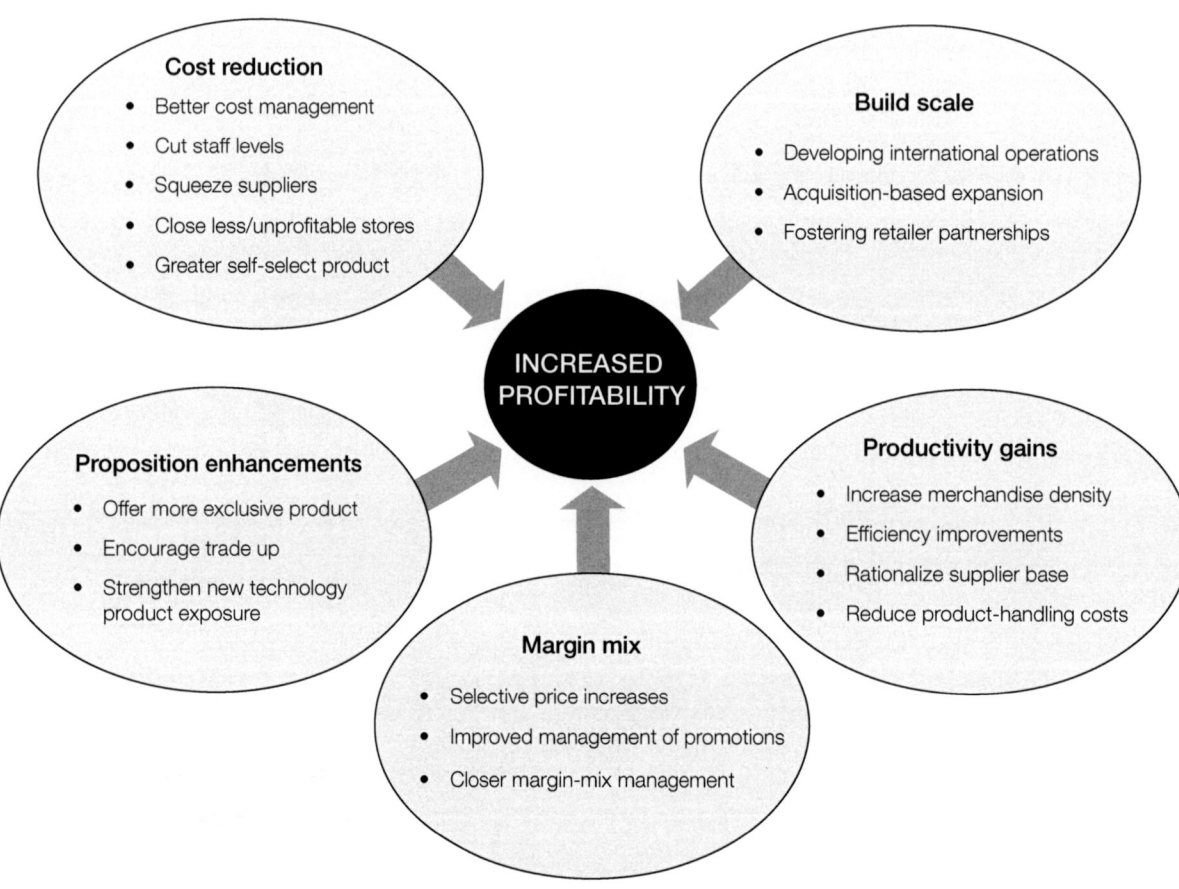

Figure 3 Routes to stronger profitability for electricals retailers
Source: Verdict Analysis

Should you be in this directory? See the form at the back for new entries and amendments

20

Table 1: Total consumer expenditure on electrical goods 1998–2002

	Current prices £m	Y-o-Y change %	Constant 1995 prices £m	Y-o-Y change %
1998	16,605	4.9	19,258	12.4
1999	17,731	6.8	21,953	14.0
2000	18,516	4.4	25,281	15.2
2001	19,742	6.6	29,963	18.5
2002	20,770	5.2	34,232	14.2
% change				
1997–2002	31.2		99.9	
1992–2002	60.8		185.3	

Source: ONS, Verdict Analysis

The recent difficulties experienced by Powerhouse highlights the harsh trading conditions that are currently found in much of the sector. Much of the sector is operating on wafer-thin margins – which have been reduced further owing to the Competition Commission (CC) investigation into extended warranties (EW). The more regulated environment for the sale of extended warranties that will ensue from this enquiry, allied with how consumer demand for these insurance products changes, will have significant repercussions on the economics of electricals retailing in the UK. Whatever the outcome of the enquiry, we expect sales of EWs to fall and electricals retailers to lose profit as a result. Those retailers that are especially reliant on EW sales will need to make up the shortfall from other areas.

As the short-term outlook is for increasingly difficult trading conditions, retailers need to shore up profitability through a combination of tactical and potentially more strategic measures. This will involve looking at several areas, such as closer margin-mix management, offering more exclusive product and rationalizing the supplier base. Additionally, of course, selective price increases will need to be made. Given the challenging retail environment, we believe that Powerhouse has not been the only retailer experiencing difficulties.

MORE INFORMATION ON THIS MARKET AND ITS RETAILERS CAN BE FOUND IN 'ELECTRICALS RETAILERS 2003' AND IN 'FORECAST ELECTRICALS TO 2008'.

Should you be in this directory? See the form at the back for new entries and amendments

21

FURNITURE

Verdict defines the market for furniture and floorcoverings using consumer expenditure data from the Office of National Statistics (ONS) and industry sources. The combined market was worth £14.0 billion in 2002. Furniture represents the bulk of this – some £11.7 billion in 2002, and was the more robust market in the year, ahead by 4.2 per cent on 2001 levels. By contrast, the floorcoverings market only achieved a modest increase of 1.2 per cent to reach a value of £2.3 billion.

Furniture has been the stronger performer over the past 10 years by some distance, more than doubling in value over 1992–2002. Much of this growth was attributable to strong performances in the first half of the decade. Building society windfall payments in 1996 and 1997 provided the sector with a major fillip, as consumers sought to spend their new-found wealth on big-ticket items for the home.

By contrast, floorcoverings has shown comparatively little growth over the past 10 years, growing just 17.6 per cent over the period. During this time value has been taken out of the market, as retailers have struggled to convince consumers of the benefits of carpets, while (cheaper) laminate floorcoverings and bare boards have grown in popularity at their expense.

This retail sector is heavily biased towards higher than average ticket prices. As such, its fortunes are influenced more than most other sectors by external economic factors that buffet consumer confidence and which can result in deferred and aborted spending decisions. However, it is all too easy for these factors to be used as excuses covering internal weaknesses.

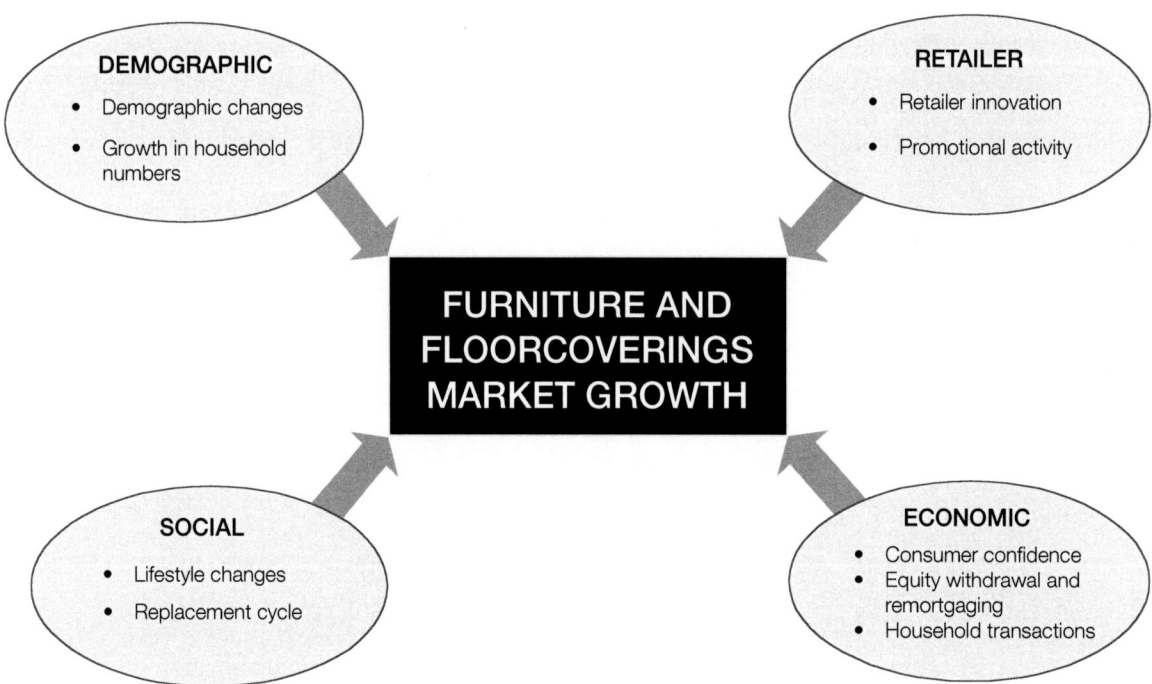

Figure 4 Key influences on the furniture and floorcoverings market
Source: Verdict Analysis

Should you be in this directory? See the form at the back for new entries and amendments

22

Table 2: Traditional and added-value retailer habits

Traditional behaviour

- Excessive retailer focus on promotional offers and credit deals
- Store staff are order takers as opposed to transaction makers
- Undifferentiated and uninspiring in-store environments
- Poorly segmented product offers
- Limited responsiveness to emerging consumer design trends

Added-value approach

- Focus on celebrating new product attributes and customer benefits
- Greater emphasis on more contemporary modern design product ranges
- Improved after-sales service, developing better long-term customer relations and personal endorsement
- Improved standards of visual merchandising, product offer segmentation and better in-store navigation
- Greater use of room-set displays and total-room solutions
- Better communication of cost to the consumer rather than retailer-led prices
- Increased use of cross-merchandising with homewares
- Wider availability of in-store CAD facilities and home-visit interior design services
- Strong levels of staff product knowledge and advanced selling skills
- Development of online order-tracking facilities

Source: Verdict Analysis

There are two distinct types of furniture and floorcoverings consumer. The first is usually young, looking for cheaper furniture and floorcoverings solutions with which they can furnish their first home. Purchasing is closely linked to the number of housing transactions, and is highly needs-driven. By contrast, the second group of consumers is wants-driven. This group consists of older consumers in the market for replacement furniture in keeping with their evolving tastes. This market is more susceptible to purchase deferral than the first-time buyer group.

Manufacturers in this sector have been guilty of not focusing enough attention on product innovation and retailers have been culpable for placing insufficient focus on making the customer's shopping and buying experience easier, more stimulating and more gratifying. The industry at large still retains a fixation around low price and promotional deals and until it sheds this mind-set the market will continue to miss out on growth opportunities.

Furniture retailing is not just about selling product – it is about selling home-enhancement ideas. As retailers look to better inspire customers in-store, they are increasingly making stronger use of the added-value approach with room-sets and by moving towards the concept of providing total-room solutions. The retailers that have embraced this concept most strongly have been among those that have gained the most share in recent years and we expect these to continue to prosper going forward.

MORE INFORMATION ON THIS MARKET AND ITS RETAILERS CAN BE FOUND IN 'FURNITURE AND FLOORCOVERINGS RETAILERS 2003' AND IN 'FORECAST FURNITURE & FLOORCOVERINGS TO 2008'.

Should you be in this directory? See the form at the back for new entries and amendments

23

GROCERY

In 2002 the total grocery market was worth £119.8 billion, ahead by 4.0 per cent on the previous year. This represented a slowdown in growth compared with 2001, owing to a more competitive trading environment and much reduced price inflation.

The diverse nature of the offer of most grocers and superstore operators means that consumer expenditure on core food and drink does not accurately reflect the broader activities of the major retailers in the grocery sector, accounting for only part of the sales of the major players. As such we adopt a much broader definition of the grocery market, including categories such as health and beauty, music and video, and books. The core remit of the grocers is becoming ever broader, as they extend their offers into a wider range of non-food categories.

Indeed, the key growth for grocers' sales over the next five years lies in non-food sales. Put simply, if a grocer does not have a strong non-food offer, and the large stores needed to present non-food lines authoritatively, it will be confined to grocery's slow lane. We believe that four-fifths of the addditional profits that grocers will gain in 2007 compared with 2002 will be derived from non-food sales. With leading grocers already pursuing non-food with vigour, those that do not will find the going increasingly tough.

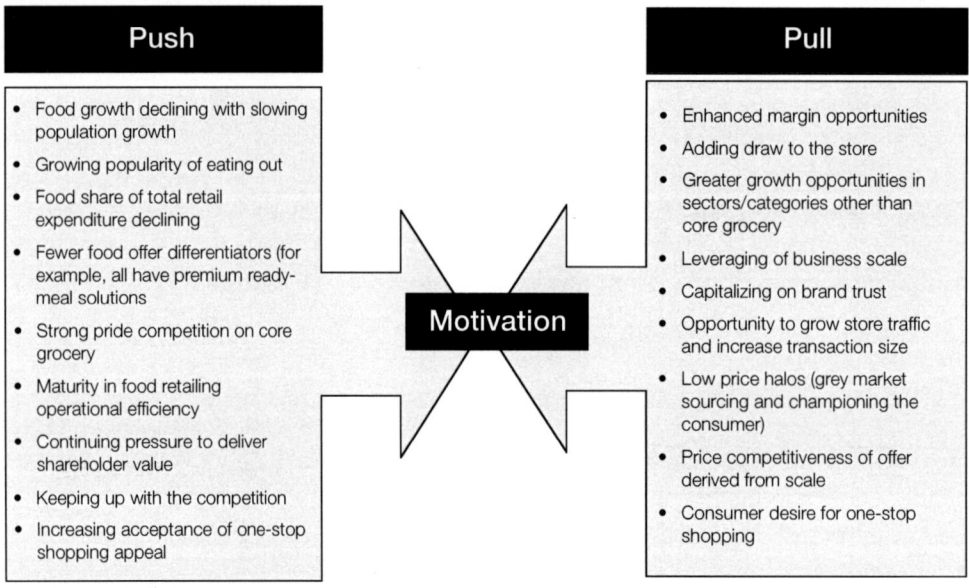

Figure 5 Main drivers of grocers move into non-food
Source: Verdict Analysis

Despite growth in non-food, grocers must not neglect opportunities to raise sales of food and groceries. These will still account for over three-quarters of grocers' sales in the coming 5 years. Grocers have already lifted volume by enhancing their range of convenience foods that can command a price premium and provide a source of differentiation from rivals. But there is much more that they can achieve by truly understanding the needs of the customer. Customer tastes have fragmented and it is retailers that recognize how advanced this process is that will reap the rewards.

Should you be in this directory? See the form at the back for new entries and amendments

24

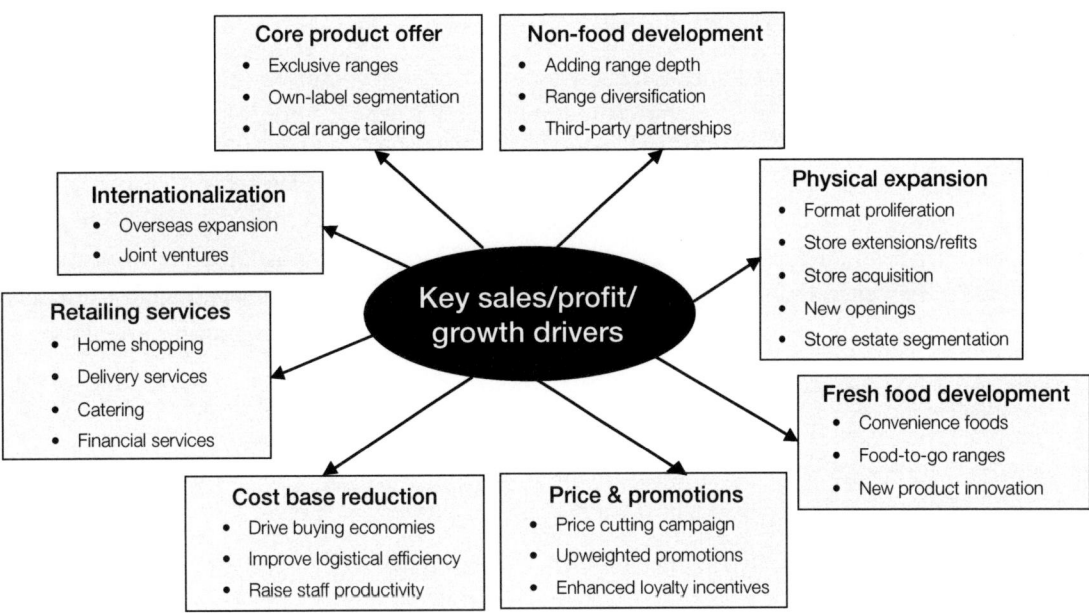

Figure 6 Key grocery sales and profit-growth drivers
Source: Verdict Analysis

The takeover of Safeway is a watershed in the history of grocery retailing. It is the most significant event since Wal-Mart's acquisition of Asda in 1999 and it is hard to envisage a future event with similarly powerful implications for the sector as a whole. It will precipitate a redistribution of sales, stores, space and market share: it will set the terms of engagement for the sector as a whole.

The most important consequence of the Safeway takeover will be a return to intense price competition. We expect prices to rise by just 0.8 per cent per year in 2003–2008, an even lower rate than the 1.3 per cent of the previous five years. Whichever of the four contenders buys Safeway, it is bound to offer lower prices. Those that lose out will seek to exploit the disruption that the ownership change will cause by initiating further bouts of price competition – to pick up Safeway shoppers with no allegiance to its new owner.

MORE INFORMATION ON THIS MARKET AND ITS RETAILERS CAN BE FOUND IN 'GROCERY RETAILERS 2003' AND IN 'FORECAST FOOD & GROCERIES TO 2008'.

Should you be in this directory? See the form at the back for new entries and amendments

25

ELECTRONIC SHOPPING

In 2001 the online market doubled and 2002 saw a period of consolidation. Market growth of 10.4 per cent still far outperformed total retail expenditure growth of 4.3 per cent but reflected a bedding down of consumer demand in the online market.

Figures for 2003 will show customer numbers growing and the major driver of value growth will be increased spend per head. However, from 2004 we believe there will be substantial new numbers coming on board as online becomes a more integral part of shopping life, and retailers will benefit from continued increase in spend as customers transfer their shopping habits to higher-value product categories such as clothing and food.

Online retail has therefore carved its position as an additional channel to market. It will not drive extra spend in the market, but simply act as another medium through which customers can make their purchases and its appeal will vary according to the attraction of physical offers.

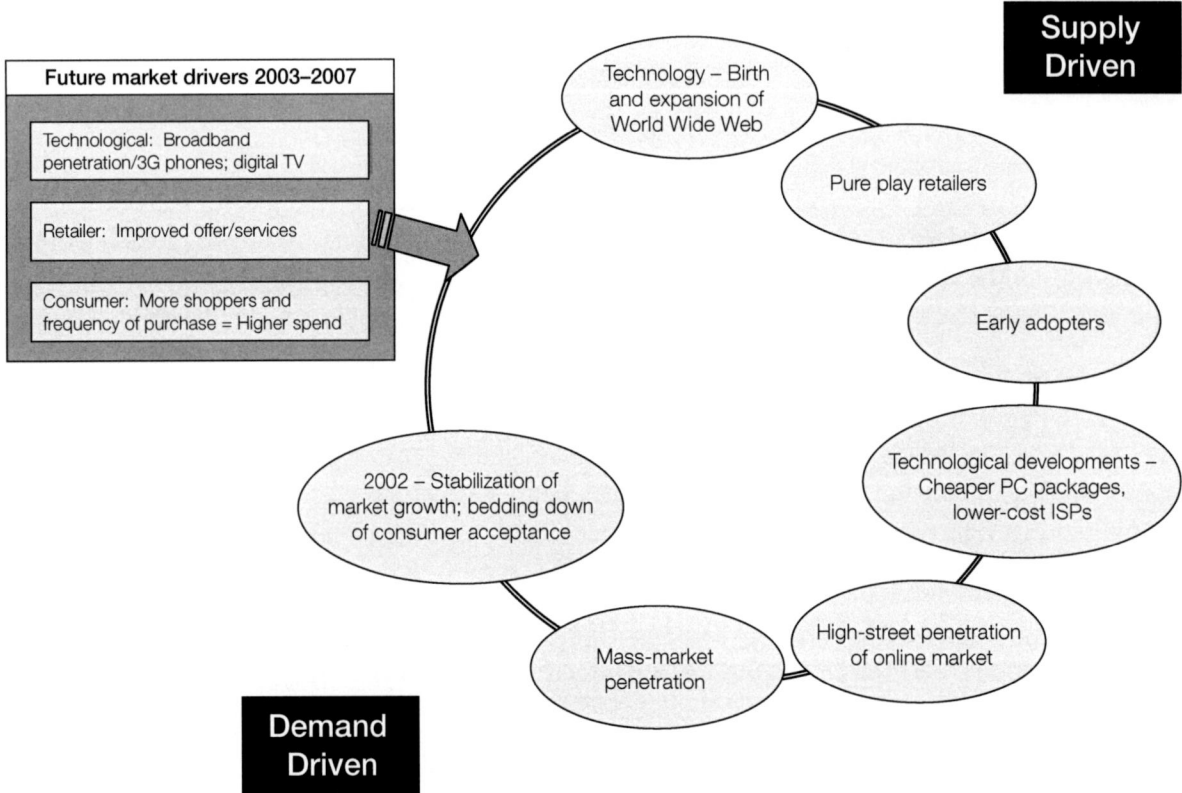

Figure 7 Online market development drivers
Source: Verdict Analysis

Should you be in this directory? See the form at the back for new entries and amendments

26

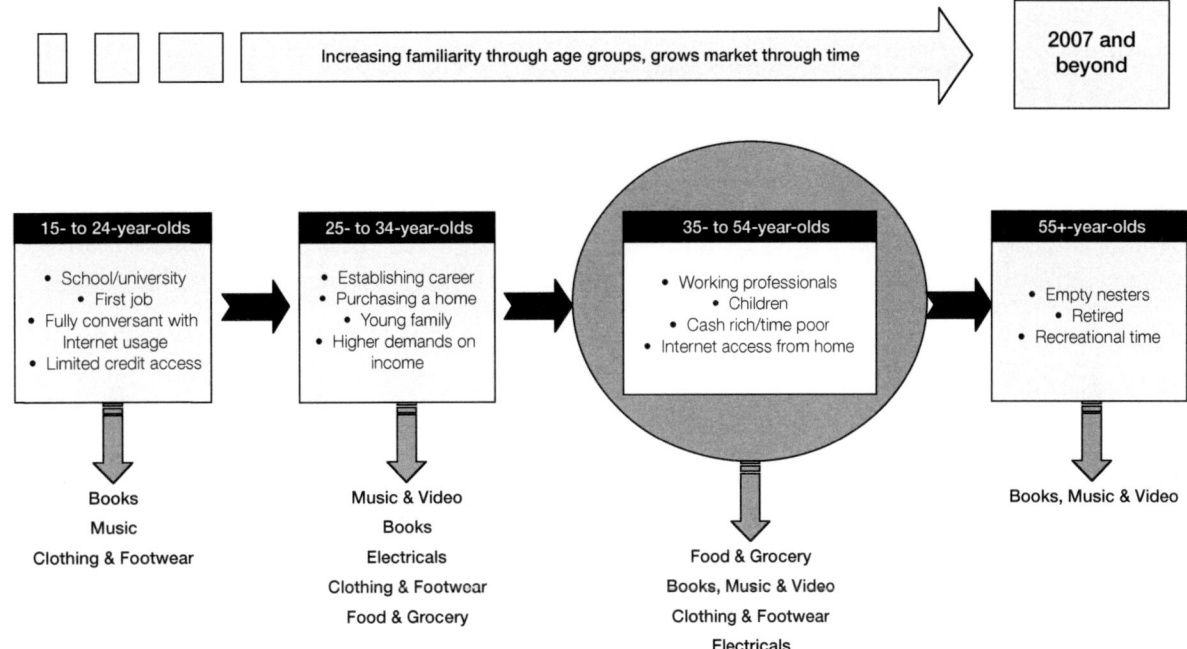

Figure 8 Core market development
Source: Verdict Analysis

So if electronic shopping is simply providing consumers with another channel from which to purchase, it begs the question: is it worth physical retailers investing in online sites and what can they do in order to encourage growth via this channel? For those retailers that do not have a wide geographical presence (such as John Lewis) it undoubtedly benefits them with an increased customer base, but they must have a fulfilment and delivery system in place that will meet the needs and demands of their customers. Retailers of all sizes are reliant on the development of new technology to expand and improve their interactive services, which in turn will provide the impetus to drive faster growth, but 2002 saw a hiatus. Although broadband offers fast access and wider services to consumers, it is expensive, not compatible with all systems and is taking longer for consumers to take up than forecast. Benefits from digital TV and 3G phones will not be seen until later in the decade and retailers are therefore restricted to using PCs as the main platform for access until these new technologies are established.

At present the most extensive users of the Internet are 15- to 24-year-olds. These shoppers make more shopping trips and spend longer online than older shoppers but have lower disposable incomes and spend less per visit. The 35–44 online shopping group is still growing and developing and in this respect still provides mass potential to retailers in shopper numbers, increased spend and growing confidence in shopping habits. Experienced shoppers are less concerned about shopping with known high-street retail brands and are more concerned with reliable service. In the short term, larger retailers will achieve greater returns from targeting younger age groups, but as core shoppers mature they will bring their shopping habits with them and retailers should adapt their offers to the more mature lifestyles to retain their loyalty and spend.

MORE INFORMATION ON THIS MARKET CAN BE FOUND IN 'ELECTRONIC SHOPPING 2004'.

Should you be in this directory? See the form at the back for new entries and amendments

27

Retail Industry Services

Chip and PIN
The number's up for card fraud

Chip and PIN is on its way to the UK, as banks and retailers join forces to tackle a card fraud problem which cost UK business over £420 million last year. The new system will ensure that for every face-to-face transaction in the UK, both the card and the cardholder are genuine.

With the Northampton trial already underway, Chip and PIN is being rolled out in the UK over the next 18 months. It will mean fewer retrieval requests, less time spent checking signatures, a reduction in chargebacks and administration and, most importantly, protection from fraud for retailers and the banks.

Over the next 18 months, banks and retailers will be re-issuing cards and updating their systems in readiness for the new initiative. From January 2005, if fraud occurs, the liability will sit with whichever party is not protected.

PDQ Classic –
a compact counter-top unit with an integral PIN pad and Chip reader. Designed to carry out a small to moderate number of card transactions quickly and efficiently. Ideal for businesses processing fewer than 1,000 card transactions per year (about 2 or 3 a day).

PDQ Eclipse –
designed to be fast, flexible and future-proof. Ideal for businesses carrying out large volumes of card transactions – over 1,000 per year.

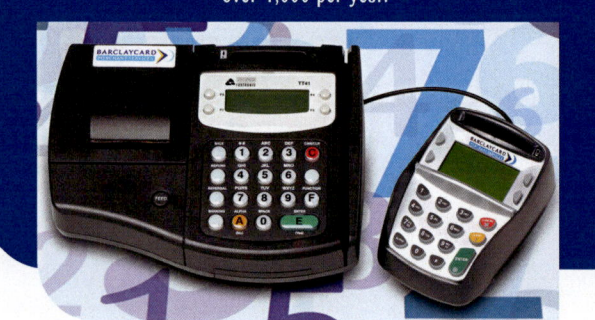

PDQ Portable –
fully equipped for Chip and PIN. The base unit supports compact handsets each with its own integral PIN pad. Ideal for hotels and restaurants as it allows staff to take the terminal to the customer.

If a customer card is Chip and PIN protected but the point-of-sale equipment is not, the retailer will be liable for any fraud losses. Industry experts predict that under the new system, fraudsters will actively target businesses that have not adopted the technology.

Having been fully involved in the Northampton town trial, Barclaycard Merchant Services is now launching a range of Chip and PIN enabled terminals to suit different business needs.

What do retailers need to do now?

Throughout 2003, Barclaycard Merchant Services is contacting all of its retailers with bank-owned terminals to arrange for their terminal to be upgraded.

If your terminal is owned by Barclaycard Merchant Services, it is simply a question of waiting for us to contact you.

However, retailers that own their EPOS equipment need to act now. Software and hardware suppliers are gearing up for the change to Chip and PIN but as the 2005 deadline approaches, order books are filling up fast. The industry-wide Chip and PIN Programme Team estimate that businesses with their own EPOS equipment will need between 12 and 18 months to install and properly test their systems.

However, while waiting for EPOS equipment to be updated to accept Chip and PIN, Barclaycard Merchant Services' PDQ terminals can be used alongside the EPOS equipment, ensuring that the retailer is protected from fraud come January 2005.

Chip and PIN

We'll point you in the right direction

If you're looking for a card processor to help you adapt to Chip and PIN as smoothly as possible, everything points to Barclaycard Merchant Services. We'll show you where to start, highlight your options and advise you on what's right for your particular environment and customers. We can aid your business, so that you're all fully prepared when Chip and PIN rolls out nationwide.

Remember, from January 2005, liability for card fraud will lie with the 'weakest link in the chain'. Don't let that be you.

Call us today on 0870 60 600 60* – or visit www.barclaycardmerchantservices.co.uk – to find out how we can help you upgrade seamlessly to Chip and PIN.

*Calls are charged at national rate and may be monitored or recorded for training purposes.

Barclaycard Merchant Services
Northampton NN4 7SG
www.barclaycardmerchantservices.co.uk

Barclaycard Merchant Services is a trading name of Barclays Bank PLC. Registered in England. Registered No. 1026167
Registered Office: 54 Lombard Street London EC3P 3AH

WWRAD 07/03

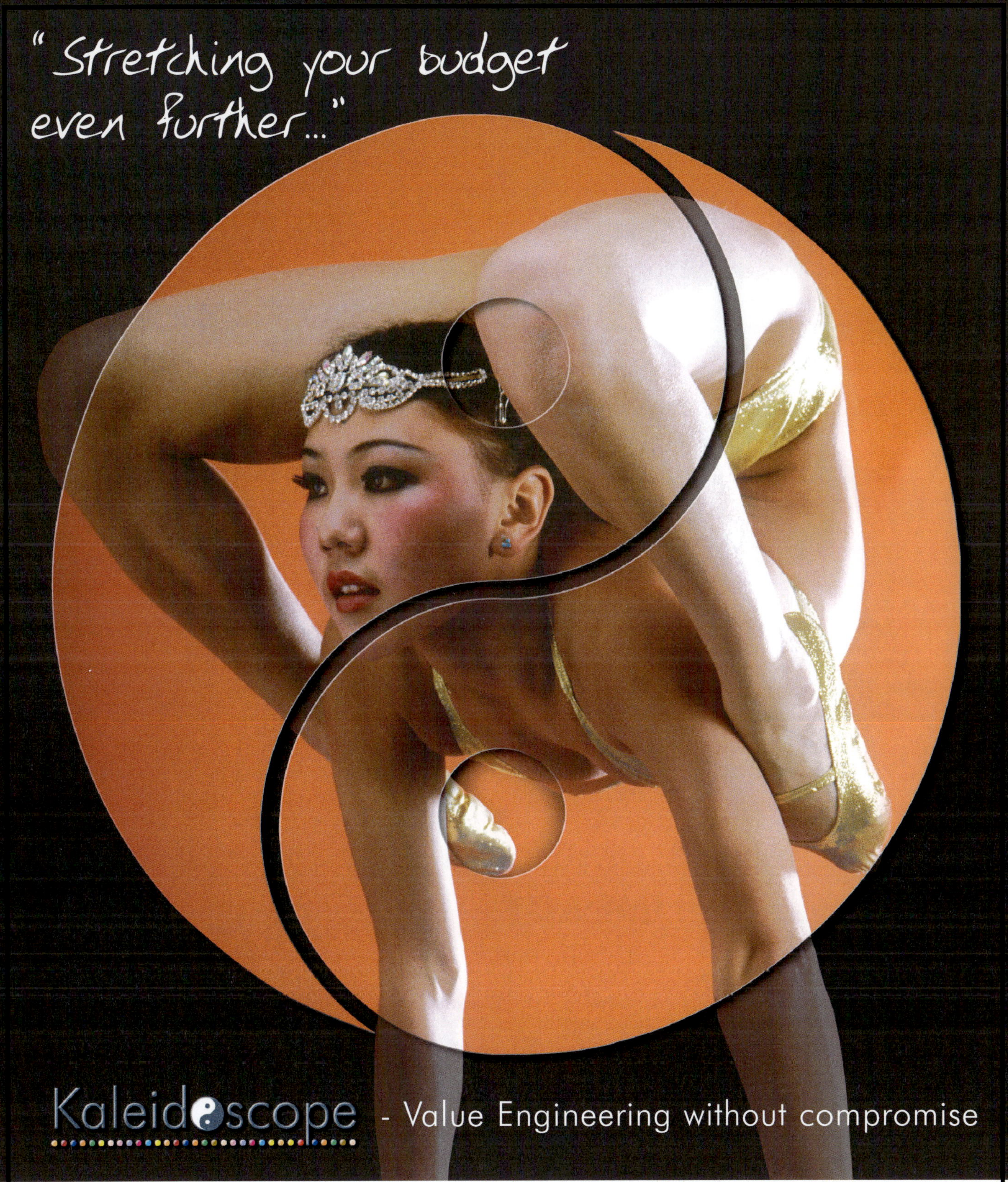
"Stretching your budget even further..."
Kaleidoscope - Value Engineering without compromise

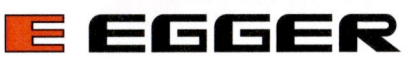

Environmental IMPACT

Research proves that creating the right in-store environment has a positive effect on sales, increases dwell time and improves loyalty. So what makes a great environment? The answer...it should appeal to all the senses. Does it look, smell, feel, taste and sound great?

Retailers put so much effort into the look of a store that they often forget that other senses, particularly hearing can have a major impact.

Music for example has an important part in all our lives, waking us up in the morning, keeping us up at night and we've all got our favourites that bring the memories flooding back.

Having such an effect on emotions, its not surprising then that music is used so often to influence and change buyer behaviour, helping sell everything from cars to beer to mortgages.

And where better to influence and change buyer behaviour than at the point of purchase?

But beware the dangers of getting it wrong. Knowing what to use and when is as important as your store design or your promotional merchandise – after all you can look away from a poorly designed poster, but you can not close your ears to an inappropriate track.

So can retailers be experts in the use of music in-store? No, that's where consultancies like DMX MUSIC come in. With 40 years of experience choosing the in-store music for many of the UK's leading retail organisations DMX MUSIC has an in-depth knowledge of how music and systems can help improve the retail experience.

So next time you walk into one of your stores, close your eyes and think about what you can hear – is it saying stay, enjoy, spend or leave, leave, leave. And then give a company like DMX MUSIC a call.

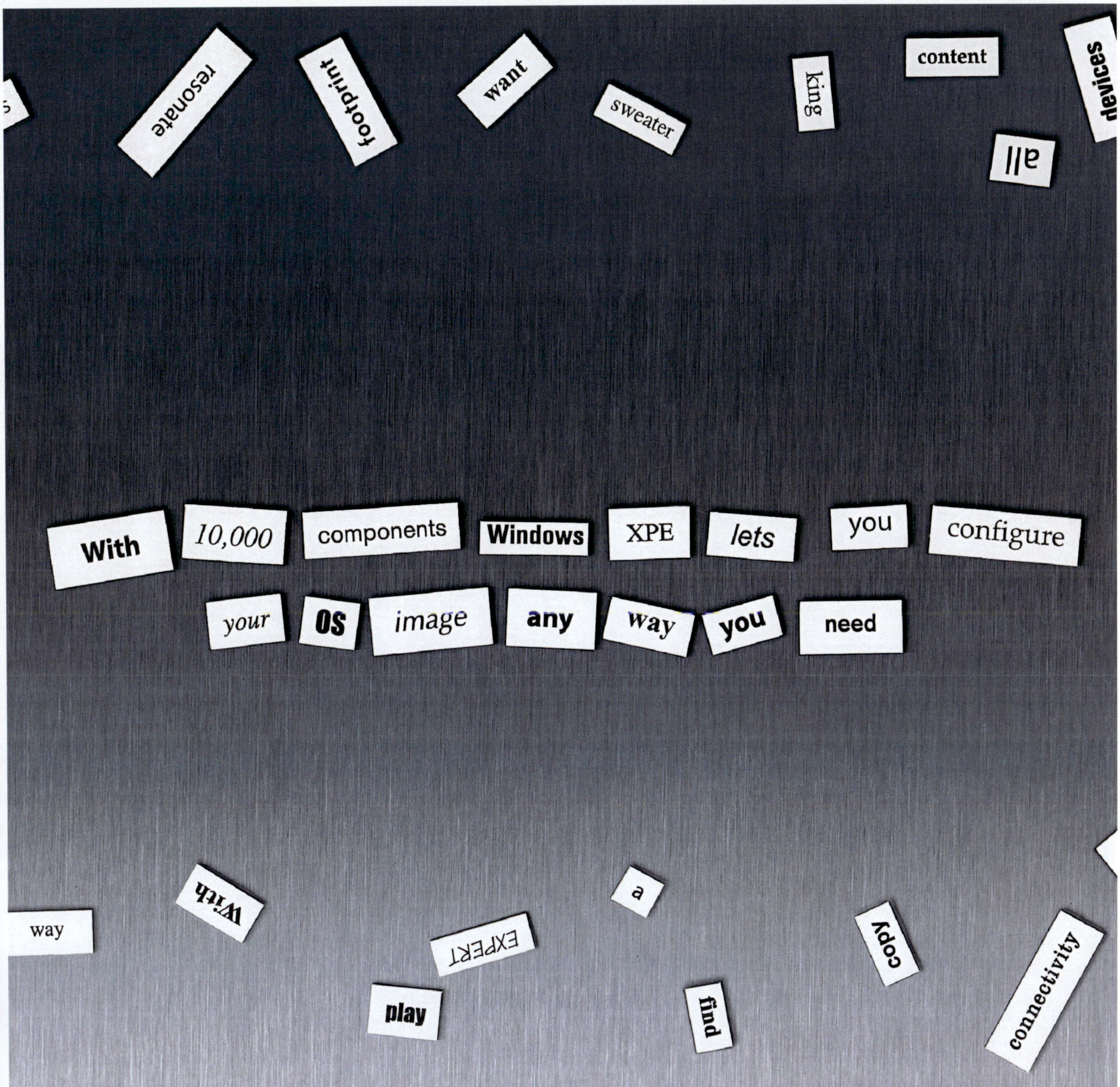

With 10,000 components Windows XPE lets you configure your OS image any way you need

Introducing Windows® XP Embedded. When it comes to configuring your OS image, you don't need everything – just the right things. Devices come in all shapes and sizes, and so must the OS images that run them. Part of the Windows Embedded family, Windows XP Embedded allows you to assemble exactly the components you need to build the device with the functionality you want.

With over 10,000 individual OS components from the latest desktop OS, Windows XP Professional, and a powerful end-to-end toolset, Windows XP Embedded gives you the flexibility to quickly configure your OS image the way you see fit. And that flexibility means less time configuring and more time building innovative applications – and a much richer user experience.

Windows XP Embedded enabling next generation PoS; Windows XP, the retail hardened platform, with support designed to meet your retail requirements. **Visit www.microsoft.com/uk/business/industry/retail** or call 0870 6010100. Software for the Agile Business.

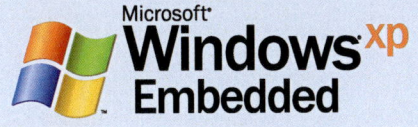

Microsoft®
Windows XP
Embedded

Microsoft®

Forward thin

ALPHABETICAL LISTING BY

Surname

RETAILERS

Acheson, Paul (Mr)
Sales Director, Shellys Shoes Ltd

Ackroyd, Martin (Mr)
Finance Director, Wm Morrison Supermarkets Plc

Adams, David (Mr)
Deputy Chief Executive and Group Finance Director, House of Fraser Plc
Tel: 020 7963 2427
DOB: 12/11/54
Marital Status: Married

Adams, Dean (Mr)
A/V Purchasing and Marketing Director, Bennetts Retail Ltd

Adams, George (Mr)
Commercial and Marketing Director, B & Q Plc

Adams, Michael Percy (Mr)
Non-Executive Director, Alexon Group Plc

Adams, Robert (Mr)
Financial Director, Poundland Ltd

Adderly, Will (Mr)
Managing Director, Dunelm (Soft Furnishings) Ltd

Adlestone, Mark (Mr)
Joint Managing Director, Beaverbrooks the Jewellers Ltd

Adshead, John (Mr)
Group Human Resources and Information Systems Director, J Sainsbury Plc

Afkami, Amir (Mr)
Finance Director, Evans, Arcadia Group Ltd
Employment History:
Corporate Finance Director at Arcadia Group; Business Development Director at Wickes
Awards: ACA

Ager, Rowley (Mr)
Company Secretary, Tesco Stores Ltd

Ahern, June (Mrs)
Customer Services, Morley's Stores Ltd

Ainley, Harvey (Mr)
Finance Director, Allders Department Stores Limited

Al Fayed, Mohammed (Mr)
Chairman, Harrods Limited

Aldis, Peter (Mr)
Managing Director, Holland & Barrett Retail Ltd
Tel: 024 7624 4422   **Fax:** 024 7632 0135
Personal Email: p.aldis@nbty.com
DOB: 17/06/64
Marital Status: Married

Alexander, Ian David (Mr)
Finance Director, John Lewis Plc
Tel: 020 7592 6398
DOB: 21/03/50
Employment History:
Civil Servant at Department of Health and Social Security (1971–87); Director of Personnel at John Lewis Plc (1991–2000); Development Director at John Lewis Plc (2000–01); Finance Director at John Lewis Plc (2001–)
Additional Directorships:
Citizens Advice UK

Alexander, Rod (Mr)
Communications Director, Budgens Stores Ltd

Alexander, Sandy (Mr)
Founding Director, Schuh Ltd

Alldis, Michelle (Ms)
Head of Customer Services, Vision Express UK Ltd

Alldridge, Steve (Mr)
Finance Director, Bon Marché Ltd

Alldritt, Nigel (Mr)
Financial Director, Majestic Wine Warehouses Ltd

Allen, Dave
Financial Controller, Wine Cellar Ltd

Allen, Martin (Mr)
Finance Director, Thorntons Plc
Tel: 01773 542240   **Fax:** 01773 542496
DOB: 11/10/50

Allen, Paul (Mr)
Chief Executive, Jacques Vert Plc

Alleston, David (Mr)
Retail Operations Manager, Stead & Simpson

Alliance, David (Sir)
Chairman, N Brown
Awards: CBE

Allister, Justine (Ms)
Head of Public Relations, Debenhams Plc

Allkins, Ian (Mr)
Commercial Director, Bhs Plc

Should you be in this directory? See the form at the back for new entries and amendments

41

Allman, Andrew (Mr)
Senior Manager, Financial Planning and Analysis in Europe, Gap

Anders, Jill (Ms)
Company Secretary, Fenwick Ltd

Anderson, Rob (Mr)
Chief Executive, UK, Signet Group Plc

Andreini, Guiseppe (Mr)
Product Director, Benetton Retail 1988 Ltd

Andrew, Ian (Mr)
Company Secretary, Grattan Plc

Andrews, Barry (Mr)
Executive Chairman, Moss Pharmacy Ltd

Angelides, Christos (Mr)
Group Product Director, Next Plc

Antcliff, Richard (Mr)
Marketing Manager, Dunelm (Soft Furnishings) Ltd

Antony, Martyn (Mr)
Acting Head of Retail Operations, T-Mobile (UK)

Apthorp, John (Mr)
Chairman, Majestic Wine Warehouses Ltd

Archer, Bill (Mr)
Chairman and Chief Executive Officer, Focus Wickes
Memberships:
Chairman of the DIY Federation; Member of the IOD
Personal Leisure Interests: Painting; walking; golf; tennis; swimming

Armstrong, David (Mr)
Purchasing and Marketing Director, Unwins Wine Group Ltd

Ashby, Diane (Ms)
Head of Logistics Projects, The Body Shop International Plc

Ashley, Michael (Mr)
Proprietor, Sports World International Ltd

Ashworth, Neil (Mr)
Supply Chain Director, Woolworths Plc

Assanand, Raj (Mr)
Managing Director, Harrods Limited

Atkinson, Peter (Mr)
Operations Director, John David Group Plc
DOB: 23/12/65
Marital Status: Married

Atterton, Charlie (Mr)
Financial Director, Jigsaw
Personal Email: csja@jigsaw-uk.co.uk
DOB: 11/11/56
Marital Status: Married with three children
Memberships:
Member of Worshipful Company of Founders

Auld, Phillip (Mr)
George UK Director, George (Asda)

Avens, Jez (Mr)
Deputy Managing Director, Richer Sounds Plc

Avis, Alice (Ms)
Group Director of Marketing and E-Commerce, Marks & Spencer Plc

Aylward, Chris (Mr)
Business Development Director, Moss Pharmacy Ltd

Aylwin, Mark (Mr)
Supply Chain Director, Safeway Plc

Back, Steven (Mr)
Group Finance Director, Somerfield Stores Ltd
Tel: 020 8966 6156   **Fax:** 020 8423 2263
Personal Email: steve.back@budgens.co.uk
DOB: 30/09/60
Personal Leisure Interests: Canoeing; gardening; music; touring country and historical locations

Bacon, Chrissie (Ms)
Financial Controller, House of Fraser Plc

Bacon, Paul (Mr)
Buying Director, QS Plc

Bagot, Andrew (Mr)
Managing Director, Le Riches Stores Limited

Bailey, Colin (Mr)
Finance Director, River Island

Bailey, Fiona (Ms)
Culture Director, Safeway Plc

Bains, Tony (Mr)
Buying Director, Aldi Stores Ltd

Baker, Richard (Mr)
Deputy Chief Operating Officer, Asda Stores Ltd
Personal Email: r4baker@asda.co.uk

Baker, Richard (Mr)
Chief Executive, Boots Group Plc

Balfour Lynn, Richard (Mr)
Chairman, Liberty

Should you be in this directory? See the form at the back for new entries and amendments

Ball, Colin (Mr)
Group Commercial Services Director and E-Commerce, Focus Wickes
Tel: 01270 507276   **Fax:** 01270 250504
Marital Status: Married

Bamford, Peter (Mr)
Chief Marketing Officer, Vodafone Ltd

Bannister, Roger (Mr)
Senior Buyer, TK Maxx

Barber, Angela (Ms)
Trading and Marketing Director, Costcutter Supermarkets Group Limited

Barber, Kevin (Mr)
Purchasing Director, Netto Foodstores Ltd

Barbour, Caroline (Mrs)
Office Manager, Cash Converters UK Ltd

Barclay, Andrew (Mr)
Marketing Manager, Moss Bros Group Plc

Barcley, Elizabeth (Ms)
Director and Company Secretary, Jenners Limited

Barcroft, Tony (Mr)
General Manager of Bakers Oven, Greggs Plc

Barczyk, Julian (Mr)
Purchasing Director, Stokes Plc

Barker, Steve (Mr)
Development Director, Choices Video

Barlow, Martin (Mr)
Project and Property Manager, MK One

Barnes, Richard (Mr)
Group Finance Director, Waterford Wedgwood Retail Ltd

Barr, Garry (Mr)
IT Director, Budgens Stores Ltd

Barr, Gill (Ms)
Business Development Director, Woolworths Plc

Barrett, Craig (Mr)
Retail Operations Executive, Russell & Bromley

Barrett, Nick (Mr)
Chairman, Apollo 2000 Ltd

Bartle, Ken (Mr)
Managing Director, A Jones & Sons Ltd

Barton, Daniel (Mr)
Head of Marketing, Diesel

Basnett, Keith (Mr)
Customer Services Director, N Brown

Batchellor, Lance (Mr)
Marketing Director, Vodafone Ltd

Bate, Jennifer (Ms)
Acting Commercial Director, Littlewoods Stores, Littlewoods Stores Ltd

Bateman, Paul (Mr)
Group Operations Director, Boots Group Plc

Baxter, Joanna (Ms)
Head of Press and Public Relations, Monsoon Accessorize Ltd

Baxter, Paul (Mr)
Marketing Director, TM Retail Ltd
DOB: 01/01/60

Beale, Nigel (Mr)
Chairman, J E Beale Plc

Beardsley, Chris (Mr)
Business Development Director, Waterford Wedgwood Retail Ltd

Beaumont, Martin (Mr)
Chief Executive, Co-operative Group (CWS) Limited

Beddoe, Paul (Mr)
Marketing Director, J H Leeke & Sons Ltd

Bedford, Terry (Mr)
Sales Director, Londis (Holdings) Ltd
Tel: 020 8481 9209   **Fax:** 020 8783 1346
DOB: 21/06/53
Marital Status: Married

Beecham, Robin (Mr)
Financial Director, C & J Clark International

Beere, Sacha (Mr)
Finance Director, ScS Upholstery Plc

Beever, David (Mr)
Non-Executive Director, JJB Sports Plc

Begley, Michelle (Ms)
Head of Marketing, Pets at Home Ltd

Begum, Luthfa
Marketing Manager, Borders UK Ltd

Bell, James (Mr)
Chief Accountant, Mackays Stores Ltd

Bell, Les (Mr)
Chairman, Bells Stores Limited

Should you be in this directory? See the form at the back for new entries and amendments

Bell, Norman (Mr)
Group Strategy Director, The Big Food Group Plc

Bell, Steven (Mr)
Joint Managing Director, Bells Stores Limited

Bellamy, Adrian (Mr)
Chairman, The Body Shop International Plc

Benge, Alex (Mr)
Property Director, Unwins Wine Group Ltd

Bennett, Neil (Mr)
Merchandising Director, Mackays Stores Ltd

Bennett, Paul (Mr)
Property Director, TM Retail Ltd

Benson, David (Mr)
Director, Buying and Distribution, E H Booth & Co. Ltd

Bentley, Phil (Mr)
Non-Executive Director, Kingfisher Plc

Berlyn, John (Mr)
Finance Director, Apollo 2000 Ltd

Berry, John (Mr)
Group Company Secretary, Matalan plc

Best, Roger (Mr)
Managing Director, John David Group Plc

Bester, Barry (Mr)
Executive Chairman, Topps Tiles Plc

Bettley, Tim (Mr)
Buying and Merchandising Director, The Peacock Group Plc

Bevin, Bryan (Mr)
Vice-President International Operations, Blockbuster Entertainment Ltd
Tel: 01895 866311   **Fax:** 01895 819655
Personal Email: bryan.bevin@blockbuster.com
DOB: 02/02/63
Marital Status: Married
Memberships:
Director of the Video Standards Council

Bews, Colin (Mr)
Company Secretary and Accountant, Stokes Plc

Bielby, Peter (Ms)
Head of Business Development, Cargo Homeshop

Biggs, Janet (Ms)
Director of Trading, New Look Retailers Ltd

Bilton, Howard (Mr)
Purchase Director, American Golf Discount Centre Ltd

Binder, Joanna (Ms)
Head of Merchandising, Burberrys

Binks, Jeanette (Ms)
Customer Services Manager, Tulchan Group

Bird, Jeremy
Trading Director, Wickes, Focus Wickes

Bird, Richard
Managing Director, Focus Wickes

Bish-Jones, Trevor (Mr)
Chief Executive, Woolworths Plc
Tel: 01442 353566   **Fax:** 01442 353499
DOB: 23/04/60
Marital Status: Married
Memberships:
Member of the Marketing Society
Personal Leisure Interests: Golf; motor cycling; squash; travel; children

Bishko, Roy (Mr)
Co-Chairman, Tie Rack Ltd

Bisset, Alick (Mr)
Finance Director, Global Video Ltd

Bittner, Beverly (Ms)
Director of Strategy and New Business, J Sainsbury Plc
Tel: 020 7695 3491   **Fax:** 020 7695 3491
Personal Email: beverly.bittner@aol.com
DOB: 10/05/65
Quals/Educ: BEng Engineering and Science and BA Spanish at Rutgers University (1983–88); MBA General Management at Harvard Business School (1989–91)
Employment History:
Operations Planner at Johnson & Johnson (1987–89); Senior Associate at Booz Allen & Hamilton (1991–93); Business Planning Manager at Pepsico Inc (1993–95); Business Director at Campbell Soup Company (1995–96); Principal at Cobra Group (1996–99); Strategy and Development Director at Kingfisher Plc (1999–2001); Director of Strategy and Business Development at Sainsbury's Supermarkets Ltd (2001–)
Personal Leisure Interests: Reading; cooking; spending time with family

Blackhurst, Malcolm (Mr)
Financial Director, John David Group Plc

Should you be in this directory? See the form at the back for new entries and amendments

44

Blackledge, Graham (Mr)
Joint Managing Director, Bodycare (Health & Beauty) Limited

Blackledge, Margaret (Ms)
Joint Managing Director, Bodycare (Health & Beauty) Limited

Blackmore, Steve (Mr)
Head of Retail, Spar (UK) Limited

Blackwell, Phillip (Mr)
Chief Executive, Blackwell's UK

Blair, Ken (Mr)
Chief Executive, Shops Division, British Heart Foundation, Shops Division

Blake, Nigel (Mr)
Plc Director, Courts Plc
Tel: 020 8410 9221   **Fax:** 020 8410 9373
Personal Email: nblake@courts.plc.uk
DOB: 30/03/50
Marital Status: Married
Memberships:
Financial Institute of Management
Personal Leisure Interests: Scuba diving; opera; shooting; golf

Blank, Victor (Sir)
Chairman: Burberrys; GUS

Blundell, Chris (Mr)
Business Development Director, Wm Morrison Supermarkets Plc

Blythe, Peter (Mr)
Finance Director, Burberrys

Bolliger, Peter (Mr)
Chief Executive, C & J Clark International
DOB: 1945

Bolton, Ivan (Dr)
Director and Company Secretary, Findel Plc
DOB: 29/12/43
Marital Status: Married

Bond, Andy (Mr)
Managing Director, George (Asda); **Trading Director, Non-Food**, Asda Stores Ltd

Boot, Terry (Mr)
Financial Director, Brantano UK Ltd

Booth, Edwin (Mr)
Chairman, E H Booth & Co. Ltd

Bostock, Kate (Ms)
Design Director, George (Asda)

Bosworth, Dave (Mr)
Customer Services Manager, Wilkinson Hardware Stores Limited

Botterill, James (Mr)
Managing Director, Botterills Convenience Stores Ltd

Bottomley, John (Mr)
Marketing Director, Thermawear Limited (t/a Damart)

Bowe, Julia (Ms)
Marketing Director, Harvey Nichols Group Plc
Tel: 020 7584 0011   **Fax:** 020 7235 9507
DOB: 03/05/60
Memberships:
Member of the Marketing Society
Personal Leisure Interests: Theatre; music; opera; country pursuits; sports; golf; tennis; eating out; fine wine

Bowes, John (Mr)
Chief General Manager, Marketing, Co-operative Group (CWS) Limited
Tel: 0161 827 5183   **Fax:** 0161 827 5541
Personal Email: john.bowes@co-op.co.uk
Marital Status: Married

Bowie, Jonathan (Mr)
Managing Director, Bowie-Castlebank Group Ltd

Bowles, Glenn (Mr)
Retail Managing Director, Asda Stores Ltd
DOB: 28/03/57
Marital Status: Married

Bowness, Ian Francis (Mr)
Finance Director, DFS Furniture Company plc
Tel: 01302 330365
DOB: 28/03/57
Marital Status: Married with two children
Quals/Educ: Kimbolton School (1968–75); BA Economics at Sheffield University (1975–78)
Employment History:
Auditor and Assistant Manager at Price Waterhouse Cooper (1978–84); Head of Retail Accounts at Foster Menswear Ltd (1984–86); Finance Director at Adams Childrenswear Ltd (1986–93); Group Financial Controller at Sears Plc (1993–94); Finance Director at DFS Furniture Company plc (1995–)

Should you be in this directory? See the form at the back for new entries and amendments

Additional Directorships:
Kingston Hall Management Ltd
Memberships:
Fellow of the Institute of Chartered Accountants in England and Wales
Personal Leisure Interests: Golf; football; rugby; opera; theatre

Boyd, Gary (Mr)
Finance Director, Northern Electric Retail

Boyd, Walker (Mr)
Group Financial Director, Signet Group Plc
DOB: 21/04/52
Marital Status: Married with three sons
Personal Leisure Interests: Golf

Boyes, Andrew (Mr)
Joint Managing Director, W Boyes & Company

Boyes, Timothy (Mr)
Joint Managing Director, W Boyes & Company

Bradburn, Jeremy (Mr)
Chief Executive and Financial Director, all:sports Retail Ltd

Bradbury, Richard (Mr)
Managing Director, River Island

Bradford, Suzanne (Ms)
Operations Manager, Ottakar's Plc

Bradley, Hugh (Mr)
Communications Director, Debenhams Plc
Tel: 020 7408 3632   **Fax:** 020 7408 3568
Marital Status: Married

Bralsford, Martin (Mr)
Chief Executive, Le Riches Stores Limited

Brandon, Sally (Ms)
Customer Services Manager, Habitat UK Limited

Brass, Sarah (Ms)
Head of Marketing, Whittard of Chelsea Plc

Bratt, Andrew (Mr)
Property Director, Furnitureland Holdings Ltd
Tel: 020 8768 7135
Personal Email: andrewbratt@furnitureland.co.uk
DOB: 21/10/70
Memberships:
RICS
Personal Leisure Interests: Mountaineering

Bravo, Rose Maria (Ms)
Chief Executive, Burberrys

Brayton, Norman
Marketing Director, WCF Retail

Brenna, Sean (Mr)
Company Secretary, Carpetworld Manchester Ltd

Brian, Rachel (Ms)
Merchandise Director, La Senza

Briant, Jerry (Mr)
Managing Director, Land of Leather

Brick, Alex (Mr)
Marketing and Property Director, Speciality Retail Group Plc

Brick, Brian (Mr)
Managing Director, Speciality Retail Group Plc

Bridge, Mark (Mr)
Marketing Director, American Golf Discount Centre Ltd

Bright, Neil (Mr)
Group Financial Director, HMV Group Plc

Bromley, Peter (Mr)
Chairman and Joint Managing Director, Russell & Bromley

Bromley, Roger (Mr)
Joint Managing Director, Russell & Bromley

Brookfield, Barry (Mr)
Chairman, Ponden Mill Ltd

Broughall, David (Mr)
Managing Director, Apollo 2000 Ltd

Broughton, David S (Mr)
Managing Director, Broughton Brothers Ltd

Brown, Andrew (Mr)
Joint Managing Director, Beaverbrooks the Jewellers Ltd

Brown, Barry (Mr)
Chief Executive, John David Group Plc

Brown, Gary (Mr)
Joint Finance Director, Brown & Jackson

Brown, Gordon (Mr)
Managing Director, Wilkinson Hardware Stores Limited
Personal Email: browng@wilko.co.uk
DOB: 22/09/50
Marital Status: Married
Personal Leisure Interests: Scuba diving; sailing

Should you be in this directory? See the form at the back for new entries and amendments

Brown, Roy (Mr)
Deputy Chairman, HMV Group Plc

Brown, Steve (Mr)
Finance Director, Shoe Zone Ltd

Brown, Tony (Mr)
Retail Director, Bhs Plc

Browne, Mike (Mr)
Deputy Chairman, ScS Upholstery Plc

Brozetti, Gianluca (Mr)
Retail Director, Asprey & Garrard Ltd

Bryant, Keith (Mr)
Group Finance Director, The Peacock Group Plc
Personal Email: keith.bryant@peacocks.co.uk
DOB: 02/04/62
Personal Leisure Interests: Golf; football; badminton

Buckley, Steve (Mr)
Managing Director, UK Specialities, Alpha Retail

Budd, Alastair (Mr)
Property Controller, Stationery Box Holdings Ltd

Budge, Paul (Mr)
Finance Director, Arcadia Group Ltd

Bugler, Mike (Mr)
Marketing Director, Clinton Cards

Bull, George (Sir)
Non-Executive Chairman, J Sainsbury Plc
DOB: 1936
Personal Leisure Interests: Golf; photography

Bullaf, Mike (Mr)
Merchandise Director, N Brown

Buller, Denise (Ms)
Commercial Director, Londis (Holdings) Ltd

Bullock, Gordon (Mr)
Chief Executive Officer, TK Maxx

Bullock, Jackie (Ms)
Head of Business Development, HMV Group Plc

Bunnell, Matt (Mr)
Director, Magnet Ltd

Burden, Paul (Mr)
Communications Director, John Lewis Plc

Burdon, Peter (Mr)
Chief Executive, Thorntons Plc

Burford, Chris (Mr)
Finance Manager, Hamleys Plc

Burke, Peter (Mr)
Human Resources Director, Littlewoods Stores Ltd

Burman, Terry (Mr)
Group Chief Executive, Signet Group Plc
DOB: 14/10/45
Marital Status: Married
Memberships:
Member of World Presidents' Organization (1996–)

Burnes, Neil (Mr)
IT and Logistics Director, The Peacock Group Plc

Burnley, Roger (Mr)
Supply Chain Director, Matalan plc

Burrows, Dawn (Ms)
Customer Services Manager, Etam Plc

Burton, Nigel (Mr)
Development and Services Director, Waitrose Ltd
DOB: 06/04/47
Memberships:
Past President of the British Council of Shopping Centres
Personal Leisure Interests: Breeding native ponies and Aberdeen Angus cattle

Butler-Wheelhouse, Keith (Mr)
Non-Executive Director, J Sainsbury Plc

Buttle, George (Mr)
Deputy Managing Director, Wm Morrison Supermarkets Plc
DOB: 1937

Calderbank, Tom (Mr)
Managing Director, Alfred Jones Ltd

Caldwell, Graham (Mr)
Managing Director, Maplin Electronics Ltd

Campbell, Amanda (Ms)
Head of Strategic Marketing, Adams Childrenswear

Canning, Nick (Mr)
Marketing Director, The Big Food Group Plc

Cantello, Tina (Ms)
Marketing Director, The Body Shop International Plc

Carberry, Mark (Mr)
Customer Services Director, Phones 4u

Carney, Seaun (Mr)
Finance Director, Waterstone's Booksellers Ltd

Should you be in this directory? See the form at the back for new entries and amendments

Carr, Martin (Mr)
Operations Director, Waterstone's Booksellers Ltd

Carr, Rosemary (Ms)
Marketing Services Director, C & J Clark
International
Tel: 01458 843039
DOB: 09/04/64
Marital Status: Married
Personal Leisure Interests: Travel; hiking;
swimming; gardening; literature

Carr, Tony (Mr)
Retail Operations Director, Mothercare Plc
DOB: 12/04/66
Personal Leisure Interests: Football; skiing; water-
skiing; keepfit; travel; good food; reading

Carroll, Brian (Mr)
Finance Director, Waitrose Ltd
Tel: 01344 824473   **Fax:** 01344 824488

Carroll, Ray (Mr)
Retail Operations Director, Ethel Austin Ltd

Carter, Nick (Mr)
Finance and Property Director, Halfords Limited

Carter, Phillip (Sir)
Chairman, Kookai

Carter, Shaun (Mr)
Manager, Mole Valley Farmers

Cartright, T (Mrs)
Customer Services Manager, Stead & Simpson

Cashmore, Anita (Ms)
Financial Director, Kookai

Cassar, Stefan (Mr)
Finance Director, Shoe Studio Group Ltd

Cathcart, Alun (Mr)
Chairman, Selfridges & Co

Caudwell, John (Mr)
Chairman and Chief Executive, Phones 4u

Caunce, Steve (Mr)
Finance Director, Phones 4u

Cavenagh, Pamela (Ms)
Senior Vice-President, Accessories, Burberrys

Cavern, Kevin (Mr)
Managing Director, Savers Health & Beauty Plc

Ceirnduff, Ken (Mr)
Joint Managing Director, Internacionale Limited

Cèzar, Marcel (Mr)
Chairman, Vision Express UK Ltd

Chapman, Keith (Mr)
Chairman, Findel Plc

Charlton, David (Mr)
Chairman, The Officers Club Ltd

Cheesewright, David (Mr)
Deputy Trading Director, Asda Stores Ltd

Chellingsworth, William (Mr)
Store Operations Manager, Burberrys

Cherry, Mark (Mr)
Head of Property, Allders Department Stores
Limited

Cheshire, Ian (Mr)
Chief Executive of International Development,
Kingfisher Plc
DOB: 1960

Chick, Sarah (Ms)
Sales Development Executive, Costcutter
Supermarkets Group Limited

Chopping, Lynton (Mr)
Finance Director, Ponden Mill Ltd

Christensen, Lawrence (Mr)
Logistics Director, Safeway Plc
Tel: 020 8756 2111   **Fax:** 020 8561 0709
Personal Email:
lawrence_christensen@safeway.co.uk
DOB: 18/06/43
Marital Status: Married
Awards: CBE
Memberships:
FILT
Personal Leisure Interests: Reading; swimming;
country pursuits

Church, Johnathon (Mr)
Finance Director, Church & Co. Footwear Ltd

Church, William (Mr)
Production Director, Church & Co. Footwear Ltd

Clare, John (Mr)
Chief Executive, DSG Retail Ltd

Clark, Andrew (Mr)
Retail Operations Director, Stationery Box
Holdings Ltd

Clark, Jack (Mr)
Finance Director, Furniture Village Plc

Should you be in this directory? See the form at the back for new entries and amendments

48

Clark, Murray (Mr)
Head of Retail Finance, T-Mobile (UK)

Clarke, Andy (Mr)
Group Retail Director, Matalan plc

Clarke, David (Mr)
Finance Director, G T Retail

Clarke, John (Mr)
Retail Operations Director, Ann Summers Ltd

Clarke, John (Mr)
Head of Direct Businesses, Waitrose Ltd

Clarke, Philip (Mr)
Finance Director, Selfridges & Co
Tel: 01992 644925   **Fax:** 01992 644381
DOB: 1960
Marital Status: Married

Clarke, Philip (Mr)
IT and Logistics Director, Tesco Stores Ltd

Clarkson, Ian (Mr)
Property Manager, Globus Office World Plc

Clayton, John (Mr)
Merchandise Manager, Russell & Bromley

Clifford, Neil (Mr)
Chief Executive, Kurt Geiger

Clifford-King, Martin (Mr)
Group Financial Director, MFI Furniture Centres
Limited
Fax: 01708 558612
DOB: 31/12/63

Coakley, Paul (Mr)
Finance Director, Bhs Plc

Coates, Peter (Mr)
Group Chief Accountant, Fenwick Ltd

Cochrane, Fiona (Miss)
Head of Marketing, Schuh Ltd

Cochrane, James (Mr)
Customer Services Manager, Botterills Convenience
Stores Ltd

Cogman, Rowland (Mr)
Company Secretary, Roys (Wroxham) Ltd

Cohen, Andrew (Mr)
Director, Courts Plc

Cohen, Bruce (Mr)
Chief Executive, Courts Plc
Tel: 020 8410 9372   **Fax:** 020 8410 9400

Personal Email: bruce@courts.plc.uk
DOB: 12/12/39
Marital Status: Married with five children
Quals/Educ: Clifton College Bristol (1953–58); MA
and LLM at Jesus College Cambridge (1959–62)
Employment History:
Managing Director and Chief Executive at Courts Plc
(1964–)
Memberships:
Fellow of the Institute of Chartered Accountants in
England and Wales
Personal Leisure Interests: Tennis; golf; skiing;
travel; theatre; sport

Cohen, Steven (Mr)
UK Managing Director, Courts Plc

Coleman, Chris (Mr)
Financial Director, Broughton Brothers Ltd

Coleman, John (Mr)
Non-Executive Director, Clinton Cards
DOB: 17/06/52
Marital Status: Married with two children

Coleman, John (Mr)
Chief Executive, House of Fraser Plc
DOB: 25/08/35
Marital Status: Married with two children
Personal Leisure Interests: Theatre; opera

Collier, Richard (Mr)
Group Property Director, Carphone Warehouse Plc
Tel: 0116 280 6800   **Fax:** 0116 280 6996
Personal Email: richard.j.collier@sears.co.uk
DOB: 23/09/60
Marital Status: Married
Personal Leisure Interests: Reading; football; golf;
tennis

Collinge, Louise (Ms)
Merchandise and Marketing Director, Borders UK
Ltd

Collins, John (Sir)
Chairman, DSG Retail Ltd

Collins, Les (Mr)
Financial Director, Fortnum & Mason Plc

Collins, Richard (Mr)
Director for Retail Properties, Allders Department
Stores Limited

Connell, Bob (Mr)
Finance and Warranties Director, MFI Furniture
Centres Limited

Should you be in this directory? See the form at the back for new entries and amendments

Tel: 01707 362000   **Fax:** 01707 338629
Personal Email: bob.connell@mfi.co.uk
DOB: 30/01/52
Memberships:
HCIMA; CMA
Personal Leisure Interests: Football; golf

Constantine, Clem (Mr)
Property and Retail Planning Director, Arcadia Group Ltd

Coogan, Mike (Mr)
Marketing Director, Toys R Us Limited

Cook, David (Mr)
Finance Director, Laura Ashley

Cook, Diane (Ms)
Director, J H Leeke & Sons Ltd

Cook, Julie (Ms)
Retail Operations and Marketing Director, Moss Bros Group Plc
Tel: 020 7200 2909
DOB: 16/07/63

Cook, Kevin (Mr)
Director, HPJ UK Ltd

Cooke, Malcolm (Mr)
Group Managing Director, La Senza

Cooper, Derek (Mr)
Purchasing Director, Apollo 2000 Ltd

Cooper, Heather (Ms)
Marketing Director, Etam Plc

Cooper, Ian (Mr)
Multi-Channel Director, Adams Childrenswear

Cooper, Julia (Ms)
Divisional Director, Merchandise, Toys R Us Limited

Cooper, Patrick E (Mr)
Chairman, Alexon Group Plc

Copas, Kegan (Mr)
Internet Manager, Whittard of Chelsea Plc

Copeland, Avril (Ms)
Executive Finance Director, Russell & Bromley

Corbett, Gerald (Mr)
Chairman, Woolworths Plc

Cordrey, Scott (Mr)
UK Property Manager, IKEA Ltd

Cormosh, Phillip (Mr)
Finance Director, all:sports Retail Ltd

Cornish, Phillip (Mr)
IT Director, all:sports Retail Ltd

Corridan, Sandra (Ms)
Marketing Director, Morley's Stores Ltd

Cotton, Fran (Mr)
Managing Director, Cotton Traders Ltd

Coulter, John (Mr)
Director, Warren James Ltd

Coupe, Mike (Mr)
Managing Director, The Big Food Group Plc
Tel: 0113 241 8822   **Fax:** 0113 241 8960
Personal Email: mike.coupe@asda.co.uk
DOB: 26/09/60
Marital Status: Married

Cox, Lesley
Non-Executive Director, HMV Group Plc

Cox, Phil (Mr)
Commercial Director, Allders Department Stores Limited
DOB: 01/07/50

Cox, Russel (Mr)
Group Financial Director, TM Retail Ltd

Coyle, Kelvin (Mr)
Commercial Director, Index, Littlewoods Stores Ltd

Crabtree, John (Mr)
Finance Director, Jessops

Craddock, John (Mr)
Marketing and Merchandise Director, James Beattie PLC
DOB: 1949

Craig, Allan (Mr)
Financial Director, Botterills Convenience Stores Ltd

Craig, Lizette (Ms)
Retail Operations Director, Botterills Convenience Stores Ltd

Craig, Stephen (Mr)
Marketing Director, USC Group Plc

Criado-Perez, Carlos (Mr)
Chief Executive, Safeway Plc

Cribb, James (Mr)
Finance Director, Rosebys Ltd

Should you be in this directory? See the form at the back for new entries and amendments

Croft, Frank (Mr)
Chairman, Shoefayre Ltd

Crompton, David (Mr)
Managing Director, Retail, Northern Electric Retail
DOB: 1954
Marital Status: Married
Personal Leisure Interests: Football; running; squash; family

Cronie, Andy (Mr)
Operations Director, Lillywhites

Crookshank, L P (Mr)
Non-Executive Director, Robert Dyas Holdings Ltd

Crossland, Roy (Mr)
Group Chief Executive, The Outdoor Group Ltd

Crowley, Kieran (Mr)
Finance Director, Time Group Ltd

Crutchley, Mark (Mr)
Finance Director, Schuh Ltd
Personal Email: mark@schuh.co.uk
DOB: 20/02/67
Marital Status: Married

Currier, Jon (Mr)
Financial Director, Richer Sounds Plc

Cushen, John (Mr)
General Manager, Supply Chain, John Lewis Plc

Cussani, Barbara
Non-Executive Director, Marks & Spencer Plc

Dahlvig, Andres (Mr)
Group President, IKEA Ltd

Dalby, Simon
Managing Director, Agency, Shop Direct Group Ltd

Danielsson, Anders (Mr)
Marketing Director, IKEA Ltd

Darbershire, Susan (Ms)
Marketing Director, Spar (UK) Limited

Darke, Bob (Mr)
Business Unit Head, Comet Group Plc

Darrington, Michael (Mr)
Managing Director, Greggs Plc

Darroch, Jeremy (Mr)
Finance Diretor, DSG Retail Ltd

Darrouzet, Jean-Claude (Mr)
Chief Executive Officer, Etam Plc

Darwin, Keith (Mr)
Chairman, Co-operative Group (CWS) Limited

Davey, Christ (Mr)
Managing Director, Disney Consumer Products

Davidson, Karen (Ms)
Financial Director, Joseph

Davie, Steve (Mr)
Finance Director, Harrods Limited

Davies, Annie (Ms)
Design Director, Eastex, Alexon Group Plc

Davies, Peter (Mr)
Chief Executive, Rubicon

Davies, Timothy (Mr)
Strategy Director, Debenhams Plc
Tel: 020 7408 3259   **Fax:** 020 7408 3874
Personal Email: timothy.davies@debenhams.com
DOB: 16/09/71
Quals/Educ: BA Hons Physics at Oxford University (1990–94)
Employment History:
Consultant at Marakon Associates (1994–2000); Head of Corporate Intelligence at Debenhams Plc (2000–02); Head of Business and Commercial Development at Debenhams Plc (2002); Director of Strategy at Debenhams Plc (2002–)

Davis, Bill (Mr)
Non-Executive Chairman, Time Group Ltd

Davis, Fiona (Ms)
Brand Marketing Director, Early Learning Centre

Davis, Jane (Ms)
Buying Director, Liberty

Davis, Matthew (Mr)
Finance Director, Pets at Home Ltd

Davis, Nigel (Mr)
Managing Director, Shoe Studio Group Ltd

Davis, Peter (Sir)
Group Chief Executive, J Sainsbury Plc
Tel: 020 7695 2740   **Fax:** 020 7695 2741
Personal Email: spjd@tao.sainsburys.co.uk
DOB: 23/12/41
Marital Status: Married
Awards: Knighted, New Year's honours for Services to Training and Industry (1997)
Memberships:
Chairman of the Welfare to Work New Deal Task Force

Should you be in this directory? See the form at the back for new entries and amendments

Davis, Philip (Mr)
Marketing Director, Asprey & Garrard Ltd

Dawson, Nick (Mr)
Financial Director, William Jackson & Son Ltd

Day, Gill (Mr)
Finance Director, Holland & Barrett Retail Ltd

Day, Philip (Mr)
Chief Executive, Edinburgh Woollen Mill Ltd

de Mellow, Steve (Mr)
Marketing Director, Majestic Wine Warehouses Ltd
DOB: 1959

De Moller, June (Ms)
Non-Executive Director, J Sainsbury Plc

De Nunzio, Tony (Mr)
President and Chief Operating Officer (Wal-Mart UK), Asda Stores Ltd

Dean, Graham (Mr)
Retail Operations and Logistics Director, Heal's Plc

Dee, Chris (Mr)
IT and Marketing Director, E H Booth & Co. Ltd

Dejardin, Galleran (Mr)
Financial Director, Vision Express UK Ltd

Delamare, Lee (Mr)
Head of Logistics and Distribution, Le Riches Stores Limited

Deller, Ben (Mr)
Marketing Manager, World News, Alpha Retail

Denham, P (Mr)
IT Manager, Northern Electric Retail

Deve, Francoise (Mr)
Catalogue Director, Redcats UK (Brands) Ltd

Dibb, Graham (Mr)
Property Director, Moss Bros Group Plc

Dignum, Tony (Mr)
Chairman, QS Plc

Dillane, Mark (Mr)
Head of Property Department, Claire's Accessories
Tel: 0121 682 8000   **Fax:** 0121 250 8949
Personal Email: mark.dillane@claires.co.uk

Din, Richard (Mr)
Managing Director, Hennes & Mauritz

Dixon, Tom (Mr)
Head of Design, Habitat UK Limited

Dobinson, Ken (Mr)
Sales Director, C & J Clark International

Dodd, David (Mr)
Chief Executive, Poundland Ltd

Dodd, Howard (Mr)
Chief Financial Officer, Boots Group Plc

Doherty, Pat (Ms)
Senior Vice-President, Marketing, Burberrys

Dolce, Deborah (Ms)
Marketing Director, TK Maxx
Tel: 01923 475765   **Fax:** 01923 235851
DOB: 1967

Dolman, Steve (Mr)
Buying Director, Stationery Box Holdings Ltd

Donnelly, Mike (Mr)
Merchandising Director, all:sports Retail Ltd

Doohan, John (Mr)
Finance Controller, Bowie-Castlebank Group Ltd

Dorkin, Sue (Ms)
Logistics Director, Early Learning Centre

Dormer, Sarah (Ms)
Human Resources Director, Waterstone's Booksellers Ltd

Doughty, Stephen (Mr)
Finance Director, United News Shops

Douglas, Brian (Mr)
Operations Director, T J Hughes Plc

Douglas, David (Mr)
Director, USC Group Plc

Douty, Philip (Mr)
Trading Director, Thorntons Plc

Downer, Phillip (Mr)
Managing Director, Borders UK Ltd
DOB: 1943

Downing, Bill (Mr)
IT Director, TK Maxx

Drake, Louise (Miss)
Customer Services Manager, QD Stores Ltd

Dreesmann, Bernard (Mr)
Chairman, Morley's Stores Ltd

Should you be in this directory? See the form at the back for new entries and amendments

52

Dregent, Patricia (Ms)
Company Secretary, Carpetright Plc
Fax: 01708 526738

Drennan, Padraig (Mr)
Senior Director, IT and Finance in Europe, Gap

Drury, Mike (Mr)
Head of Finance, AJT Trading Ltd

Drury, Romney (Mr)
Marketing Director, Bhs Plc

Duddy, Terry
Chief Executive, Argos Retail Group, GUS

Duff, Donal (Mr)
Group Director of Finance, Le Riches Stores Limited

Duffy, Charles (Mr)
Retail Operations Director, Bay Trading, Alexon Group Plc

Duley, Ian (Mr)
Financial Director, Lloyd Shoe Co Ltd

Duley, Jacques (Mr)
Managing Director, Oddbins UK Ltd

Duncan, Steve (Mr)
Managing Director, Moss Pharmacy Ltd

Dundas, Bruce (Lord)
Chairman and Chief Executive, Asprey & Garrard Ltd

Dundas, Jamie (Mr)
Non-Executive Director, J Sainsbury Plc

Dunn, Barry (Mr)
Property Director, JJB Sports Plc
DOB: 1956

Dunne, Philip (Mr)
Chairman, Ottakar's Plc
Tel: 020 7655 7795   **Fax:** 020 7655 7399
DOB: 14/08/58
Marital Status: Married

Dunstone, Charles (Mr)
Chief Executive Officer, Carphone Warehouse Plc
Personal Email: cdunstone@cpw.co.uk
DOB: 21/11/64
Quals/Educ: Uppingham School
Employment History:
Founder of the Carphone Warehouse Plc (1989)
Additional Directorships:
Non-Executive Director of HBOS Plc and the Daily Mail General Trust; Chairman of the Princes Trust Trading Board
Personal Leisure Interests: Skiing; sailing

Durkin, John (Mr)
Trading Director, Safeway Plc

Dutton, Phil (Mr)
Group Finance Director, Matalan plc

Dyson, Mark (Mr)
Company Secretary, Rosebys Ltd

Eaglesham, Graham (Mr)
Financial Director, Bennetts Retail Ltd

Earl, Belinda (Ms)
Chief Executive, Debenhams Plc
DOB: 1961
Quals/Educ: University of Wales, Aberystwyth
Employment History:
Buying and Merchandising Director for Womenswear, Lingerie, Accessories and Childrenswear at Debenhams Plc (1985–99); Trading Director at Debenhams Plc (1999–2000); Chief Executive at Debenhams Plc (2000–)
Additional Directorships:
Chair of Skillsmart

Ebert, Roger (Mr)
Executive Vice-President, Chevron Texaco

Edgar, John (Mr)
Trading and Marketing Finance Manager, House of Fraser Plc

Edwards, Neil (Mr)
Commercial Manager, Ponden Mill Ltd

Elliott, Colin (Mr)
Finance Director, Hennes & Mauritz

Empson, David (Mr)
New Brands Director, Adams Childrenswear
DOB: 1951

Esom, Steven (Mr)
Managing Director, Waitrose Ltd
Tel: 01344 824396   **Fax:** 01344 824488
Personal Email: steven_esom@waitrose.co.uk
DOB: 13/11/60
Marital Status: Married

Etheridge, Stephen (Mr)
Chief Executive, Church & Co. Footwear Ltd

Etherington, Andy (Mr)
Chief Executive Officer, Globus Office World Plc

Should you be in this directory? See the form at the back for new entries and amendments

Evans, Brian A (Mr)
Chairman, Wyevale Garden Centres Plc
DOB: 24/02/44

Evans, Christine (Ms)
Director of Merchandise, Adams Childrenswear

Evans, Keith (Mr)
Director of Non-Foods, J Sainsbury Plc

Evans, Nicholas (Mr)
Chief Executive, The MW Group Ltd

Evenson, Chris (Mr)
Development Director, Wm Morrison
Supermarkets Plc

Faith, Jonathan (Mr)
Managing Director, Faith Footwear

Faith, Samuel (Mr)
Chairman, Faith Footwear

Faley, R (Mr)
Finance Director, W Boyes & Company

Farmer, Patrick (Mr)
Non-Executive Director, Timpson Ltd

Farnsworth, Patrick (Mr)
Joint Managing Director, William Jackson & Son
Ltd

Farrar-Hockley, Rebecca (Mrs)
Buying Director, Kurt Geiger
Tel: 020 7546 1801   **Fax:** 020 7546 1760
Personal Email:
rebecca.farrarhockley@kurtgeiger.co.uk
DOB: 26/09/71
Marital Status: Married
Quals/Educ: BA Hons English and Philosophy at
University of Essex (1990–93)
Employment History:
Head of Buying, Mens Formalwear at Selfridges
(1998–2000); Head of Buying, Ladies Accessories,
Shoes and Jewellery at Selfridges (2000–02); Buying
Director at Kurt Geiger (2002–)
Personal Leisure Interests: Travelling; art; film

Farrell, John (Mr)
Development Director, Pets at Home Ltd

Farrington-Smith, Justin
Trading Director, Focus, Focus Wickes

Favell, Gary (Mr)
Managing Director, Magnet Ltd

Fawson, Pat (Mr)
Corporate Affairs Director, MFI Furniture Centres
Limited

Fearnley, Stephen (Mr)
Chairman, United News Shops

Feeney, Amon (Mr)
Finance Director, Blockbuster Entertainment Ltd

Fellows, Johnathan (Mr)
Finance Director, American Golf Discount Centre
Ltd

Felwick, David (Mr)
Deputy Chairman, John Lewis Plc
DOB: 1946

Fenwick, Adam (Mr)
Deputy Chairman, Bentalls

Fenwick, John (Mr)
Deputy Chairman, Fenwick Ltd

Fenwick, Mark (Mr)
Group Chairman, Fenwick Ltd
Tel: 020 7629 9161   **Fax:** 020 7629 1186
Personal Email: markfenwick@mfw.demon.co.uk
DOB: 11/05/48
Additional Directorships:
Afirax Inc; Roger Waters Touring Ltd
Personal Leisure Interests: Music; outdoor
activities

Ferguson, Andy (Mr)
Operations Director, Dollond & Aitchison Group
Plc

Ferguson, George (Mr)
Operations Director, Slater Menswear

Ferguson, John (Mr)
Retail Operations Controller, MK One
Fax: 020 8896 1321
DOB: 29/06/62

Ferguson, Lyn (Ms)
Personnel Director, Schuh Ltd

Ferrier, Cathy (Ms)
Trading Director, Poundland Ltd

Ferry, Joe (Mr)
Customer Services Manager, Slater Menswear

Finlan, Steve (Mr)
Managing Director, Gap

Finlay, Lyle (Mr)
Chief Executive, Claire's Accessories

Should you be in this directory? See the form at the back for new entries and amendments

54

Finnigan, Norman (Mr)
**Human Resources and Customer Services
Director**, Grattan Plc

Fisher, Nigel (Mr)
Finance Director, Select Retail Plc

Fitzgerald, Deborah (Ms)
Marketing and Communications Director, Liberty

Fletcher, Neil (Mr)
IT Manager, Holland & Barrett Retail Ltd

Flowers, Pamela (Miss)
**Human Resources and Customer Services
Manager**, Savers Health & Beauty Plc

Foley, Paul (Mr)
Managing Director, Aldi Stores Ltd

Foot, Peter (Mr)
Financial Director, Stead & Simpson

Ford, Dominic (Mr)
Food and Beverage Director, Harvey Nichols Group
Plc
Tel: 020 7584 0011   **Fax:** 020 7823 1571
Personal Email: dominic.ford@harveynichols.co.uk
DOB: 22/09/63
Marital Status: Married
Memberships:
Member of the Institute of Directors; Committee
Member of the Restaurant Association of Great Britain

Foreftier, Marc (Mr)
Administrative Director, Joseph

Forman, Chris (Mr)
Merchandising Controller, Poundland Ltd

Forrest, Kenneth (Mr)
Managing Director, Fortnum & Mason Plc

Forsey, Dave (Mr)
Managing Director, Lillywhites

Fortune, Andrew (Mr)
Financial Director, Tulchan Group
Tel: 01524 878102   **Fax:** 01524 272950
Personal Email: afortune@sockshop-group.co.uk
DOB: 05/11/53
Marital Status: Married
Personal Leisure Interests: Skiing; outdoors

Foster, George (Mr)
Chief Executive, T J Hughes Plc

Foster, Martin A (Mr)
Managing Director, Miller Brothers Group Ltd

Foster, Rose (Ms)
UK Managing Director, Monsoon Accessorize Ltd

Foster-Brown, Tania (Miss)
Director of Public Relations and Special Events,
Arcadia Group Ltd

Foulser, Steve (Mr)
Vice-President, Blockbuster Entertainment Ltd
DOB: 13/11/63
Marital Status: Married
Memberships:
Member of the Marketing Society
Personal Leisure Interests: Keep fit; cinema; music

Fowle, Adam (Mr)
Director of Retail Operations, J Sainsbury Plc

Fowler, Mike (Mr)
Finance Director, J H Leeke & Sons Ltd

Fox, Simon (Mr)
Managing Director, Comet Group Plc

Fox, Sue (Ms)
Retail Director, Kookai

France, Mike (Mr)
Managing Director, Early Learning Centre
Tel: 01793 443103
Personal Email:
mike.france@earlylearningcentre.co.uk
DOB: 13/05/56
Marital Status: Married with two children
Memberships:
Member of the Institute of Directors

Franchini, Marco (Mr)
Chief Executive, Bally UK Sales Ltd

Francis, Rick (Mr)
IT Director, Safeway Plc

Frangi, Simone (Ms)
Co-Chairman, Tie Rack Ltd

Franks, Bob (Mr)
Finance Director, News Shops Ltd

Fraser, Craig (Mr)
Operations Director, The Stationers Ltd

Fraser, Ian (Mr)
**Director of Sales and Distribution, Personal and
Small Business**, Orange Plc

Free, John (Mr)
Head of Retail, Time Group Ltd
DOB: 1968

Should you be in this directory? See the form at the back for new entries and amendments

Marital Status: Married with one son
Personal Leisure Interests: Fishing; shooting

Freed, Norman (Mr)
Managing Director, Jane Norman

Freedman, Cyril (Mr)
Non-Executive Director, Stead & Simpson

Freedman, Jonathan (Mr)
Finance Director, Speciality Retail Group Plc

Friend, Jason (Mr)
Advertising Manager, Burberrys

Frost, Graham (Mr)
Chairman, Alpha Retail

Frost, Graham (Mr)
Deputy Chairman, Monsoon Accessorize Ltd
DOB: 1950

Fryatt, Andrew (Mr)
Managing Director, T-Mobile (UK)

Fuller, Neil
Finance Director, Homebase Ltd

Gallant, Ken (Mr)
Development Director, Alfred Jones Ltd

Galloway, Mike (Mr)
Customer Services Manager, Bowie-Castlebank Group Ltd

Gardiner, John (Mr)
Non-Executive Director, Tesco Stores Ltd

Gardner, Diane (Ms)
Managing Director, Choices Video

Garratt, Nick (Mr)
Director, Marketing Operations, MFI Furniture Centres Limited

Garrett, Kevin (Mr)
Customer Services Manager, Waitrose Ltd

Garton, John (Mr)
Head of Marketing, Le Riches Stores Limited

Gaskell, Paul
Managing Director, Wine Cellar Ltd

Gaston, Sue (Ms)
Customer Services Manager, William Jackson & Son Ltd

Gates, Stuart (Mr)
Managing Director, Fortnum & Mason Plc
Fax: 020 7437 4021

Memberships:
Chairman of the Guild of Fine Food Retailers

Gavin, Gerard (Mr)
Marketing Manager, Internacionale Limited

Gawthorne, Mark (Mr)
Financial Director, Game Stores Group Ltd

Gay, Colin (Mr)
Retail Director, Europe, Waterford Wedgwood Retail Ltd
DOB: 09/05/56
Personal Leisure Interests: Family; archaeology

Gaynor, Alan (Mr)
Chief Executive, Stationery Box Holdings Ltd

Gearty, Tony (Mr)
Chief Executive, Lyndale Foods Ltd

Geary, Phil (Mr)
Marketing Director, Holland & Barrett Retail Ltd
DOB: 01/07/71
Personal Leisure Interests: Ice hockey; parachuting

Geddes, Paul (Mr)
Marketing Director, Argos Ltd

Gee, Ernie (Mr)
Director, W Boyes & Company

Gee, Peter (Mr)
Managing Director, Stylo Plc

Gee, Richard (Mr)
Property Director, River Island

Geitner, Thomas (Mr)
Chief Technical Officer, Vodafone Ltd

Gent, Christopher (Sir)
Life President, Vodafone Ltd

Genthialan, Laurent (Mr)
Finance Director, Oddbins UK Ltd

George, Joanna (Ms)
Head of Corporate Communications, Debenhams Plc

Gerhrad, Tim (Mr)
Finance Director, Unwins Wine Group Ltd

Gerrard, Paul (Mr)
Logistics Manager, Jacques Vert Plc

Ghinn, Sarah (Ms)
Corporate Communications, Courts Plc

Should you be in this directory? See the form at the back for new entries and amendments

Gibbons, David (Mr)
Distribution Director, Asda Stores Ltd

Gibson, Geoff (Mr)
Group Finance Director, Austin Reed Group Plc
DOB: 1955
Marital Status: Married with two children
Personal Leisure Interests: Golf; reading; travel;
theatre

Gilbert, David (Mr)
Chief Operating Officer, Central Operations, DSG
Retail Ltd

Giles, Alan James (Mr)
Chief Executive Officer, HMV Group Plc
Fax: 01628 818305
DOB: 04/06/54
Marital Status: Married with two children
Quals/Educ: MA Physics at University of Oxford
(1972–75); MSc Management at Stanford University
Graduate School of Business (1987–88)
Employment History:
Buyer at Boots Group Plc (1975–79); Assistant
Merchandise Controller at Boots Group Plc (1980–82);
Retail Development Manager at W H Smith Retail Ltd
(1982–85); General Manager for Books at W H Smith
Retail Ltd (1985–88); Operations and Development
Director at Do It All (1988–92); Managing Director at
Waterstone's (1993–98); Chief Executive at HMV
Group Plc (1998–)
Additional Directorships:
Somerfield Plc
Memberships:
Society of Bookmen
Personal Leisure Interests: Football; cycling; music;
skiing

Giles, Andy (Mr)
Commercial Director, Gilesports Plc

Giles, Howard (Mr)
Chairman, Gilesports Plc

Gilmore, Meg (Ms)
Director of Marketing, House of Fraser Plc

Gimpel, Oliver (Mr)
Marketing Director, Redcats UK (Brands) Ltd

Gladwin, Rob
Operations Director, Focus Wickes

Glanfield, Cliff (Mr)
Head of Property, Etam Plc

Glanville, Richard (Mr)
Finance Director, Oasis Stores Plc

Glew, Stephen (Mr)
Finance Director, Mothercare Plc
Tel: 01933 371677
DOB: 09/05/57
Marital Status: Married

Goddard, John (Mr)
Property Director, Early Learning Centre
Tel: 01793 443107   **Fax:** 01793 443132
Personal Email:
john.goddard@earlylearningcentre.co.uk
DOB: 11/04/51
Marital Status: Married
Memberships:
Associate of Royal Institution of Chartered Surveyors
Personal Leisure Interests: Football

Godfrey, Brian (Mr)
Managing Director, Roys (Wroxham) Ltd

Gold, Jacqueline (Miss)
Chief Executive and Managing Director, Ann
Summers Ltd

Goldsbrough, Sandy (Ms)
Merchandise Director, Karen Millen
DOB: 1965
Personal Leisure Interests: Travel; film; theatre;
fitness

Goldsmith, Mark (Mr)
Retail Director, Kuwait Petroleum Ltd
Personal Leisure Interests: Golf; travel

Goodfellow, Mark (Mr)
Retail Operations Manager, Lakeland Limited

Goodman, Cliff (Mr)
Trading Director, Budgens Stores Ltd

Goody, Andy (Mr)
Finance Director, T J Hughes Plc

Gordon, Ann (Ms)
Trading Director, House of Fraser Plc

Gordon, Ben (Mr)
Chief Executive, Mothercare Plc
Tel: 020 7514 9711   **Fax:** 020 7514 9757
DOB: 08/08/59
Marital Status: Married
Memberships:
Board member of the Atlanta Chamber of Commerce;
Member of Forward Europe

Goring, Mike (Mr)
Group Operations Director, Arcadia Group Ltd
DOB: 1953

Should you be in this directory? See the form at the back for new entries and amendments

Gosling, Sue (Ms)
Marketing Director, PRG Powerhouse Retail Ltd

Gott, Julian (Mr)
Property Director, United News Shops
Personal Leisure Interests: Sailing; rugby; walking

Grabiner, Anthony (Lord)
Chairman, Arcadia Group Ltd

Grabiner, Ian (Mr)
Chief Operating Officer, Arcadia Group Ltd
DOB: 12/05/59
Personal Leisure Interests: Football; tennis

Graham, David (Mr)
Joint Managing Director, Bells Stores Limited

Graham, Douglas (Mr)
Chairman, News Shops Ltd
Awards: DL
Personal Leisure Interests: Shooting

Graham, John (Mr)
Head of Marketing, Apollo 2000 Ltd

Grailey, Tracey (Ms)
General Manager, Asda Stores Ltd

Grant, Jim (Mr)
Operations Director, Littlewoods Stores Ltd

Grant, Kenneth (Mr)
Buying and Marketing Director, Jenners Limited
Tel: 0131 260 2324 **Fax:** 0131 226 1549
Personal Email: k.grant@jenners.com
Marital Status: Married

Gravells, David (Mr)
Chairman, B & M Retail Ltd

Graves, Colin (Mr)
Managing Director, Costcutter Supermarkets Group Limited

Graves, Ian (Mr)
Marketing Manager, Costcutter Supermarkets Group Limited

Gray, Elaine (Ms)
Group Buying and Merchandising Director, MK One

Gray, Liz (Ms)
Human Resources Director, House of Fraser Plc

Green, Andrew (Mr)
Marketing Manager, Allied Carpets Group

Green, Christopher (Mr)
Deputy Chairman, Timpson Ltd

Green, Geoff (Mr)
Head of Property, Oasis Stores Plc

Green, Linda
Managing Director, Direct, Shop Direct Group Ltd

Green, Marianne (Ms)
Finance Director, Redcats UK (Brands) Ltd
Tel: 01274 763723 **Fax:** 01274 731721
DOB: 07/11/54
Marital Status: Married

Green, Mark (Mr)
Marketing Director, Lloyds Pharmacy

Green, Nigel (Mr)
Marketing Director, N Brown

Green, Peter (Mr)
Managing Director, Phones 4u

Green, Philip (Mr)
Owner: Arcadia Group Ltd; Bhs Plc; **Chief Executive**, MK One

Green, Terry (Mr)
Chief Executive, Allders Department Stores Limited
DOB: 1952
Marital Status: Married
Personal Leisure Interests: Wine connoisseur

Greener, George (Mr)
Non-Executive Chairman, The Big Food Group Plc

Greenhalgh, Michael (Mr)
Group Marketing Director, Magnet Ltd

Greenwood, Anthony (Mr)
Finance Director, Claire's Accessories

Greenwood, David (Mr)
Finance Director and Company Secretary, JJB Sports Plc
DOB: 1945

Greenwood, Stuart (Mr)
Chief Executive, B & M Retail Ltd

Grey, Jon (Mr)
Group Logistics Director, The Big Food Group Plc

Grieves, John (Mr)
Chairman, New Look Retailers Ltd

Griffiths, David (Mr)
Finance Director, Early Learning Centre
Tel: 01793 443128

Should you be in this directory? See the form at the back for new entries and amendments

Personal Email:
david.griffiths@earlylearningcentre.co.uk
DOB: 28/02/60
Marital Status: Married
Memberships:
Member of ACMA
Personal Leisure Interests: Football; sport; cinema;
travelling

Griffiths, Matthew (Mr)
Marketing Director, French Connection

Grimsdale, Simon (Mr)
Retail Operations Manager, Shell Retail UK

Grimsey, Bill (Mr)
Chief Executive, The Big Food Group Plc
DOB: 1952
Marital Status: Married
Personal Leisure Interests: Motorcycling; skiing;
theatre

Grindlay, Gary (Mr)
Supply Chain Director, Shellys Shoes Ltd

Ground, Andrew (Mr)
Director of Consumer Marketing, J Sainsbury Plc

Gudgeon, Richard (Mr)
Finance Director, Magnet Ltd

Guerard, Annie (Ms)
Finance Director, Diesel

Guillaume, Jane
Personnel Director, Debenhams Plc

Gunter, Kevin (Mr)
Chief Executive, Frozen Value Ltd

Gustavesson, Kent (Mr)
Operational Director, Hennes & Mauritz

Guthrie, Adrian (Mr)
Head of Human Resources, Carphone Warehouse
Plc

Hadfield, Caroline (Ms)
Director of Product, The Body Shop International
Plc

Halford, Emma (Miss)
Marketing Manager, A Jones & Sons Ltd

Halford, Seamus (Mr)
Store Operations Director, Primark

Halkett, Peter (Mr)
Chairman and Chief Executive, PRG Powerhouse
Retail Ltd

Hall, Andy (Mr)
Group Finance Director, The Outdoor Group Ltd
DOB: 31/07/55
Marital Status: Married
Awards: First Prize for Elements of Financial
Decisions (1978)
Memberships:
Fellow of Institute of Chartered Accountants
Personal Leisure Interests: Tennis; football
coaching; family outings

Hall, Graham (Mr)
Customer Services Manager, Thermawear Limited
(t/a Damart)

Hall, Jo (Ms)
Commercial Director, Woolworths Plc

Hallam, Geoff (Mr)
Managing Director, A F Blakemore & Son Ltd

Halliday, Mike (Mr)
Merchandising Director, Jacques Vert Plc

Halliday, Ross (Mr)
Trade Marketing Director, Londis (Holdings) Ltd

Halton, Sara (Ms)
Financial Director, Borders UK Ltd

Hamblin, Nick (Mr)
Retail Director, Cotton Traders Ltd

Hamburger, Paul (Mr)
Marketing Director, Phones 4u

Hamid, David (Mr)
Chief Operating Officer, Retail Operations, DSG
Retail Ltd

Hamid, David (Mr)
Chief Executive, Halfords Limited
DOB: 1954

Hamill, Keith (Mr)
Chairman, Moss Bros Group Plc
DOB: 12/07/52
Memberships:
Member of CBI Companies; Member of UITF;
Treasurer of Nottingham University

Hampson, Stuart (Sir)
Executive Chairman, John Lewis Plc
Tel: 020 7592 6117   **Fax:** 020 7592 6342
Personal Email: chairman@johnlewis.co.uk
DOB: 1947
Marital Status: Married with two children
Awards: Knight Bachelor in the Queen's Birthday

Should you be in this directory? See the form at the back for new entries and amendments

Honours (1998); Honorary Doctorate in Business
Administration from Kingston University (1998)
Memberships:
Chairman of Royal Society of Arts (1999)

Hamwee, Nikki (Mrs)
Brand Director, Accessorize, Monsoon Accessorize
Ltd

Hancock, John (Mr)
Chief Executive, MFI Furniture Centres Limited
DOB: 1949

Hancox, Mike
Chief Operating Officer, Shop Direct Group Ltd

Handley, Roger (Mr)
Marketing Director, Furnitureland Holdings Ltd

Handover, Richard
Chairman, W H Smith Retail Ltd

Hanly, Patrick (Mr)
Commercial Director, Harvey Nichols Group Plc

Hanns, Dennis (Mr)
Head of Retail, Oddbins UK Ltd
Tel: 020 8944 4400   **Fax:** 020 8944 4483
Personal Email: mark_dence@oddbins.com
DOB: 30/09/66
Personal Leisure Interests: Golf; football; sailing;
skiing; antiques

Hansell, Debbie (Ms)
Commercial Director, Superdrug Stores

Harding, Jim (Mr)
Managing Director of UK Sales, Waterford
Wedgwood Retail Ltd

Harding, Michael (Mr)
Financial Director, F Hinds Ltd

Hardy, Robert (Mr)
Director of Property, House of Fraser Plc

Hardy, Russell (Mr)
Chief Executive, Dollond & Aitchison Group Plc

Hare, Richard (Mr)
Legal and Human Resources Director, Budgens
Stores Ltd

Hargreaves, Jamey (Mr)
Director of Category and Brand Marketing,
Matalan plc

Hargreaves, John (Mr)
Chairman, Matalan plc
DOB: 1944

Hargreaves, Martin (Mr)
Chairman, Hargreaves Sports

Hargreaves, Robin (Mr)
Managing Director, Hargreaves Sports

Harlow, E D
Director and Company Secretary, Alfred Jones Ltd

Harrington, Neil (Mr)
Finance Director, George (Asda)

Harris, Martin (Mr)
Director of Buying, Carpetright Plc
DOB: 1960

Harris, Ray (Mr)
Customer Services Manager, Bentalls

Harris of Peckham, (Lord)
Chairman and Chief Executive, Carpetright Plc
Tel: 01708 527730   **Fax:** 01708 630970
DOB: 15/09/42
Marital Status: Married with three sons and one
daughter
Quals/Educ: Streatham Grammar School
Employment History:
Chairman of Harris Queensway (1964–88); Chairman
of Westminster Abbey Fundraising Appeal Committee
(1987–96); Chairman of Guy's and Lewisham NHS
Trust (1991–93)
Awards: Hambro Businessman of the Year (1983);
Knighted (1985); Freeman of City of London (1992);
Elevated to the Peerage (1996)
Additional Directorships:
Chairman of Harris Ventures Ltd; Chairman of
Prostate Cancer Charity's Investing in Life Campaign;
Chairman of the Generation Trust at Guy's Hospital,
London; Chairman of Governors and Trustee of The
Academy at Peckham
Memberships:
British Showjumping Association; University College
London Council
Personal Leisure Interests: Tennis; football; cricket;
showjumping
Other Biographical Details:
Sponsor of the Harris City Technology College in
Croydon; sponsor of the Bacon CTC in Southwark;
founder of The Phillip and Pauline Harris Charitable
Trust

Harrison, Peter (Mr)
Managing Director, Furniture Village Plc
Tel: 01753 897720   **Fax:** 01753 897730
DOB: 19/08/46
Marital Status: Married
Awards: Entrepreneur of the Year (1999); winner of

Should you be in this directory? See the form at the back for new entries and amendments

60

the Southern Regional Retail Section
Personal Leisure Interests: Family; rugby

Hart, Kevin (Mr)
Joint Managing Director, Operations, TM Retail Ltd

Hartley, Stephen (Mr)
Operations Controller, Speciality Retail Group Plc

Hartog, Barry (Mr)
Finance Director and Company Secretary, Clinton Cards
DOB: 1947

Harvey, Hugh (Mr)
Deputy Managing Director, Commercial, Comet Group Plc

Harvey, Martyn (Mr)
Supply Chain Development Director, Londis (Holdings) Ltd

Harvey, Peter (Mr)
Director of Commercial Finance, Thresher Group

Haughney, Mark (Mr)
Sales Director, ScS Upholstery Plc

Hawker, Michael L (Mr)
Chief Executive: Grattan Plc; Freemans Plc

Hawkins, Kevin (Mr)
Communications Director, Safeway Plc

Hawkins, Terry (Mr)
Merchandise Director, Multiyork Furniture Ltd

Haworth, Melanie (Ms)
Buying and Merchandising Director, Claire's Accessories

Hay, Brian (Mr)
Operations Director, Whittard of Chelsea Plc

Hayman, Jane (Ms)
Marketing Director, Principles, Rubicon

Hazelebach, Gerard (Mr)
Managing Director, Superdrug Stores

Headington, Steve (Mr)
Retail Operations Director, Thresher Group
Tel: 020 8242 8271　　**Fax:** 020 8242 8514
Personal Email: steve.headington@signet.co.uk
DOB: 31/01/59
Marital Status: Married

Healy, J (Mr)
Store Operations Manager, Harrods Limited

Heard, Eric (Mr)
Managing Director, Farmfoods Freezer Centre

Hearsay, Peter (Mr)
Company Secretary, House of Fraser Plc
Tel: 020 7963 2421
Personal Email: phearsey@hof.co.uk
DOB: 04/06/65

Heath, Reg (Mr)
Chairman, Merchant Retail Group Plc
DOB: 05/06/41

Heathcote, Dawn (Mrs)
Customer Services Manager, Netto Foodstores Ltd

Heaton, Mark (Mr)
Merchandising Director, JJB Sports Plc

Heaviside, John A (Mr)
Production Director, Mackays Stores Ltd

Helfgott, Maurice (Mr)
Business Unit Director, Menswear, Marks & Spencer Plc

Helm, Andrew (Mr)
Marketing Director, John David Group Plc

Henderson, Dennis (Mr)
Group Operations Director, Virgin Retail Group Limited

Henderson, Paul (Mr)
Marketing Director, Ottakar's Plc

Hendry, David (Mr)
Finance Director, TK Maxx

Heneage, James (Ms)
Managing Director, Ottakar's Plc
DOB: 1957
Personal Leisure Interests: Reading; skiing; walking; cartoon drawing; piano playing

Hepher, Michael (Mr)
Non-Executive Director, Kingfisher Plc

Hepton, Richard (Mr)
Property Director, Alexon Group Plc

Hepworth, Malcolm (Mr)
Chief Operating Officer, Co-operative Group (CWS) Limited

Herbert, Claire (Ms)
Head of Property, Allied Carpets Group

Herbert, Sarah (Ms)
Marketing Director, Multiyork Furniture Ltd

Should you be in this directory? See the form at the back for new entries and amendments

Heuck, Andrew (Mr)
Sales and Marketing Director, Heron Frozen Foods Ltd

Heuck, David (Mr)
Finance Director, Heron Frozen Foods Ltd

Hewitt, Paul (Mr)
Chief Financial Officer, Co-operative Group (CWS) Limited

Hewitt, Robert J (Mr)
Chief Executive, Wyevale Garden Centres Plc

Hibbert, Steve (Mr)
Operations Director, House of Fraser Plc

Hickford, Alan (Mr)
Buying Director, Harveys Furnishing Group

Hide, Belinda (Ms)
Head of Marketing, Bentalls

Higgins, Joanne (Miss)
Customer Services Manager, Timberland UK Ltd

Higginson, Andrew (Mr)
Finance Director, Tesco Stores Ltd
Personal Email: andrew.higginson@tesco.com
DOB: 1957

Higham, Winston (Mr)
Marketing Director, JJB Sports Plc

Higton, John (Mr)
Group Financial Director, Multiyork Furniture Ltd

Hill, Andy (Mr)
Managing Director, Thermawear Limited (t/a Damart)
DOB: 1957
Personal Leisure Interests: Motorcycling; cycling; music

Hill, Ian (Mr)
Chief Executive, Shoefayre Ltd

Hill, Lewis (Mr)
Managing Director, Fraser Hart Ltd

Hill, Peter (Mr)
Finance Director, HMV Group Plc

Hill, Phill (Mr)
Managing Director, Homeform Group Ltd

Hill, Richard (Mr)
Finance Director, Spar (UK) Limited

Hinchcliff, Mike (Mr)
Marketing Manager, Netto Foodstores Ltd

Hinchliffe, John (Mr)
Marketing and Strategy Director, N Brown

Hind, John (Mr)
Trading Director, Arcadia Group Ltd

Hinds, Andrew (Mr)
Buying Director, F Hinds Ltd
Memberships:
Fellow of Gemmological Association

Hinds, David (Mr)
Managing Director, F Hinds Ltd

Hinds, Neil (Mr)
Property Director, F Hinds Ltd

Hinds, Roy (Mr)
Chairman, F Hinds Ltd
DOB: 10/09/32
Marital Status: Married
Memberships:
Member of the Moor Park Golf Club

Hine, Derek (Mr)
Chief Executive, Jessops
Tel: 0116 2326006   **Fax:** 0116 2326255
Personal Email: dhine@jessops.com
DOB: 08/06/52
Employment History:
Productivity Director at Fine Fare Ltd (1969–87); Operations Director at Dixons Financial Services Ltd (1987–88); Retail Director at RHM Retail Ltd (1988–91); Group Managing Director at In Shops Plc (1991–94); Group Managing Director at B&Q (1994–97); Managing Director then Chief Executive at Jessops (1998–)
Personal Leisure Interests: Reading; sports

Hiremath, Raju (Mr)
Finance Director, Adminstore Ltd

Hirth, Garry (Mr)
Finance Director, Furnitureland Holdings Ltd

Hislop, Mark (Mr)
Retail Operations Director, Habitat UK Limited

Hitchcott, Paul (Mr)
Property Director, New Look Retailers Ltd
DOB: 1957
Personal Leisure Interests: Sports; football; horse riding; running; marathons

Hobbs, Michael (Mr)
Chief Executive, Adams Childrenswear
DOB: 1961

Should you be in this directory? See the form at the back for new entries and amendments

62

Personal Leisure Interests: Keep fit; rugby; entertaining

Hobdey, John (Mr)
Merchandise Systems Executive, J E Beale Plc

Hobhouse, William (Mr)
Non-Executive Chairman, Whittard of Chelsea Plc
Personal Email: will.hobhouse@whittard.co.uk
DOB: 24/09/56
Marital Status: Married
Memberships:
Member of Young Presidents Organisation
Personal Leisure Interests: Fishing

Hodge, Mike (Mr)
Executive Director, Stylo Plc

Hodges, Boo (Mr)
Womenswear Director, Timberland UK Ltd

Hodkinson, Jim (Mr)
Chairman, Furniture Village Plc

Hodson, Beverley (Mrs)
Managing Director, W H Smith Retail Ltd
Tel: 01793 616161   **Fax:** 01793 562746
Personal Email: beverley.hodson@whsmith.co.uk
DOB: 14/06/51
Marital Status: Married
Awards: Midlands Business Woman of the Year (1994)
Memberships:
WACL
Personal Leisure Interests: Tennis; horse riding; skiing; water sports; mountain biking; roller blading; walking; reading; arts; wine; food; antiques; family; friends

Hoerner, John (Mr)
Chief Executive, Clothing, Tesco Stores Ltd

Hogan, Brian (Mr)
Sales Director, Lloyd Shoe Co Ltd

Hogg, James (Mr)
Franchise Director, Dollond & Aitchison Group Plc

Hogg, Sally (Mrs)
Merchandise Director, Asprey & Garrard Ltd

Hogsted, Peter (Mr)
Managing Director, IKEA Ltd

Holes, Eric (Mr)
Group Finance Director, QS Plc

Holliman, Alan (Mr)
Store Development and Property Manager, Robert Dyas Holdings Ltd

Holme, Jane (Ms)
Property and Operations Manager, QS Plc

Holmes, Chris (Mr)
Brand Director, Austin Reed, Austin Reed Group Plc

Holmes, Roger (Mr)
Chief Executive, Marks & Spencer Plc
Employment History:
Chief Executive at Marks & Spencer Plc (2002–)

Holmes, Tony (Mr)
Property Controller, Bewise Ltd

Hood, John (Mr)
Managing Director, Brantano UK Ltd

Hood, John (Mr)
Finance Director, Lloyds Pharmacy
Tel: 02476 432020   **Fax:** 02476 841877
Personal Email: john.hood@lloydspharmacy.co.uk
DOB: 17/11/52
Marital Status: Married with two children
Employment History:
Senior Group Accountant at Marley Plc (1978–83); Finance Director at Payless DIY Ltd (1983–89); Finance Director at Do It All Ltd (1989–94); Finance Director at Dillons the Bookstore (1994–98); Finance Director at Lloyds Pharmacy (1998–)
Memberships:
Member of the Institute of Chartered Accountants in England and Wales; Member of Institute of Directors
Personal Leisure Interests: Golf; travel

Hook, Jonathan (Mr)
Retail Director, Carphone Warehouse Plc

Horgan, Mark (Mr)
Executive Director, UK Retail, MFI Furniture Centres Limited

Horn-Smith, Julian (Mr)
Chief Operating Officer, Vodafone Ltd

Hoskins, Bill (Mr)
Group Finance Director, The Big Food Group Plc
DOB: 1953
Personal Leisure Interests: Sport in general; watching cricket

Hoskinson, Philip E (Mr)
Chief Executive, Ethel Austin Ltd

Should you be in this directory? See the form at the back for new entries and amendments

63

Hotson, David (Mr)
Customer Services Manager, Time Group Ltd

Hourston, Gordon (Sir)
Chairman, Rosebys Ltd
DOB: 24/07/34

Houston, David (Mr)
Financial Director, Edinburgh Woollen Mill Ltd

How, Timothy (Mr)
Managing Director, Majestic Wine Warehouses Ltd
DOB: 29/12/50
Marital Status: Married with four daughters
Additional Directorships:
Non-Executive Director, Austin Reed Group Plc

Howard, Caroline (Ms)
Marketing Director, J E Beale Plc

Howard-Allen, Flic (Ms)
Director of Communications, Marks & Spencer Plc

Howes, Clare (Ms)
Buying Director, Shoe Zone Ltd

Howling, Mark (Mr)
Finance Controller, Cotton Traders Ltd

Hubbold, Colin (Mr)
Marketing Manager, Lyndale Foods Ltd

Hudson, Dave (Mr)
Operations Director, Motorworld Ltd

Hudson, Kevin (Mr)
Finance Director, L Rowland & Co (Retail) Ltd

Hughes, David E (Mr)
Chairman, all:sports Retail Ltd

Hughes, Robert (Mr)
Managing Director, Hughes Electricals

Hume, Simon (Mr)
Human Resources Director, Moss Pharmacy Ltd

Humphries, Ann (Ms)
Director of Retail Development, John Lewis Plc

Hunter, Tom (Mr)
Chief Executive, AJT Trading Ltd

Hutchinson, Clive (Mr)
Chief Executive, Allied Carpets Group

Hydon, Ken (Mr)
Group Finance Director, Vodafone Ltd

Hyson, Martin (Mr)
Chief Executive Officer, Budgens Stores Ltd

Idun, B
Stores Director, Argos Ltd

Imani, Mazz (Miss)
Customer Service Manager, Hennes & Mauritz

Imrie, David (Mr)
Trading Director, Furniture Village Plc

Ingle, Matthew (Mr)
Managing Director, Howden Joinery, MFI
Furniture Centres Limited

Ingram, Colin (Mr)
Finance Director, Bewise Ltd

Inman, Chris (Mr)
Group Finance Director, Rubicon

Irwin, John (Mr)
Customer Sevices Director, Asda Stores Ltd

Ivel, Nick (Mr)
Finance Director, Costcutter Supermarkets Group
Limited

Izard, Olivier (Mr)
Managing Director, Redcats UK (Brands) Ltd

Jackson, A (Mr)
Chief Executive, Mole Valley Farmers

Jackson, Keith (Mr)
New Business Development Director, Somerfield
Stores Ltd

Jackson, Phil (Mr)
Sales and Marketing Director, Northern Electric
Retail

Jackson, Richard (Mr)
Managing Director, Bennetts Retail Ltd

Jacques, David (Mr)
Chairman, Jack Loggin Ltd

Jacques, Peter (Mr)
Managing Director, Jack Loggin Ltd

Jagger, Denise (Ms)
Company Secretary, Asda Stores Ltd
Personal Email: denise.jagger@asda.co.uk
DOB: 07/09/58
Marital Status: Married with two children

James, Tim (Mr)
Managing Director, Index, Littlewoods Stores Ltd

Jani, Anita (Mrs)
Marketing Executive, British Heart Foundation,
Shops Division

Should you be in this directory? See the form at the back for new entries and amendments

Jarvis, Peter (Mr)
Chairman, Debenhams Plc
DOB: 01/07/41
Marital Status: Married
Employment History:
Director at Whitbread (1979–85); Group Managing
Director at Whitbread (1985–90); Group Chief
Executive at Whitbread (1990–97); Chairman at
Debenhams Plc (1997–)
Awards: CBE
Additional Directorships:
Director of The Rank Group Plc
Memberships:
Vice-President of the Brewers and Licensed Retailers
Association; Fellow of the Institute of Grocery
Distribution; Governor of Bolton School

Jefferson, John C (Mr)
Finance Director, Joplings Ltd

Jeffreys, Penny (Ms)
IT Director, Allders Department Stores Limited

Jenkins, Jean (Mr)
Retail Operations Director, Blockbuster
Entertainment Ltd

Jenkins, Steven (Mr)
Customer Service Manager, Globus Office World
Plc

Jennings, Roger (Mr)
Chief Executive, Austin Reed Group Plc

Jermine, John (Mr)
Chairman, Furnitureland Holdings Ltd

John, Garry (Mr)
**Senior Director, Real Estate and Store
Development in Europe**, Gap
DOB: 18/04/64
Marital Status: Married

Johnson, D (Mr)
Financial Director, A Jones & Sons Ltd

Johnson, Gill (Ms)
Customer Services Adminstrator, Gilesports Plc

Johnson, P
Non-Executive Director, Ethel Austin Ltd

Johnson, Rachel (Ms)
Regional Marketing Director, Levi Strauss (UK) Ltd

Johnson, Tony (Mr)
Chief Executive, Findel Plc

Johnson-Flint, James (Mr)
Director, Richer Sounds Plc

Johnston, Clare (Ms)
Head of Design, Liberty
Tel: 020 7573 9427   **Fax:** 020 7573 9493
Personal Email: cjohnston@liberty-of-london.com
DOB: 07/08/51
Awards: RSA Winner for Fashion Textiles (1972)
Personal Leisure Interests: Theatre; film; dance;
sport

Jones, Ann (Ms)
Director, Warren James Ltd

Jones, Christopher (Mr)
Managing Director, James Beattie PLC
DOB: 1944

Jones, David (Mr)
Chairman, Cotton Traders Ltd

Jones, David (Mr)
Chairman, Next Plc
DOB: 02/02/43
Marital Status: Married with three children
Personal Leisure Interests: Snooker; golf

Jones, Helen (Ms)
Company Secretary, Kingfisher Plc

Jones, John (Mr)
Finance Director, Littlewoods Stores Ltd

Jones, Johnathon A (Mr)
Chairman, Alfred Jones Ltd

Jones, Malcolm (Mr)
Managing Director and Chairman, Total UK Ltd

Jones, Mark (Mr)
Retail Speciality Manager, Timberland UK Ltd
DOB: 01/01/62
Personal Leisure Interests: Sport

Jones, Martyn (Mr)
Senior Trading Director, Wm Morrison
Supermarkets Plc

Jones, Mike (Mr)
Commercial Director, Bennetts Retail Ltd

Jones, Nadia (Ms)
Design Director, Oasis Stores Plc

Jones, Peter
Operations Director, Homebase Ltd

Jones, Terry (Mr)
Group Design Director, J H Leeke & Sons Ltd

Should you be in this directory? See the form at the back for new entries and amendments

Kaikobad, Farida (Ms)
Buying Director, River Island

Kane, Mike (Mr)
Director, Retail, MFI Furniture Centres Limited

Kappler, David (Mr)
Non-Executive Director, HMV Group Plc

Karia, Nilesh (Mr)
Senior Merchandiser, Faith Footwear

Karia, Rohit
Finance Director, Hobbs Limited

Kavanagh, Carol (Ms)
Human Resources Director, Argos Ltd
Tel: 01908 600827   **Fax:** 01908 204447
Personal Email: carol.kavanagh@argos.co.uk
DOB: 30/03/62
Quals/Educ: BA Hons at Manchester University
(1980–83); MA Dist at Nottingham University
(1994–95)
Employment History:
Human Resources Head at Ladbroke Group
(1988–91); Human Resources Director at Safeway
(1991–98); Group Human Resources Director at
Storehouse (1998–2001); Human Resources Director
at Argos Ltd (2001–)
Memberships:
IPD
Personal Leisure Interests: Swimming; horse
riding; walking

Kears, Norman (Mr)
Partnership Director, Budgens Stores Ltd

Keating, Brian (Mr)
Information Systems Director, Safeway Plc

Keeley, Mark (Mr)
Buying Director, Spar (UK) Limited

Keen, Jill
Marketing Director, Focus Wickes

Keen, Nigel (Mr)
Property Director, John David Group Plc
DOB: 11/07/65
Personal Leisure Interests: Squash; running;
swimming; weights training

Keenan, Jack (Mr)
Non-Executive Director, Marks & Spencer Plc
Employment History:
Non-Executive Director at Marks & Spencer Plc (2001–)
Additional Directorships:
Chief Executive Officer of Grand Cru Consulting Ltd;

Non-Executive Director of The Body Shop
International Plc; Non-Executive Director of Tomkins
Plc; Non-Executive Director of General Mills Inc;
Patron of the advisory board of the Centre for
International Business and Management at Cambridge
University

Keens, David (Mr)
Group Finance Director, Next Plc
Tel: 0116 284 2202   **Fax:** 0116 286 7178
Personal Email: evey_klein@next.co.uk
DOB: 1953
Marital Status: Married with two children

Kelly, J (Mr)
General Manager, Fraser Hart Ltd

Kelly, Pat (Mr)
Deputy Managing Director, Harveys Furnishing
Group

Kelly, William (Mr)
Finance Director, James Beattie PLC
DOB: 1959

Kendall-Smith, Michael (Mr)
Finance Director, Savers Health & Beauty Plc

Kendrick, Mark (Mr)
Distribution Director, Holland & Barrett Retail Ltd

Kennedy, Neil (Mr)
Finance and Planning Director, Debenhams Plc

Kennedy, Ray (Mr)
Operations Finance Director, QS Plc

Kennedy, Sandy (Mr)
Business Development Director, Bowie-Castlebank
Group Ltd

Kenny, Emma (Ms)
Corporate Marketing Director, Vodafone Ltd

Kernan, Will (Mr)
Director of Finance and IT, New Look Retailers Ltd

Kershaw, Michelle (Ms)
Customer Director, Lakeland Limited

Khan, Michael (Mr)
IT Director, Specsavers Optical Group

Khayat, Jana (Ms)
Chairman, Fortnum & Mason Plc

Kilcourse, Mike (Mr)
Group Marketing Director, The Stationers Ltd
Personal Leisure Interests: Golf; squash; football;
cinema; opera

Should you be in this directory? See the form at the back for new entries and amendments

Killen, Tracey (Ms)
Personnel Director, John Lewis Plc

Kincade, Steve (Mr)
Commercial Director, Virgin Retail Group Limited

King, David (Mr)
Executive Director and Managing Director of Alpha Retail Shopping, Alpha Retail

King, George (Mr)
Managing Director, G 101 Off Sales Ltd

King, Howard (Mr)
Property Director: John Lewis Plc; Waitrose Ltd

King, John (Mr)
Chief Executive, Matalan plc

King, Justin
Chief Executive Officer, J Sainsbury Plc

King, Justin (Mr)
Food Director, Marks & Spencer Plc

Kirby, Tom (Mr)
Chairman and Chief Executive, Games Workshop Group Plc

Kirk, Richard (Mr)
Chief Executive Officer, The Peacock Group Plc
Tel: 029 2027 0204   **Fax:** 029 2027 0220
Personal Email: richard.kirk@peacocks.co.uk
DOB: 16/11/45
Marital Status: Married with three children

Kirkham, Graham (Lord)
Executive Chairman, DFS Furniture Company plc
DOB: 14/12/44
Personal Leisure Interests: Art collecting; horse riding; charity work

Kirton, Tony (Mr)
Merchandise Director, Alexon Group Plc

Kiss, Martin (Mr)
Buying Controller, TM Retail Ltd
Fax: 01277 375742

Kitching, John (Mr)
Managing Director, Carpetright Plc
DOB: 1952

Kliner, Francesco
Chief Financial Officer, Church & Co. Footwear Ltd

Knight, David (Mr)
Chief Executive, ScS Upholstery Plc

Knight, Thomas (Mr)
Chief Executive, JJB Sports Plc
DOB: 1952
Marital Status: Married
Personal Leisure Interests: Motor racing; football

Knighton, Edward (Mr)
Finance Director and Company Secretary, Ottakar's Plc

Knott, Steve (Mr)
Managing Director, HMV Europe, HMV Group Plc

Kopacz, Greg (Mr)
Manufacturing Director, Budgens Stores Ltd

Kowalski, Tim (Mr)
Finance Director, N Brown

Kramer, Hammut
Non-Executive Director, Kingfisher Plc

Labroue, Jean Nöel
Chief Executive: KESA Electricals Plc; Kingfisher Plc

Ladha, Hashim (Mr)
Business Development Director, New Look Retailers Ltd

Laffin, Simon (Mr)
Finance Director, Safeway Plc
Tel: 020 8756 2954   **Fax:** 020 8848 1390
Personal Email: simon_laffin@safeway.co.uk
DOB: 1959
Marital Status: Married with three children

Laidlaw, John (Mr)
Marketing Director, Staples UK Ltd

Lamont, Chris (Mr)
Finance Director, Merchant Retail Group Plc

Lancaster, James (Mr)
Chief Executive, TM Retail Ltd
DOB: 19/02/48
Marital Status: Married with three children

Larkin, Simon (Mr)
Finance Director, The Stationers Ltd

Lassiter, Robin (Ms)
Director of Central Retail Operations, J Sainsbury Plc

Law, Michael (Mr)
Directory Operations Director, Next Plc

Should you be in this directory? See the form at the back for new entries and amendments

67

Lawlor, June (Ms)
Buying and Merchandising Director, House of Fraser Plc

Lawton, Christopher (Mr)
Direct Marketing Manager, Holland & Barrett Retail Ltd

Lawton, Kenton (Mr)
Marketing Director, Londis (Holdings) Ltd

Leahy, Nigel (Mr)
Marketing Director, W H Smith Retail Ltd

Leahy, Terry (Sir)
Chief Executive, Tesco Stores Ltd

Leake, J D (Mr)
Non-Executive Director, Robert Dyas Holdings Ltd

Leath, Warren
Operations Manager, Wine Cellar Ltd

Lee, Chris (Mr)
Company Secretary, Courts Plc

Lee, Kerry (Miss)
Head of Retail Marketing, Virgin Retail Group Limited

Leek, Marcus (Mr)
Financial and IT Director, Bells Stores Limited

Leeke, Anne-Marie (Mrs)
Chairperson, J H Leeke & Sons Ltd

Leeke, Emma (Ms)
Director of Commercial Operations, J H Leeke & Sons Ltd

Leeke, Gerald (Mr)
Managing Director, J H Leeke & Sons Ltd

Leeke, Stephen J (Mr)
Vale Complex Managing Director, J H Leeke & Sons Ltd

Leeke, Stuart (Mr)
Director and Company Secretary, J H Leeke & Sons Ltd
Tel: 01443 667703   **Fax:** 01443 667704
Personal Email: ajohn@leekes.co.uk
DOB: 09/03/50
Marital Status: Married
Personal Leisure Interests: Travel; jogging; tennis; cycling

Leibe, Sharon (Ms)
Customer Services Manager, Waterford Wedgwood Retail Ltd

Leigh, Carmel (Ms)
Buying and Merchandising Director, Edinburgh Woollen Mill Ltd
Tel: 01387 382770
DOB: 14/10/62
Quals/Educ: BA Hons Maths and Economics at Essex University (1981–84)
Employment History:
Merchandise Buyer and Buying Controller at River Island (1984–92); Buying and Merchandising Director at River Island (1992–99); Merchandise Division Director at Edinburgh Woollen Mill Ltd (1999–)

Leighton, Allan (Mr)
Chairman, Bhs Plc
DOB: 1953
Marital Status: Married with one daughter and two sons
Personal Leisure Interests: Morris dancing; football; cricket; running

Lemmon, Mark (Mr)
Director of Operations, South, Cash Converters UK Ltd

Lenk, Toby (Mr)
Head of Online Sales Division, Gap

Letrilliart, Thierry (Mr)
Managing Director, Joseph

Levene of Portsoken, (Lord)
Non-Executive Director, J Sainsbury Plc

Leverett, Peter (Mrs)
Estates Manager, Jaeger Ltd
Tel: 020 7200 4118   **Fax:** 020 7200 4001
Personal Email: peter.leverett@jaeger.co.uk
DOB: 21/01/67
Quals/Educ: BSc Urban Land Economics at Sheffield City Polytechnic (1986–91); MBA Business Administration at University of Nottingham (1997–98)
Employment History:
Assistant Estates Surveyor at Bass Leisure Ltd (1988–90); Assistant Estates Manager at Augustus Barnett Wine Merchants Ltd (1991–93); Estates Surveyor at Bass Plc (1993–94); Estates Surveyor at Next Plc (1994–97); Acquisition Surveyor at Gap (1998–99); Estates Manager at Jaeger Ltd (1999–)
Memberships:
MRICS; ACIArb; Rotary International
Personal Leisure Interests: Skiing; motorcycling; running

Should you be in this directory? See the form at the back for new entries and amendments

68

Lewin, Clinton (Mr)
Managing Director, Clinton Cards
DOB: 1963

Lewin, Debbie (Ms)
Product Development Director, Clinton Cards

Lewin, Donald (Mr)
Chairman, Clinton Cards
Tel: 020 8502 8242   **Fax:** 020 8502 8240
DOB: 11/06/33
Employment History:
Chairman and Founder of Clinton Cards (1968–)
Awards: Entrepreneur of the Year; OBE; Freeman of the City of London
Additional Directorships:
Strand Cards; Greeting Store Group
Memberships:
Royal Society of St George Livery; Institute of Directors; Masonic Lodges; Royal British Legion
Personal Leisure Interests: Swimming; music; tai chi; keep fit

Lewis, Ashley (Mr)
Finance Director, Homeform Group Ltd

Lewis, Bernard (Mr)
Retail Director, River Island

Lewis, Chris (Mr)
Buying Director, Spar (UK) Limited

Lewis, Clive (Mr)
Chief Executive, River Island
Tel: 020 8991 4500   **Fax:** 020 8810 8699
DOB: 04/12/56

Lewis, Julian (Mr)
Director, River Island

Lewis, Leonard (Mr)
Managing Director, River Island

Lewis, Patrick (Mr)
Supply Chain Director, John Lewis Plc

Lewis, Robin (Mr)
Director of Human Resources, New Look Retailers Ltd

Lewis, Steve (Mr)
Retail Director, Majestic Wine Warehouses Ltd
DOB: 1952

Lewis, Wendy (Ms)
Marketing Director, Shoe Zone Ltd

Liggett, Andrew (Mr)
Finance Director, Topps Tiles Plc

Lilly, Doreen (Ms)
Customer Services Manager, Walmsley Furnishing Plc

Linton, Cred (Miss)
Customer Services Manager, Schuh Ltd

Little, Jill (Ms)
Merchandise Director, John Lewis Plc

Lock, Steven (Mr)
Customer Services Manager, French Connection

Lockyer, David (Mr)
Chief Executive, Stead & Simpson
Tel: 0116 269 1327   **Fax:** 0116 264 0713
Personal Email:
david.lockyer@steadandsimpson.co.uk
DOB: 22/03/46
Marital Status: Married
Memberships:
Fellow of the Institute of Management
Personal Leisure Interests: Reading; walking; the countryside; soccer

Loft, Paul
Managing Director, Homebase Ltd

Logue, Anne (Miss)
Customer Service Manager, Royal Doulton Plc

Loizou, Rina
Merchandise Director, Kookai

Long, Chris (Mr)
Finance Director, Lakeland Limited
Tel: 01539 440709   **Fax:** 01539 488200
Personal Email: chris.long@lakelandlimited.co.uk
DOB: 19/01/52

Long, Ian (Mr)
Merchandising & Logistics Manager, A Jones & Sons Ltd

Long, Jon (Mr)
Director of Property, PRG Powerhouse Retail Ltd

Long, Martin (Mr)
Chairman, Game Stores Group Ltd

Longdon, Steve (Mr)
Business Unit Director, Womenswear, Marks & Spencer Plc

Lord, Hugo (Mr)
Director, Specsavers Optical Group

Loring, Philip (Mr)
Business Planning Director, Thresher Group

Should you be in this directory? See the form at the back for new entries and amendments

69

Lovell, David (Mr)
Non-Executive Deputy Chairman, Stylo Plc

Lovelock, Derek (Mr)
Chief Executive, Oasis Stores Plc
Tel: 020 7452 1024
DOB: 01/01/50
Marital Status: Married

Lovering, John (Mr)
Chairman, The Peacock Group Plc

Lowbridge, David (Mr)
Managing Director, Country Casuals and Austin Reed, Austin Reed Group Plc
Tel: 020 7416 4761　　**Fax:** 020 7287 4184
Personal Email:
david.lowbridge@countrycasuals.co.uk

Lowden, Robert (Mr)
Buying and Merchandising Director, Brantano UK Ltd

Lowe, Tim (Mr)
Buying and Merchandising Director, The Officers Club Ltd

Lustman, Meg (Ms)
New Business Director, Oasis Stores Plc

Lymath, Mike (Mr)
Human Resources Director, HMV Group Plc

Lynch, Tom (Mr)
Retail Operations Director, Schuh Ltd

Lynn, Brian (Mr)
Chief Executive, Time Group Ltd

Lyons, Joe (Mr)
Marketing Director, UK, The Body Shop International Plc

Macari, Gilian (Ms)
Marketing Manager, Schuh Ltd

Macario, Anna (Ms)
Director of Marketing, Game Stores Group Ltd
Tel: 01344 464000　　**Fax:** 01344 464007

Macaskill, Bridget (Ms)
Non-Executive Director, J Sainsbury Plc

MacDonald, Gordon (Mr)
Chief Operating Officer, MFI Furniture Centres Limited
Tel: 020 8913 5345　　**Fax:** 020 8913 5388
Personal Email: gordon.macdonald@mfi.co.uk

Mackay, F (Mr)
Development Director, Morning, Noon & Night

Mackay, Francis (Mr)
Chairman, Kingfisher Plc

Mackenzie, Andrew (Mr)
Group Chief Executive, Jaeger Ltd

Mackness, Sue (Ms)
Human Resources Director, Adams Childrenswear

MacLaurin of Knebworth, (Lord)
Chairman, Vodafone Ltd

Macloud-Smith, Amanda (Ms)
Sales and Operations Director, Country Casuals, Austin Reed Group Plc

MacNab, Peter (Mr)
Commercial Director, Savers Health & Beauty Plc

Macritchie, Ian (Mr)
Chairman, Birthdays Group Ltd

Maddox, Chris (Mr)
Managing Director, Remainders Ltd

Magowan, Trisha (Ms)
Brand Director, Evans, Arcadia Group Ltd

Makepiece, John (Mr)
General Manager, National Co-operative Chemists Ltd

Maker, Vicky (Ms)
Customer Services Manager, Moss Bros Group Plc

Makin, David (Mr)
Buying and Merchandising Director, John David Group Plc
DOB: 1965

Malcolm, Simon (Mr)
Head of E-Marketing: Grattan Plc; Freemans Plc

Mallinson, Peter (Mr)
Chief Executive, Multiyork Furniture Ltd
Fax: 01842 751378
DOB: 25/04/56
Marital Status: Married
Personal Leisure Interests: Football; golf; rugby

Maloney, Vince (Mr)
Operations Director, Budgens Stores Ltd

Mardon, Crispin (Mr)
Managing Director, Kurt Geiger
Tel: 020 7546 1763　　**Fax:** 020 7546 1760
Personal Email: crispin.mardon@kurtgeiger.co.uk
DOB: 21/07/59
Marital Status: Married with two children

Should you be in this directory? See the form at the back for new entries and amendments

Quals/Educ: BA Hons Business Studies at University of Hertfordshire

Employment History:
Finance Director at Mexx UK Ltd (1990–92); Vice-President, Marketing and Business Development at DFS Ltd (1992–95); Retail Marketing Director at Shoe Express (1996); Finance and Operations Director at Conran Collection (1997–99); Finance and Property Director at Kurt Geiger (2000–03); Managing Director at Kurt Geiger (2003–)

Memberships:
Institute of Chartered Accountants in England and Wales

Personal Leisure Interests: Fitness; family; football

Marie, Steve (Mr)
Property Director, Le Riches Stores Limited

Marinker, Simon (Mr)
Property Director, W H Smith Retail Ltd

Markham, David (Mr)
Financial Controller, Shoefayre Ltd

Marks, Stephen (Mr)
Chief Executive, French Connection

Marriott, J (Ms)
Human Resources Director, TK Maxx

Marshall, Catriona (Ms)
Trading Director, Pets at Home Ltd

Martin, Chris (Mr)
Chief Executive, Mothercare Plc
DOB: 1962

Martin, Geoff (Mr)
Finance Director, Royal Doulton Plc

Martin, J (Mr)
Chairman, Ethel Austin Ltd

Martin, Jim (Mr)
Financial Director, N Brown

Martin, Karl (Mr)
Buying Director, The Big Food Group Plc

Martin, Leigh
Trading Director, Homebase Ltd

Martin, Peter (Mr)
Group Director, Human Resources, J H Leeke & Sons Ltd

Martin, Steven
IT Director, Church & Co. Footwear Ltd

Martindale, Kirsty (Ms)
National Sales Manager, Tulchan Group

Marwood, Joey (Mr)
Managing Director, Spar (UK) Limited

Mason, Neil (Mr)
Finance Director, Stationery Box Holdings Ltd

Mason, Tim (Mr)
Marketing and E-Commerce Director, Tesco Stores Ltd

Mason, Tony (Mr)
Trading Director, Majestic Wine Warehouses Ltd

Massey, Jon (Mr)
Chief Operating Officer, DFS Furniture Company plc
DOB: 22/02/49

Mather, Nick (Mr)
Finance Director, Liberty
Fax: 020 7399 7001
DOB: 07/06/58

Matheson, Marie (Ms)
Human Resources Director, ScS Upholstery Plc

Matthews, Roger (Mr)
Group Finance Director, J Sainsbury Plc

Maxwell, Jeremy (Mr)
Director of Strategy, Kingfisher Plc

May, Andrew (Mr)
Finance Director, Monsoon Accessorize Ltd
Tel: 020 8601 4046   **Fax:** 020 8601 4050
Personal Email: amay@monsoon.co.uk
DOB: 26/07/50
Marital Status: Married
Memberships:
Institute of Chartered Accountants; Member of the MCC, DHO, Member of Richmond RFC; Member of Riverside Tennis Club; Member of the RTC
Personal Leisure Interests: All country pursuits; tennis; golf; watching rugby; cricket; skiing; breeding horses

May, Joy (Ms)
Human Resources Director, Remainders Ltd

Mayes, Kieron (Mr)
Format Director, Somerfield Stores Ltd

Mayfield, Charlie (Mr)
Development Director, John Lewis Plc

Mayhew, Luke (Mr)
Managing Director, John Lewis Plc

Should you be in this directory? See the form at the back for new entries and amendments

Mayor, Robert (Mr)
Joint Managing Director, Bargain Booze Limited

McAdam, James (Mr)
Chairman, Signet Group Plc
DOB: 10/12/30
Awards: CBE
Personal Leisure Interests: Theatre; gardening

McAulay, Janet (Ms)
Publications Catalogue Director, Grattan Plc

McCafferty, Mark (Mr)
Non-Executive Director, HMV Group Plc

McCann, Jane
Retail Operations Director, Church & Co.
Footwear Ltd

McCann, Tony (Mr)
Senior Non-Executive Director, ScS Upholstery Plc

McCarthy, Don (Mr)
Chairman and Chief Executive Officer, Shoe
Studio Group Ltd

McCaskey, Ian (Mr)
IT and Customer Services Manager, QS Plc

McClymont, Sally (Ms)
Retail Operations Director, Principles, Rubicon

McComas, Jill (Ms)
Marketing Director, Somerfield Stores Ltd

McDonald, Andrew (Mr)
Marketing and Retail Director, Bon Marché Ltd

McDonald, Chris (Mr)
Retail Operations Director, American Golf
Discount Centre Ltd

McFarland, Roy (Mr)
Finance Director, Bodycare (Health & Beauty)
Limited

McGarvie, Murray (Mr)
Chief Finance Officer, Fraser Hart Ltd

McGeoch, Iain (Mr)
Managing Director, Mackays Stores Ltd

McGeorge, Alastair (Mr)
Group Chief Executive, Littlewoods Stores Ltd

McGettigan, Eoin (Mr)
Chairman, Budgens Stores Ltd

McGinlay, Steve (Mr)
Director of Supply Chain and Technology, Marks
& Spencer Plc

McGlade, David (Mr)
Managing Director, O2

McGlenn, Sarah (Ms)
New Channels Finance Director, Thresher Group
Personal Email: sarah.mcglenn@firstquench.co.uk

McGonigle, Jim (Mr)
Retail Director, AJT Trading Ltd

McIntyre, Kay (Ms)
Buying Director, Select Retail Plc

McKee, Leo (Mr)
Chief Executive, Ponden Mill Ltd

McKenna, Charles (Mr)
Sales Director, Slater Menswear

McKenna, Judith (Ms)
Chief Financial Officer, Asda Stores Ltd

McKimmie, Matthew Richard (Mr)
Financial Director, Mackays Stores Ltd
Personal Email: mmckimmie@macaysstores.co.uk
Quals/Educ: BAcc Accountancy at Glasgow
University (1974–77); Chartered Accountancy at
Institute of Chartered Accountants (1977–80)
Additional Directorships:
William McIvory Swindon Ltd; Laroque Ltd; Mackays
Financial Services Ltd; Mackays Group Trustees Ltd
Memberships:
Institute of Chartered Accountants in Scotland
Personal Leisure Interests: Golf; football

McLaughan, Roger (Mr)
Sales and Marketing Director, Barratts, Stylo Plc

McLaughlin, Brian (Mr)
Chief Operating Officer, HMV Media, HMV Group
Plc
DOB: 1949

McLaughlin, Brian (Mr)
Chairman and Managing Director, Waterstone's
Booksellers Ltd

McLaughlin, Graham (Mr)
Head of Finance, T J Morris Ltd

McLean, Donna (Ms)
Operations Manager, Jacques Vert Plc

Mcleod, Ian (Mr)
Director of Trading, Halfords Limited

McLernon, Ian (Mr)
Marketing Director, Unwins Wine Group Ltd

Should you be in this directory? See the form at the back for new entries and amendments

McMahon, Mick (Mr)
Retail Director, Shell Retail UK

McManus, Jim (Mr)
Property Director, MFI Furniture Centres Limited

McMenemy, Mark (Mr)
High Street Finance Director, W H Smith Retail Ltd

McPhail, Carl (Mr)
Group Operations Director, New Look Retailers
Ltd

McRae, Heather (Ms)
Finance Director, Alpha Retail

McReady, Willy (Mr)
Property Director, Farmfoods Freezer Centre

Megson, Angela (Ms)
Buying Director, Waitrose Ltd

Melnyk, Marie (Ms)
Joint Managing Director, Wm Morrison
Supermarkets Plc
Tel: 01924 875282 **Fax:** 01924 875220
DOB: 10/06/58

Melton, S
Supply Chain Director, Argos Ltd

Melville, Margaret (Ms)
Buying Director, Brown & Jackson

Memory, David (Mr)
Financial Director, Tie Rack Ltd

Merry, Sue (Mrs)
Customer Service Manager, Shoefayre Ltd

Metcalf, Harry (Mr)
Commercial Manager, Blackwell's UK

Metcalfe, Amanda (Ms)
Head of Customer Management, Debenhams Plc

Metson, Stephanie (Ms)
Marketing Manager, J H Leeke & Sons Ltd

Middleditch, Morton (Mr)
Chairman, Spar (UK) Limited

Middleton, Pam (Mrs)
Customer Services Manager, ScS Upholstery Plc

Miekle, Alexander (Mr)
Finance Director, G 101 Off Sales Ltd

Miles, Chris (Mr)
Retail Director, The Peacock Group Plc

Miles, Lesley (Ms)
Marketing Director, Waterstone's Booksellers Ltd

Millar, Richard (Mr)
Head of Marketing and UK Retailing, Habitat UK
Limited
DOB: 18/08/65
Memberships:
RSA

Miller, Alaistair (Mr)
Finance Director, New Look Retailers Ltd

Miller, Andrew Douglas (Mr)
Deputy Chairman and Development Director,
Jenners Limited
Tel: 0131 260 2324 **Fax:** 0131 226 1549
Personal Email: adm@jenners.com
DOB: 29/09/63
Marital Status: Married
Personal Leisure Interests: Fishing

Miller, Deborah (Ms)
UK Franchise Manager, Levi Strauss (UK) Ltd

Miller, James R (Mr)
Marketing Director, Miller Brothers Group Ltd

Miller, Jim N (Mr)
Chairman and Joint Managing Director, Miller
Brothers Group Ltd

Miller, Jonathan (Mr)
Finance Director, TM Retail Ltd

Miller, Peter (Mr)
Group Trading Director, Spar (UK) Limited

Miller, Robert (Mr)
Joint Managing Director, Miller Brothers Group Ltd

Miller, Robert Douglas (Mr)
Chairman, Jenners Limited

Miller, Simon J (Mr)
Director, Miller Brothers Group Ltd

Milling, Judith
Managing Director, Shellys Shoes Ltd

Mills, Dave (Mr)
Head of IT, Allied Carpets Group

Milner, Zoe (Ms)
Trade Marketing Manager, Bon Marché Ltd

Milton, David (Mr)
Finance Director, Internacionale Limited

Should you be in this directory? See the form at the back for new entries and amendments

73

Milward, Phil (Mr)
Business Development Director, Stead & Simpson

Mitchell, C
Director, Morning, Noon & Night

Mitchell, Stuart (Mr)
Managing Director of Sainsburys Supermarkets Ltd, J Sainsbury Plc

Mitchensen, Pat (Ms)
Marketing Director, Timberland UK Ltd

Mohammed, Tariq (Dr)
Marketing Director, Time Group Ltd

Mohsan, Tahir (Mr)
Managing Director, Time Group Ltd

Molle, Andrew (Mr)
Marketing Director, Specsavers Optical Group

Monk, Andy (Mr)
IT Director, Somerfield Stores Ltd

Montgomery, David (Mr)
Merchandising Manager, Fashion and Household, Joplings Ltd

Montgomery, Linda (Ms)
Retail Manager, Thermawear Limited (t/a Damart)

Moody, N (Mr)
Customer Services Manager, Fortnum & Mason Plc

Moody-Stewart, Mark (Sir)
Chairman, Shell Retail UK

Moore, Tessa (Ms)
Vice-President of Marketing, Disney Consumer Products

Moorhead, Robert (Mr)
Finance Director, Specsavers Optical Group

Morgan, Lisa (Ms)
Commercial Director, Game Stores Group Ltd

Morgan, Martin (Mr)
Deputy Chairman, Tie Rack Ltd
DOB: 23/04/54

Morgan, Robert (Mr)
Chairman, G T Retail

Morley, Octavia (Ms)
Marketing Director, Woolworths Plc

Morrice, I (Mr)
Managing Director, Warehouses, B & Q Plc

Morris, Andrew (Mr)
Customer Service Manager, Jaeger Ltd

Morris, Barry (Mr)
Non-Executive Director, Stylo Plc
Tel: 020 7268 8450   **Fax:** 020 7268 2106
DOB: 20/06/47
Marital Status: Married
Memberships:
Chairman of British-Israel Chamber of Commerce
Personal Leisure Interests: Golf; tennis; motor racing; cinema; theatre

Morris, J (Mr)
E-Commerce and Marketing Director, T J Morris Ltd

Morris, Tom (Mr)
Managing Director, T J Morris Ltd

Morrison, Angus (Mr)
Managing Director, USC Group Plc

Morrison, Ken (Sir)
Chairman, Wm Morrison Supermarkets Plc
Fax: 01274 494831
DOB: 1931
Marital Status: Married with three daughters and one son
Awards: Honorary Degree from the University of Bradford (1988); CBE for Services to Retailing (1990); Knighted (2000)
Personal Leisure Interests: Horticulturalist; agriculture; outdoor sport; walking

Morrison, Mike (Mr)
Marketing Director, Brown & Jackson

Morriss, David (Mr)
Head of Property, Comet Group Plc
Tel: 01482 592062   **Fax:** 01482 592388
Personal Email: david.morriss@comet.co.uk
Marital Status: Married with two children
Quals/Educ: BSc at Portsmouth Polytechnic (1981–84); MRICS at Royal Institution of Chartered Surveyors (1986)
Employment History:
Portfolio Manager at Abbey Life Investment Services (1984–89); Development Manager at B&Q Plc (1989–91); Development Manager at Comet Group Plc (1991–97); Head of Property at Comet Group Plc (1997–)
Personal Leisure Interests: Squash; skiing; football

Morton, Clive (Mr)
Finance Director, Harvey Nichols Group Plc

Should you be in this directory? See the form at the back for new entries and amendments

74

Morton, Paul (Mr)
Sales Director, Apollo 2000 Ltd

Moss, Chris (Mr)
Finance Director, Notcutts Nurseries

Mountford, Cheryl (Miss)
Operations Manager, Stationery Box Holdings Ltd

Mountford, Philip (Mr)
Group Trading Director, Moss Bros Group Plc

Mousell, John (Mr)
Managing Director, Motorworld Ltd

Moxam, Graham (Mr)
Finance Director, QD Stores Ltd

Muller, Mark (Mr)
Finance Director, Courts Plc

Munro, Gordon (Mr)
Retail Marketing Director, Esso Petroleum Co. Ltd

Murfin, Stephen (Mr)
Finance Director and Company Secretary,
Wyevale Garden Centres Plc

Murphy, Gerry M (Mr)
Chief Executive Officer, Kingfisher Plc
Tel: 020 7644 1038   **Fax:** 020 7644 1244
Quals/Educ: BSc Food Science at University College
Cork (1972–76); PhD Food Technology at University
College Cork (1976–80); MBS Marketing at
University College Dublin (1981–83)
Employment History:
Chief Executive Officer at Greencore Group Plc
(1991–95); Chief Executive Officer at Exel Plc
(1995–2000); Chief Executive Officer at Carlton
Communications Plc (2000–03); Chief Executive
Officer at Kingfisher Plc (2003–)
Additional Directorships:
Noval Plc
Memberships:
Institute of Directors; Chartered Management Institute

Murray, Dean (Mr)
Chief Operating Officer, Adams Childrenswear
DOB: 17/11/62
Marital Status: Married with two children
Personal Leisure Interests: Rugby; motorcycling;
golf; horse riding

Murray, Roddy (Mr)
Financial Director, Moss Bros Group Plc

Murray, Susan (Ms)
Acting Managing Director, Littlewoods Stores,
Littlewoods Stores Ltd

Muzika, Frank (Mr)
Finance, Admin and Logistics Director, Toys R Us
Limited
Tel: 01628 414616   **Fax:** 01628 414093
DOB: 24/11/54
Marital Status: Married
Memberships:
ACA

Myatt, Sue (Ms)
Retail Marketing Director, Next Plc

Myers, Dominic (Mr)
Managing Director, Blackwell's UK
Tel: 01865 333115   **Fax:** 01865 333991
Personal Email: dominic.myers@blackwell.co.uk
DOB: 13/08/62
Quals/Educ: MA Hons at Wadham College, Oxford
University (1981–84)
Employment History:
Head of Marketing at Somerfield (1993–98);
Managing Director at Hasbro Interactive International
(1999–2001)

Mylum, Gary (Mr)
Group Director of Marketing, Royal Doulton Plc

Myners, Paul (Mr)
Non-Executive Director, Marks & Spencer Plc
Employment History:
Non-Executive Director at Marks & Spencer Plc
(2002–)
Additional Directorships:
Chairman of Aspen Insurance Holdings Ltd;
Chairman of Guardian Media Group Plc; Non-
Executive Director of the Bank of New York; Non-
Executive Director of mmO2
Memberships:
Financial Reporting Council; Trustee of the Tate;
Trustee of Glyndebourne

Nairn, Iain (Mr)
Retail Operations Director, Laura Ashley
Tel: 020 7880 5201   **Fax:** 020 7880 5595
Marital Status: Married

Naismith, Roy (Mr)
Finance Director, French Connection

Nardini, Gordon (Mr)
Head of Retail Marketing, Carphone Warehouse Plc

Nash, C (Mr)
Non-Executive Director, Stokes Plc

Naskey, M J (Mr)
Non-Executive Director, Robert Dyas Holdings Ltd

Should you be in this directory? See the form at the back for new entries and amendments

Navarednam, Rebecca (Ms)
Joint Chief Executive, Laura Ashley

Naylor, Graham (Mr)
Retail Director, Superdrug Stores

Naylor, Lawrence (Mr)
Purchasing Director, Domestic Appliances,
Bennetts Retail Ltd

Neil, Michael (Mr)
Marketing Director, Blackwell's UK

Neilly, Brian (Mr)
Finance Director, Land of Leather

Nelson, John (Mr)
Deputy Chairman, Kingfisher Plc

Nelson, Michael (Mr)
Finance Director, Bally UK Sales Ltd
Tel: 020 8747 1606   **Fax:** 020 8742 7822
DOB: 15/10/40
Marital Status: Married
Personal Leisure Interests: Film; theatre; skiing;
swimming; tennis

Nelson, Stephen (Mr)
Trading Director, J Sainsbury Plc

Netherton, Derek (Mr)
Director, Greggs Plc
DOB: 11/04/45

Nevitt, Sean (Mr)
Purchasing Director, Sports World International Ltd

Newlands, David
Chairman, KESA Electricals Plc

Newman, Richard (Mr)
Director of Retail Operations, C & J Clark
International

Newnham, Mike (Mr)
UK Group Finance Director, Orange Plc

Newton, Philip (Mr)
Chief Executive, Merchant Retail Group Plc
DOB: 01/02/49
Marital Status: Divorced
Personal Leisure Interests: Horse racing and
breeding

Nicholson, Brian (Mr)
Finance Director, Beaverbrooks the Jewellers Ltd

Nicholson, Deryck (Mr)
Executive Chairman, Shoprite Group Plc

Nicholson, Ian (Mr)
Managing Director, Shoprite Group Plc

Nicholson, Kevin (Mr)
Head of Finance, Carpetright Plc

Nicoli, Eric (Mr)
Chairman, HMV Group Plc

Nightingale, Robert (Mr)
Customer Services Manager, Broughton Brothers
Ltd

Nolan, Jacki (Ms)
Retail Director, Oasis Stores Plc

Nordahl, Jens (Mr)
Managing Director, Habitat UK Limited

Norgrove, David R (Mr)
Director, Clothing, Outlets and International,
Marks & Spencer Plc
Employment History:
Director at Marks & Spencer Plc (2000–)
Additional Directorships:
Governor of the National Institute of Economic and
Social Research Inc; Non-Executive Director of the
Strategic Rail Authority

Norris, Terry (Mr)
Chairman, Remainders Ltd

North, Andrew (Mr)
UK Customer Service Manager, IKEA Ltd

Northover, Malcolm (Mr)
Chief Financial Officer, Globus Office World Plc

Norton, Damian (Mr)
Information Systems Director, DSG Retail Ltd

Norton, Tony (Mr)
Managing Director, American Golf Discount Centre
Ltd

Notcutt, Charles (Mr)
Chairman, Notcutts Nurseries

Notcutt, William (Mr)
Group Managing Director, Notcutts Nurseries

Nuesser, Bernard (Mr)
Marketing Director, Vision Express UK Ltd

Nurse, Paul (Mr)
Director General, Cancer Research UK

Nutbeen, Wayne (Mr)
Chief Executive, Royal Doulton Plc

Should you be in this directory? See the form at the back for new entries and amendments

76

O'Connor, Sharon (Ms)
Merchandising Director, Oasis Stores Plc

O'Donahue, Breege (Ms)
Personnel and Advertising Director, Primark

O'Hara, John (Mr)
IT Director, Mackays Stores Ltd

O'Neill, Cathy (Ms)
Personnel Administration and Services Director,
Fortnum & Mason Plc
DOB: 17/01/62
Marital Status: Divorced

O'Neill, Paul (Mr)
Retail Director, Faith Footwear
Fax: 020 8930 3476
DOB: 18/05/63
Marital Status: Married

O'Reilly, Dave (Mr)
Chairman and Chief Executive Officer, Chevron
Texaco

O'Reilly, David (Mr)
Marketing Director, Maplin Electronics Ltd

O'Reilly, Tony (Mr)
Chief Executive Officer, Waterford Wedgwood
Retail Ltd

O'Rourke, Richard (Mr)
European Managing Director, Timberland UK Ltd

O'Sullivan, Alana (Ms)
Corporate Communications, Comet Group Plc

O'Sullivan, Rita (Ms)
Retail Operations Director, Kookai

Oakes, Martin (Mr)
**Director, Logistics and New Business
Development**, Somerfield Stores Ltd

Oakley, Graham (Mr)
**Group Secretary and Head of Corporate
Governance**, Marks & Spencer Plc
Employment History:
Head of Legal Department at Marks & Spencer Plc
(1990–97); Company Secretary at Marks & Spencer
Plc (1997–); Head of Corporate Governance at Marks
& Spencer Plc (2002–)

Ogden, Ian (Mr)
Retail Director, Claire's Accessories

Oliver, Clare (Ms)
Marketing Manager, Edinburgh Woollen Mill Ltd

Oliver, Michael (Mr)
Company Secretary, Boots Group Plc

Ordman, David (Mr)
Managing Director, Morley's Stores Ltd

Ormsby, David (Mr)
Managing Director, Walmsley Furnishing Plc

Orton, Tim J (Mr)
Company Secretary, Shoefayre Ltd

Osborn, John (Mr)
Chief Executive Officer, Alexon Group Plc

Osbourne, Alan (Mr)
Retail Operations Director, New Look Retailers Ltd

Osmond, Mike (Mr)
Retail Director, Kwik Save, Somerfield Stores Ltd
Tel: 0117 935 6103

Otto, Michael (Dr)
Chairman, Grattan Plc

Ouellette, Jean-Louis (Mr)
Finance and Operations Director, IKEA Ltd
Personal Email: ouel@memo.ikea.com
Quals/Educ: BAA Finance and Administration at
University of Sherbrooke in Canada (1984);
Chartered Accountant at Canadian Institute of
Chartered Accountants (1986); Management
Accountant at Canadian Corporation of Certified
Management Accountants (1986)
Employment History:
Finance and Administration Manager at IKEA Ltd
Canada (1988–91); Finance and Administration
Manager at IKEA Distribution France (1991–93);
Managing Director at IKEA Distribution France
(1993–94); Finance and Operations Director at IKEA
Ltd (UK) (1994–)

Oughtred, Chris (Mr)
Chairman and Joint Managing Director, William
Jackson & Son Ltd

Ounstead, Nick (Mr)
Chief Executive, Topps Tiles Plc

Owen, Roger (Mr)
Property Director, Wm Morrison Supermarkets Plc
DOB: 21/10/48
Marital Status: Married
Memberships:
FRICS
Personal Leisure Interests: Sport; gardening

Owrid, Tim (Mr)
Head of Distribution Operations, Woolworths Plc

Should you be in this directory? See the form at the back for new entries and amendments

77

Owst, Ken (Mr)
Finance Director, J E Beale Plc

Oxley, Karen (Miss)
Customer Services Manager, The Stationers Ltd

Pacey, Keith (Mr)
Chairman, Maplin Electronics Ltd

Padovan, John (Mr)
Non-Executive Director, Findel Plc
DOB: 07/05/38
Memberships:
Council Member of the City and Guilds London
School of Art
Personal Leisure Interests: Walking; sailing; golf

Page, Neil (Mr)
Financial Director, Superdrug Stores

Page, Tony (Mr)
Director, General Merchandise, Asda Stores Ltd

Paine, Nick (Mr)
Managing Director, Etam Plc
DOB: 15/10/60

Palethorpe, Simon (Mr)
Managing Director, John Lewis Direct, John Lewis
Plc

Palmer, Jeremy (Mr)
E-Commerce Director, Majestic Wine Warehouses
Ltd

Palmer, Nigel (Mr)
Retail Operations Director, Debenhams Plc

Panizzo, Paolo (Mr)
Managing Consultant, Benetton Retail 1988 Ltd

Pannell, Anthony (Mr)
Finance Director, A F Blakemore & Son Ltd

Paphitis, Theo (Mr)
Chairman, La Senza

Parkash, Dolly (Ms)
General Merchandiser, MK One

Parker, Andrew (Mr)
Property Director, Redcats UK (Brands) Ltd

Parker, Ian (Mr)
Finance Director, Hamleys Plc

Parker, Neil (Mr)
Head of Retail, Pilot Clothing

Parr, Roger (Mr)
Merchandise Director, Stead & Simpson

Parsons, Rick (Mr)
Operations Director, Thermawear Limited (t/a
Damart)

Pascoe, Eva (Ms)
Joint Managing Director, Zoom, Arcadia Group
Ltd

Patel, Jitu M (Mr)
Managing Director, Adminstore Ltd

Paterson, Jack (Ms)
Business Unit Director, Beauty and Lingerie,
Marks & Spencer Plc

Payne, David (Mr)
Brand Retail Operations Director, Alexon Group
Plc

Peace, John
Chief Executive, GUS

Peach, Steve (Mr)
Purchasing Director, Motorworld Ltd

Peacock, Ian (Mr)
Chairman, Mothercare Plc
DOB: 01/01/36

Pearce, Dominic (Mr)
Company Secretary, Miller Brothers Group Ltd

Pearson, David (Mr)
Group Commercial Director, Focus Wickes
DOB: 28/07/31

Peckham, Nigel (Mr)
Retail and Operations Director, Poundland Ltd

Peddar, Chris (Mr)
Managing Director, Furnitureland Holdings Ltd

Pedder, Roger A (Mr)
Chairman, C & J Clark International
Tel: 01458 842626　　**Fax:** 01458 446569
Personal Email: roger.pedder@clarks.com
DOB: 27/02/41
Marital Status: Married with five children
Memberships:
Reform Club
Personal Leisure Interests: Travel; wine growing

Pedder, Roger A (Mr)
Non-Executive Chairman, Robert Dyas Holdings
Ltd
Tel: 01458 842626　　**Fax:** 01458 446569
Personal Email: roger.pedder@clarks.com
DOB: 27/02/41
Marital Status: Married with five children

Should you be in this directory? See the form at the back for new entries and amendments

78

Memberships:
Reform Club
Personal Leisure Interests: Travel, wine growing

Penny, Dean (Mr)
Customer Service Manager, TK Maxx

Percival, Richard (Mr)
Director, John David Group Plc

Perkins, Doug (Mr)
Managing Director, Specsavers Optical Group

Perks, Jane
Retail Operations Director, UK, Etam Plc

Perryman, Julian (Mr)
Controller of E-Commerce, Allders Department
Stores Limited

Persson, Stefan (Mr)
Chairman, Hennes & Mauritz

Philipou, Panicko (Mr)
Managing Director, Diesel

Philips, Tim (Mr)
Marketing Manager, Trago Mills

Phillips, Doug W (Mr)
Property Manager, Thorntons Plc

Phillips, Malcolm (Mr)
Planning and Development Director, James Beattie
PLC

Phillips, Peter (Mr)
Chairman, A Jones & Sons Ltd

Philpott, Robin (Mr)
Merchandise and Distribution Director,
Goldsmiths Group Plc
DOB: 08/02/64
Marital Status: Married with one child
Quals/Educ: ACMA
Memberships:
Chartered Institute of Management Accountants
Personal Leisure Interests: Golf; rugby union

Piasecki, Jurek (Mr)
Chairman and Chief Executive, Goldsmiths Group
Plc
DOB: 18/05/46
Marital Status: Married with two children
Personal Leisure Interests: Tennis; golf

Pidgeon, David (Mr)
Managing Director, Bon Marché Ltd

Pieri, Paolo (Mr)
Financial Director, Virgin Retail Group Limited

Piggot, Robin (Mr)
Finance Director, Alexon Group Plc

Pilgrim, Colin (Mr)
Chief Executive Officer, Heal's Plc
DOB: 1948

Pilgrim, Richard (Mr)
Director of Operations, North, Cash Converters
UK Ltd

Pilling, Chris (Mr)
Marketing Director, Asda Stores Ltd

Pinnington, Lee (Mr)
Head of Home Shopping, The Big Food Group Plc

Pirie, George (Mr)
Operations Director, Morning, Noon & Night

Pitcher, Anne (Ms)
Director, Womenswear, Harvey Nichols Group Plc

Pleasance, Andrew (Mr)
Head of Home and Leisure, Wm Morrison
Supermarkets Plc

Pleeth, Christopher (Mr)
Property Director, C & J Clark International
Tel: 01458 842003   **Fax:** 01458 448320
Personal Email: chris.pleeth@clarks.com
DOB: 20/10/60
Marital Status: Married
Memberships:
Royal Institution of Chartered Surveyors; British
Retail Consortium; British Council of Shopping
Centres; Property Managers Association
Personal Leisure Interests: Family; golf; tennis;
sailing; skiing; football; travel

Pogrund, David (Mr)
IT Director, Waterstone's Booksellers Ltd

Pogson, Charlie (Mr)
Head of Marketing, Bon Marché Ltd

Pomphret, Steve (Mr)
Strategic Development Director, Mothercare Plc

Pontin, Roger (Mr)
Managing Director, Select Retail Plc

Poole, Martin (Mr)
Finance Director, Shoprite Group Plc

Poon, Dickson (Mr)
Chairman, Harvey Nichols Group Plc

Should you be in this directory? See the form at the back for new entries and amendments

79

Porte, Alan (Mr)
Distribution Director, TK Maxx

Porteous, Adrian (Mr)
Merchandising Director, Matalan plc

Porter, Colin (Mr)
Supply Chain Director, House of Fraser Plc

Possamai, Paul (Mr)
Managing Director of Alpha Inflight Retail, Alpha Retail
DOB: 1947

Potter, Melissa (Ms)
Managing Director, UK Division, C & J Clark International

Potts, David (Mr)
Retail Director, Tesco Stores Ltd

Pow, James (Mr)
Chairman and Chief Executive Officer, Tulchan Group
DOB: 01/02/51

Powell, Heather (Ms)
Head of Store Design and Development, Arcadia Group Ltd

Powell, William (Mr)
Property Director, Courts Plc
Fax: 020 8410 9465
Personal Email: bpowell@courts.plc.uk
DOB: 02/05/51
Marital Status: Married

Powers-Freeling, Laurel (Ms)
Director and Chief Executive of Financial Services, Marks & Spencer Plc
Employment History:
Director at Marks & Spencer Plc (2001–)
Additional Directorships:
Non-Executive Director of the Bank of England

Prendergast, Dominic (Mr)
Retail Director, Thorntons Plc

Pressler, Paul (Mr)
Chief Executive, Gap

Preston, Anthony (Mr)
Chairman, Pets at Home Ltd

Price, David (Mr)
Non-Executive Director, The Big Food Group Plc

Price, Glyn J (Mr)
Group Buying Director, Wyevale Garden Centres Plc

Price, Mark (Mr)
Marketing Director, Waitrose Ltd

Prosser, Andrew (Mr)
Finance Director, Moss Pharmacy Ltd

Pryer, Mark (Mr)
Managing Director and Marketing Director, Carpetworld Manchester Ltd

Pryor, Patrick (Mr)
Financial Director, Primark

Pudney, Bill (Mr)
Operations Director, Signet Group Plc

Pugh, Martin (Mr)
Marketing Director, Safeway Plc

Pye, James (Mr)
Property Director, Budgens Stores Ltd

Pynor, Liz (Ms)
Retail Director, French Connection

Pyper, Simon (Mr)
Finance Director, Budgens Stores Ltd

Quiney, Pat (Mr)
Property Director, Brown & Jackson

Quinlan, Michael (Mr)
Finance Director, Lyndale Foods Ltd

Racionzer, Terry (Mr)
Chairman, Schuh Ltd
Personal Email: terry@schuh.co.uk

Radice, Vittorio (Mr)
Director, Home, Marks & Spencer Plc
Employment History:
Managing Director and Chief Executive at Selfridges (1998–2003); Director of Home at Marks & Spencer Plc (2003–)
Additional Directorships:
Non-Executive Director of Abbey National Plc; Non-Executive Director of Shoppers Stop India

Rahamin, Michael (Mr)
Managing Director, Kookai

Rand, Stewart A (Mr)
Sales and Marketing Director, Robert Dyas Holdings Ltd

Randall, Andy (Mr)
Managing Director, Staples UK Ltd

Rasul, Maqbool H (Mr)
Managing Director, Global Video Ltd

Should you be in this directory? See the form at the back for new entries and amendments

Rasul, Z (Mr)
Director, Global Video Ltd

Rathbone, Tim (Mr)
Merchandise Director, J E Beale Plc

Rattenbury, Paul (Mr)
Head of Retail, Central UK, Allders Department Stores Limited

Rayner, Julian (Mr)
Marketing Director, Lakeland Limited

Rayner, Martin (Mr)
Purchasing Director, Lakeland Limited

Rayner, Patrick (Mr)
Property Manager, Kookai

Rayner, Sam (Mr)
Managing Director, Lakeland Limited

Read, Jan (Miss)
Customer Services Manager, Furnitureland Holdings Ltd

Reavley, Martin
Finance Director, KESA Electricals Plc

Reddish, Gillian (Mrs)
Communications Manager, Wilkinson Hardware Stores Limited

Reed, Alison (Ms)
Chief Financial Officer, Marks & Spencer Plc
Employment History:
Chief Financial Officer at Marks & Spencer Plc (2001–)
Additional Directorships:
Non-Executive Director of HSBC Bank Plc; Trustee of Whizz-Kids

Reed, Sally (Ms)
Marketing Director, Notcutts Nurseries

Reeds, Stephen (Mr)
Marketing Director, Tie Rack Ltd

Rees, Karen (Ms)
Finance Director, Frozen Value Ltd

Regan, Brendon (Mr)
Marketing Manager, Russell & Bromley

Reid, David (Mr)
Deputy Chairman, Tesco Stores Ltd

Reiss, Melvyn (Mr)
Managing Director, Cromwells Madhouse

Renwick, Iain (Mr)
Chief Executive, Liberty

Revett, Clive (Mr)
Company Secretary, Mothercare Plc

Reynolds, Hugh (Mr)
Customer Liason Manager, Austin Reed Group Plc

Reynolds, Nicola (Ms)
Marketing Manager, Austin Reed Group Plc

Rice, John (Mr)
Group IT Director, Focus Wickes

Rice, Stephanie (Ms)
Marketing Director, Budgens Stores Ltd
Tel: 020 8966 6010   **Fax:** 020 8966 6093
Personal Email: stephanie.rice@budgens.com
Marital Status: Married with one son
Awards: Winner of IGD Women in Business Award (1997); winner of Winning Women Awards (1996)
Memberships:
Marketing Society

Richards, Chris (Mr)
Operations Director, Royal Doulton Plc

Richards, Tony (Mr)
Deputy Managing Director, Rosebys Ltd

Richardson, David (Mr)
Convenience Retail Manager, UK and Ireland, Esso Petroleum Co. Ltd

Richer, Julian (Mr)
Chairman, Richer Sounds Plc
DOB: 1959

Riddy, Tony (Mr)
Retail Director, Londis (Holdings) Ltd

Ridler, Peter (Mr)
Managing Director, The Body Shop International Plc

Rigby, Simon (Mr)
Chairman and Chief Executive, Northern Electric Retail

Rimmer, Barbara (Ms)
Company Secretary, Focus Wickes

Riva, Hilary (Ms)
Managing Director, Womenswear Warehouse, Rubicon

Roach, David (Mr)
Product Director, Waterstone's Booksellers Ltd

Should you be in this directory? See the form at the back for new entries and amendments

81

Roberts, Matthew (Mr)
Finance Director, Debenhams Plc
DOB: 1964

Roberts, Paul (Mr)
Head of Finance, Pilot Clothing

Robertson, Bruce (Mr)
Chairman, Trago Mills

Robertson, David (Mr)
Financial Director, Farmfoods Freezer Centre

Robertson, Tony (Mr)
Head of Department Stores, Co-operative Group
(CWS) Limited

Robins, John (Mr)
Chairman, Austin Reed Group Plc

Robinson, David (Mr)
Group Managing Director, Richer Sounds Plc
DOB: 1966
Marital Status: Married with two sons
Personal Leisure Interests: Charity organisations;
fitness; music; reading

Robinson, Deborah (Ms)
Head of Brand Management, Co-operative Group
(CWS) Limited

Robinson, John (Mr)
Operations Director, Clinton Cards

Robinson, John (Mr)
Managing Director and Chairman, Jigsaw
DOB: 22/01/46
Personal Leisure Interests: Cycling; golf

Robinson, Paul (Mr)
Director, Benetton Retail 1988 Ltd

Robinson, Robert (Mr)
Retail Operations Director, UK, Bally UK Sales Ltd

Robinson, Stephen (Mr)
Finance Director, Argos Ltd

Robson, Simon (Mr)
Director of Buying, Stylo Plc

Rockhill, Susan (Ms)
Marketing Director, Moss Pharmacy Ltd

Rodriques, Kennedy (Mr)
Financial Manager, Orange Plc

Roelofse, Hennie (Mr)
Joint Finance Director, Brown & Jackson
Tel: 0113 254 9305   **Fax:** 0113 240 6360

Personal Email: hroelofse@poundstretcher.co.uk
DOB: 10/10/52
Marital Status: Married
Memberships:
Western Cape Society of Chartered Accountants
Personal Leisure Interests: Rugby; cricket; golf

Rogers, Chris (Mr)
Finance Director, Woolworths Plc
Tel: 01923 714495   **Fax:** 01923 714655
DOB: 21/04/60
Marital Status: Married

Rogers, David (Mr)
Head of Sales and Marketing, National Co-
operative Chemists Ltd

Rogers, Julia (Mrs)
General Manger, Central Services, Co-operative
Group (CWS) Limited
Tel: 0161 246 2171   **Fax:** 0161 827 5302
Personal Email: julia.rogers@co-op.co.uk
DOB: 24/12/64
Employment History:
Commissioned Officer in the British Army (1984–92);
various positions at Woolworths (1992–98); Head of
Security at Allsports (1998); Head of Loss Prevention
at Co-operative Group (CWS) Limited (1998–2001);
General Manager of Central Services at Co-operative
Group (CWS) Limited (2001–)

Rome, Ron (Mr)
Sales Director, all:sports Retail Ltd

Rose, Paul (Mr)
Financial Director, Slater Menswear

Rose, Richard (Mr)
Chief Executive, Whittard of Chelsea Plc

Rosenblatt, Michael (Mr)
Chief Executive, Rosebys Ltd

Rosendale, Michael (Mr)
Chairman and Chief Executive, Harveys
Furnishing Group

Ross, Keith (Mr)
Financial Director, Netto Foodstores Ltd

Rosso, Renzo (Mr)
Group Chairman, Diesel

Rostron, Chris (Mr)
Finance Director, Rubicon

Round, Steven (Mr)
Commercial Director, MFI Furniture Centres
Limited

Should you be in this directory? See the form at the back for new entries and amendments

Rowe, Stuart (Mr)
E-Commerce Director, HMV Group Plc

Rowland, John P (Mr)
Company Secretary, Robert Dyas Holdings Ltd

Roy, Edward (Mr)
Finance Director, Roys (Wroxham) Ltd

Roy, Liz (Mrs)
Customer Services Manager, Bon Marché Ltd

Roy, Paul (Mr)
Merchandising Director, Roys (Wroxham) Ltd

Roy, Peter (Mr)
Chairman, Roys (Wroxham) Ltd

Royal, Kevin (Mr)
Marketing Director, ScS Upholstery Plc

Rudd, Nigel (Sir)
Chairman, Boots Group Plc

Rudge, Alan (Sir)
Non-Executive Director, GUS

Ruitinga, Gerrit
Managing Director, Kuwait Petroleum Ltd

Rurka, David (Mr)
Chairman and Managing Director, Toys R Us
Limited

Russell, Frances (Ms)
Brand Director, Burton, Arcadia Group Ltd

Russell, Hannah (Ms)
Marketing Director, Oasis Stores Plc

Ryan, Arthur (Mr)
Chairman and Managing Director, Primark

Saaid, Ainum Mohd
Joint Chief Executive, Laura Ashley

Sadd, John (Mr)
Business Development Director, Miller Brothers
Group Ltd

Sainsbury of Preston Candover KG, (Lord)
Life President, J Sainsbury Plc

Salmon, Margaret (Ms)
Non-Executive Director, Kingfisher Plc

Salt, Geoffrey (Mr)
Distribution Director, Waitrose Ltd

Salt, Vernon (Mr)
Senior Vice-President, Blockbuster Entertainment
Ltd

Fax: 01895 866334
Personal Email: vernon.salt@blockbuster.com
DOB: 22/11/58
Marital Status: Married with two children
Memberships:
Marketing Society; Chartered Institute of Marketing
Personal Leisure Interests: Family; travel; skiing

Samuel, Nick (Mr)
Chief Executive & Joint Managing Director,
Hobbs Limited

Samuel, Philip (Mr)
Managing Director, Joplings, Merchant Retail
Group Plc

Samuels, Malcolm (Mr)
Finance Director, Courts Plc

Sandbach, Malcolm (Mr)
Managing Director, Trago Mills

Sansom, Ed (Mr)
IT Director, Edinburgh Woollen Mill Ltd

Sargent, Ron (Mr)
Chief Executive, Staples UK Ltd

Sargent, Steve C (Mr)
Financial Director, Goldsmiths Group Plc

Sarin, Arun (Mr)
Chief Executive, Vodafone Ltd

Saunders, David (Mr)
Managing Director, TM Retail Ltd
DOB: 12/10/47
Marital Status: Married with one child
Personal Leisure Interests: Travel; golf

Saunders, Mark (Mr)
Merchandising Director, Brown & Jackson

Saunders, Peter (Mr)
Customer Service Manager, Russell & Bromley

Saunders, Peter (Mr)
Chief Executive, The Body Shop International Plc

Schofield-Lawley, Peter (Mr)
Commercial Director, Diesel

Schwab, Anne-Marie (Ms)
Group Marketing Manager, Habitat UK Limited

Schwarz, Jeremy (Mr)
Director of Brand Marketing, J Sainsbury Plc

Scicluna, Terry (Mr)
Operations Director, Moss Pharmacy Ltd

Should you be in this directory? See the form at the back for new entries and amendments

83

Scott, Julia (Ms)
Purchasing Director, Jessops

Scott, Tom (Mr)
Chairman, Le Riches Stores Limited

Sealey, John (Mr)
Finance Director, Choices Video

Seaman, David (Mr)
Head of Strategic Development, Co-operative
Group (CWS) Limited

Searle, G W (Mr)
Non-Executive Director, Monsoon Accessorize Ltd

Seaton, Graham (Mr)
Property Director, Matalan plc
Tel: 01695 552524   **Fax:** 01695 554399
Personal Email: seaton_g@matalan.co.uk
DOB: 30/09/56
Quals/Educ: BSc Hons Estate Management at
Reading University (1975–79)
Employment History:
Development Manager at B&Q (1986–95)

Seigal, Jeremy (Mr)
Managing Director, The Perfume Shop, Merchant
Retail Group Plc

Selby, David (Mr)
Head of Mail Order and E-Commerce, Laura
Ashley

Senior, Adam (Mr)
Head Footwear Buyer, Lloyd Shoe Co Ltd

Senior, Stuart (Mr)
IT Director, Marks & Spencer Plc

Shah, Saj (Mr)
Chief Executive, Jane Norman

Shane, Denise (Ms)
Head of Home Business Unit, Woolworths Plc

Shannon, John (Mr)
Non-Executive Chairman, Stead & Simpson

Shapland, Darren (Mr)
Finance Director, Carpetright Plc

Sharma, Sanjay (Mr)
Finance Director, Karen Millen

Sharp, Michael
Trading Director, Debenhams Plc

Sharp, Steve (Mr)
Marketing Director, Allders Department Stores
Limited

Shawe, Jan (Ms)
Director of Group Corporate Communications,
J Sainsbury Plc

Shayer, Phil (Mr)
Merchandise Director, Toys R Us Limited

Shearer, Gwen (Mrs)
Customer Service Manager, HPJ UK Ltd

Sheffield, David (Mr)
Merchandise and Retail Controller, Shoefayre Ltd

Shenstrom, Karen (Ms)
Commercial Director, Meat and Fresh Foods,
Safeway Plc

Shepherd, David (Mr)
Brand Director, Topman, Arcadia Group Ltd

Shepherdson, Jane (Ms)
Brand Director, Top Shop, Arcadia Group Ltd

Sherwin, Michael (Mr)
Group Finance Director, Games Workshop Group
Plc

Shields, Jane (Ms)
Retail Operations Director, Next Plc

Shields, Lititia (Mrs)
Customer Service Manager, Jenners Limited

Shipley, David (Mr)
Non-Executive Director, Matalan plc

Shrager, Robert (Mr)
Chairman, Courts Plc

Shrager, Robert (Mr)
Non-Executive Director, Matalan plc

Siegman, Andreas (Mr)
Regional Managing Director, Aldi Stores Ltd

Sills, David (Mr)
Buying Director, Furnitureland Holdings Ltd

Sim, Graham (Mr)
Group Marketing Director, Monsoon Accessorize
Ltd

Simmons, Wendy (Ms)
Marketing Manager, Joplings Ltd

Simon, Peter (Mr)
Chief Executive and Chairman, Monsoon
Accessorize Ltd

Simonin, Richard (Mr)
Chief Executive Officer, Harrods Limited

Should you be in this directory? See the form at the back for new entries and amendments

Simons, Carolyn (Ms)
Group Managing Director, Harveys Furnishing Group
Fax: 01708 556900

Simons, Carolyn (Ms)
Managing Director, Rosebys, Rosebys Ltd

Simons, David (Mr)
Group Chairman, Littlewoods Stores Ltd

Simpson, Malcolm (Mr)
Financial Director, Greggs Plc

Sims, Phillip (Mr)
Sales Director, William Jackson & Son Ltd

Sinclair, Douglas (Mr)
Property Director, Holland & Barrett Retail Ltd

Singh, Tom (Mr)
Non-Executive Director, New Look Retailers Ltd

Sinnot, Mike (Mr)
Production Director, Multiyork Furniture Ltd

Siviter, Paul (Mr)
Managing Director, News Shops Ltd

Skelsey, Jim (Mr)
Merchandise Director: Grattan Plc; Freemans Plc
DOB: 08/04/51
Personal Leisure Interests: Mountaineering; football

Skilt, Anthony (Mr)
Commercial Director, Choices Video

Slater, Paul (Mr)
Managing Director, Slater Menswear

Smalley, Richard (Mr)
Real Estate Controller, Staples UK Ltd

Smart, Malcolm (Mr)
Financial Director, Robert Dyas Holdings Ltd
DOB: 1942

Smith, (Mr)
Managing Director, L Rowland & Co (Retail) Ltd

Smith, Alan (Mr)
Financial Director, Fenwick Ltd
DOB: 17/03/41
Marital Status: Married with four children
Memberships:
Brooks

Smith, Alex (Mr)
Managing Director, TK Maxx

Smith, Andy (Mr)
Group Human Resources Director, Boots Group Plc

Smith, Andy N (Mr)
Personnel Director, Halfords Limited

Smith, Anthony (Mr)
Chief Executive, Shoe Zone Ltd

Smith, Brian (Mr)
Head of Property and Central Retail Operations, Adams Childrenswear
Tel: 02476 530943 **Fax:** 02476 531654
Personal Email: brian@smith10.fsnet.co.uk
DOB: 15/10/46
Marital Status: Married
Personal Leisure Interests: Reading; travel; films

Smith, Charles (Mr)
Chief Operating Officer, Shoe Zone Ltd

Smith, Chris (Mr)
Property Manager, La Senza
Tel: 09966 145482 **Fax:** 020 7733 7977
Personal Email: smithch1@gusco.com, chriss@ncco.com
DOB: 20/02/55
Marital Status: Married

Smith, Jonathon (Mr)
Property Director, Stead & Simpson
Tel: 0116 2695981
Personal Email:
jonathan.smith@steadandsimpson.co.uk
DOB: 21/04/42
Marital Status: Married
Personal Leisure Interests: Rugby; tennis; gardening

Smith, Matthew (Mr)
Customer Services Manager, Blackwell's UK

Smith, Michael (Mr)
Chairman, Shoe Zone Ltd

Smith, Peter (Mr)
IT Director, Redcats UK (Brands) Ltd

Smith, Steve (Mr)
Finance Director, Cargo Homeshop

Smith, Steve (Mr)
Sales Director, Cotton Traders Ltd

Smith, Ted (Mr)
Stores Director, The Big Food Group Plc

Should you be in this directory? See the form at the back for new entries and amendments

Smith, Trevor
Finance Director, WCF Retail

Snook, Hans (Mr)
Non-Executive Chairman, Carphone Warehouse Plc

Soares Dos Santos, Francisco (Mr)
Chairman, Lillywhites

Souber, Carol (Ms)
Finance Controller, Cromwells Madhouse

Souber, Peter (Mr)
Managing Director, Cromwells Madhouse

Soucier, Robert (Mr)
Marketing Director, Hughes Electricals

Sparks, Alexander (Mr)
Managing Director, Blockbuster Entertainment Ltd
Fax: 01895 819938
DOB: 07/12/57

Spicer, P
Director, Frozen Value Ltd

Spindler, Angela (Mrs)
Trading and Marketing Director, Food, Asda Stores Ltd

Spink, Geoff (Mr)
Sales Director, Choices Video

Spooner, John (Mr)
International Development Director, Monsoon Accessorize Ltd
DOB: 1951

Spratley, Jim (Mr)
Finance Director, Cash Converters UK Ltd

Standish, Nick (Mr)
Head of Merchandising, Hobbs Limited

Stanford, Kevin (Mr)
Chief Executive Officer, Karen Millen
DOB: 29/07/60
Personal Leisure Interests: Family

Stansfield, Mark
Retail Director, O2

Stanway, Andrew (Mr)
Chief Executive, Homeform Group Ltd

Stark, Liz (Ms)
Sales Manager, Great Plains, French Connection

Stark, Ron (Mr)
Managing Director, Priceless Shoes, Stylo Plc

Steer, Liz (Ms)
Merchandising Director, Heal's Plc

Stevens, Chris (Mr)
Head of Finance, National Co-operative Chemists Ltd

Stevens, Richard (Mr)
Purchasing Manager, G T Retail

Stewart, Norrie (Mr)
Joint Managing Director, Internacionale Limited

Stirling, Muriel (Ms)
UK Brand Director, W H Smith Retail Ltd

Stock, Lionel (Mr)
Finance Director, Faith Footwear
Personal Email: lionels@faith.co.uk
DOB: 13/08/58
Quals/Educ: BTh at Nottingham University (1991–94)
Employment History:
Accountant and General Manager at Bogart Partnership (1983–86); Company Accountant at Faith Footwear (1986–91); Curate in the Church of England (1994–97); Priest in the Church of England (1997–2000); Project Development Manager at Faith Footwear (2000–01); Head of Finance at Faith Footwear (2001–02); Financial Director at Faith Footwear (2002–)
Additional Directorships:
The Retail Experience Ltd
Memberships:
Chartered Institute of Management Accountants; Institute of Chartered Secretaries and Administrators
Personal Leisure Interests: Croquet; rail travel
Other Biographical Details:
Ordained Deacon (1994); ordained Priest (1995)

Stocken, Oliver
Non-Executive Director, GUS

Stokes, Daniel (Mr)
Chairman, Stokes Plc

Stokes, T (Mr)
Non-Executive Director, Stokes Plc

Stokes-Johnson, Louise (Ms)
Managing Director, Stokes Plc

Storer, Jane (Ms)
Buying and Merchandising Director, House of Fraser Plc

Stott, Robert (Mr)
Joint Managing Director, Wm Morrison Supermarkets Plc
Tel: 01924 875108
DOB: 22/03/43

Should you be in this directory? See the form at the back for new entries and amendments

86

Straiton, Brian (Mr)
Operations Manager, Botterills Convenience Stores Ltd

Street, Richard (Mr)
Stores Director, W H Smith Retail Ltd

Stuart, Simon (Mr)
IT Manager, Allied Carpets Group

Styles, Kevin (Mr)
Managing Director, Marketing, Thresher Group

Suggett, Chris (Mr)
Buying Director, Bells Stores Limited

Sunderland, John (Mr)
Business Development Director, Select Retail Plc
DOB: 1951

Sunnucks, Stephen (Mr)
Chief Executive, New Look Retailers Ltd
DOB: 1958

Sutcliffe, Keith (Mr)
Customer Services Manager, Findel Plc

Sutherland, Euan (Mr)
Retail and Marketing Director, Matalan plc
Tel: 01695 552520   **Fax:** 01695 552759
Personal Email: sutherland_e@matalan.co.uk
DOB: 06/02/69
Quals/Educ: BSc Hons at Aston University (1989–93)
Employment History:
National Sales Manager at Mars Confectionery (1994–96); European Marketing Manager at Coca-Cola Co. (1996–97); General Manager at Coca-Cola & Schweppes (1997–98); Marketing Director at Currys (1998–2002); Retail and Markeing Director at Matala
Memberships:
Marketing Society

Swann, Kate (Ms)
Chief Executive Officer, W H Smith Retail Ltd
Tel: 01908 600672   **Fax:** 01908 296630
Personal Email: kate.swann@argos.co.uk
DOB: 21/12/64
Employment History:
Marketing Director at Currys; Marketing Director at Homebase Ltd; Managing Director at Homebase Ltd; Managing Director at Argos Retail Group

Swannie, Sue (Ms)
Buying Director, Mackays Stores Ltd

Swartz, Jeff (Mr)
Chief Executive, Timberland UK Ltd

Sweet, Tony (Mr)
Food Hall Director, House of Fraser Plc

Sweetenham, Paul (Mr)
Buying Director, Men's, Children's, and Shoes, TK Maxx

Swift, Michelle (Mrs)
Manager of Customer Services, Karen Millen

Swift, Roger (Mr)
Managing Director, United News Shops

Syed, Maura (Mrs)
Financial Director, Morley's Stores Ltd

Tadler, Steve (Mr)
Non-Executive Director, HMV Group Plc

Taglioni, Lara (Mrs)
Customer Services Manager, Fenwick Ltd

Tague, Stephen (Mr)
Chief Executive, Cargo Homeshop
DOB: 1955
Personal Leisure Interests: Golf

Tankard, Judith (Ms)
Customer Services Manager, Brantano UK Ltd

Tanner, Adrian (Mr)
Finance Director, Benetton Retail 1988 Ltd

Tapin, Penny (Ms)
Customer Service Manager, Staples UK Ltd

Tapp, Chris (Mr)
Buying and Merchandising Director, Birthdays Group Ltd

Tatton-Brown, Duncan (Mr)
Finance Director, B & Q Plc
Personal Email: duncan.tatton-brown@virgin.co.uk
DOB: 15/03/65
Marital Status: Married
Memberships:
ACMA

Tawns, David (Mr)
Commercial Director, Multiyork Furniture Ltd

Taylor, Caroline (Ms)
Head of International Mail Order, Whittard of Chelsea Plc

Taylor, Graham (Mr)
Marketing Manager, Robert Dyas Holdings Ltd

Should you be in this directory? See the form at the back for new entries and amendments

Taylor, John (Mr)
Trading Director, Londis (Holdings) Ltd
Tel: 01535 650202   **Fax:** 01535 654000
DOB: 01/06/59
Marital Status: Married
Memberships:
Institute of Directors
Personal Leisure Interests: Racing; motor racing

Taylor, Julie (Ms)
Head of Retail, Bon Marché Ltd

Taylor, Matt (Mr)
Marketing Manager, Borders UK Ltd

Taylor, Mike (Mr)
Development Director, Budgens Stores Ltd

Taylor, Paul (Mr)
Buying Director, B & M Retail Ltd

Taylor, Richard (Mr)
Retail Director, Cancer Research UK

Taylor, Roger (Mr)
Chief Financial Officer, Carphone Warehouse Plc

Taylor, Simon (Mr)
Property Director, Signet Group Plc

Teale, Penny
Trading Director, Homebase Ltd

Teicher, Ben
Finance Director, Disney Consumer Products

Temple, Colin (Mr)
Managing Director, Schuh Ltd

Templeman, Rob (Mr)
Chairman, Halfords Limited

Tennant, Sue (Ms)
Trading Director, Ethel Austin Ltd
Tel: 0151 207 8814   **Fax:** 0151 298 1517
DOB: 19/12/62
Marital Status: Married

Terras, Duncan (Mr)
Group Human Resources Director, Focus Wickes

Terry, Colin (Mr)
Merchandise Director, Allders Department Stores
Limited

Tesseras, Mick (Mr)
Systems Manager, Cromwells Madhouse

Tesseras, Nick (Mr)
Customer Service Manager, Cromwells Madhouse

Tesseras, Peter (Mr)
Marketing Director, Cromwells Madhouse

Testo, Paul (Mr)
Finance Director, Wilkinson Hardware Stores
Limited
DOB: 1955

Thomas, Andrew (Mr)
Chairman, Homeform Group Ltd

Thomas, Gareth (Mr)
Director of Retail Operations, John Lewis Plc
Tel: 020 7592 6100   **Fax:** 020 7592 6588
Personal Email: gareth-thomas@johnlewis.co.uk
Marital Status: Married
Personal Leisure Interests: Art

Thomas, Graham (Mr)
General Manager, Estates, The Peacock Group Plc

Thomas, Judy (Ms)
Garden Centre Manager, J H Leeke & Sons Ltd

Thomas, Les (Mr)
IT Director, Brown & Jackson

Thomas, Ray (Mr)
Property Director, Remainders Ltd

Thompson, Anthony (Mr)
Head of Childrenswear, Marks & Spencer Plc
DOB: 02/03/64
Marital Status: Married
Personal Leisure Interests: Reading; classic cars;
collecting art; gardening

Thompson, Charles (Mr)
Non-Executive Director, Matalan plc

Thompson, David (Mr)
Sales and Development Director, Costcutter
Supermarkets Group Limited
DOB: 30/08/53

Thompson, Edward (Mr)
Chief Executive, Morning, Noon & Night

Thompson, John
Operations Manager, Wine Cellar Ltd

Thompson, Leslie (Ms)
Fashion Director, Alexon Group Plc

Thompson, Maria (Ms)
Commercial Director, Argos Ltd

Thompson, Stephen (Mr)
Marketing Director, Morning, Noon & Night

Should you be in this directory? See the form at the back for new entries and amendments

88

Thompson, Thiry (Ms)
Head of Buying, Bon Marché Ltd

Thomson, Bob (Mr)
Head of Retail and Property, Ponden Mill Ltd

Thomson, David (Mr)
Finance Director, MK One

Thornley, David (Mr)
Property Director, Wilkinson Hardware Stores Limited

Thornton, John (Mr)
Chairman, Thorntons Plc

Thornton, Lisa (Ms)
Marketing Co-ordinator, Tulchan Group

Timpson, James (Mr)
Managing Director, Timpson Ltd

Timpson, John (Mr)
Chairman and Chief Executive Officer, Timpson Ltd

Tindall, Rod (Mr)
Trading Director, Alfred Jones Ltd

Tipple, Vanessa (Ms)
Head of Press Office, Carphone Warehouse Plc

Titterton, Mark (Mr)
Retail Director, G T Retail

Todd, Martin (Mr)
Retail Director, Esso Petroleum Co. Ltd

Tomey, Gill (Ms)
Customer Service Manager, Somerfield Stores Ltd

Tomlin, Jean (Ms)
Director of Human Resources, Marks & Spencer Plc

Tomlinson, Andrew (Mr)
News Development Manager, News Shops Ltd

Tomlinson, Mark (Mr)
Distribution Director, all:sports Retail Ltd

Torrance, Andy J (Mr)
Operations Director, Halfords Limited

Townsend, Jeremy (Mr)
Director of Strategy and Planning, J Sainsbury Plc

Tragen, Martin (Mr)
Finance Director, Timpson Ltd

Tranfield, Dan (Mr)
Financial Director, Gilesports Plc

Trangmar, Don (Mr)
Non-Executive Director, The Outdoor Group Ltd

Trubshaw, John (Mr)
Retail Operations Manager, B & M Retail Ltd

Trueman, Sarah (Ms)
Marketing Manager, A F Blakemore & Son Ltd

Trujillo, Solomon (Mr)
Chief Executive, Orange Plc

Tubb, Gary (Mr)
Deputy Managing Director, Courts Plc

Tucker, David (Mr)
Director, Bewise Ltd

Tucki, Julian (Mr)
Marketing Director, Remainders Ltd

Tulley, Steve (Mr)
Development Director, Londis (Holdings) Ltd

Turnball, Patrick (Mr)
Property Development and Construction Director, TK Maxx
Tel: 01923 473736   **Fax:** 01923 473506
DOB: 24/01/63
Marital Status: Married with two children
Personal Leisure Interests: Tennis; sailing; squash

Turner, Gemma (Ms)
Senior Buyer, Faith Footwear

Turner, Ken (Mr)
Chief Executive, QD Stores Ltd

Turner, Mark (Mr)
Operations Director, Alfred Jones Ltd

Turner, Mark (Mr)
Managing Director of Property, Thresher Group

Tutt, Eddie
Operations and IT Director, WCF Retail

Tyler, David
Finance Director, GUS

Tyson, Matt (Mr)
Managing Director, Super Centre, B & Q Plc

Unadkat, Ray (Mr)
Finance Director, Ann Summers Ltd

Urry, Julian (Mr)
Managing Director, Cash Converters UK Ltd

Vandenberghe, Mark (Mr)
International Director, Arcadia Group Ltd

Should you be in this directory? See the form at the back for new entries and amendments

89

Vandermeer, John (Mr)
   Finance Director, E H Booth & Co. Ltd

Vandevelde, Luc (Mr)
   Chairman, Marks & Spencer Plc
   Additional Directorships:
   Managing Director at Change Capital Partners

Vann, Paul (Mr)
   Chairman, Mackays Stores Ltd

Varley, Andrew (Mr)
   Group Property Director, Next Plc
   DOB: 27/09/50

Vernon, Claudia (Ms)
   Marketing Director, Richer Sounds Plc

Vernon, Michelle (Mr)
   Public Relations Manager, Co-operative Group
   (CWS) Limited

Verona, Mark (Mr)
   Managing Director, Lloyd Shoe Co Ltd

Vickers, Barry (Mr)
   Chief Executive Officer, Holland & Barrett Retail
   Ltd
   DOB: 1938
   Marital Status: Married with two sons and one
   daughter
   Personal Leisure Interests: Swimming; gardening

von Sprecklesen, John (Mr)
   Executive Chairman, Somerfield Stores Ltd

Wade, Charles (Mr)
   Chairman, Multiyork Furniture Ltd

Wadeley, Melanie (Ms)
   Personnel Director, Merchant Retail Group Plc
   DOB: 1970

Waedeled, Claus (Mr)
   Managing Director, Netto Foodstores Ltd

Waggett, Colin (Mr)
   Finance Director, Thresher Group

Walker, David
   IT Manager, Wine Cellar Ltd

Walker, Michael (Mr)
   Retail Operations Director, Bells Stores Limited

Walker, Philip (Mr)
   Managing Director, Product, Adams Childrenswear
   DOB: 1958
   Personal Leisure Interests: Sport; theatre; art

Walker, S (Mrs)
   Customer Services Manager, Wyevale Garden
   Centres Plc

Wallace, Andrew (Mr)
   Finance Director, Londis (Holdings) Ltd
   Tel: 020 8481 9208   **Fax:** 020 8783 1346
   Personal Email: andrew.wallace@londis-
   uk.demon.co
   DOB: 03/11/52
   Marital Status: Married
   Memberships:
   FCMA
   Personal Leisure Interests: Sailing; family

Wallbridge, Andrew (Mr)
   Human Resources Director, Claire's Accessories

Wallis, Peter (Mr)
   Non-Executive Director, MFI Furniture Centres
   Limited

Walmsley, Philip (Mr)
   Chairman, Walmsley Furnishing Plc

Walsh, Mark (Mr)
   Purchasing Director, Pilot Clothing

Walsh-Hill, Steven (Mr)
   Finance Director, Blackwell's UK

Walters, Michael (Mr)
   Financial Director, Staples UK Ltd

Walters, Nick (Mr)
   Finance Director, Birthdays Group Ltd

Walton, Graham (Mr)
   Finance Systems Manager, News Shops Ltd

Walton, Tim (Mr)
   Sales Director, Phones 4u

Wan, Joseph (Mr)
   Managing Director, Harvey Nichols Group Plc
   DOB: 1954
   Memberships:
   Fellow of the Royal Society of Arts
   Personal Leisure Interests: Spending time with family

Ward, Andrea (Ms)
   Marketing Manager, Jaeger Ltd

Ward, Michael (Mr)
   Chief Executive, Lloyds Pharmacy
   Tel: 024 7643 2251   **Fax:** 024 7643 2616
   Personal Email: michael.ward@ahh.co.uk
   DOB: 1956
   Marital Status: Married

Should you be in this directory? See the form at the back for new entries and amendments

Ward, Natasha (Ms)
Personnel Manager, Jane Norman

Ward, Paul (Mr)
General Manager, Cromwells Madhouse

Warnes, William (Mr)
Food Trading Director, Roys (Wroxham) Ltd

Warren, John (Mr)
Group Finance Director, W H Smith Retail Ltd

Watkinson, John (Mr)
Chief Executive, Hamleys Plc

Watson, Ian (Mr)
Managing Director, Timberland UK Ltd

Wattel, Jean (Ms)
Finance Director, Allied Carpets Group

Watts, Christine (Ms)
Corporate Affairs Director, Asda Stores Ltd

Wayment, Richard (Mr)
Retail Sales Director, House of Fraser Plc

Weaving, John (Mr)
Chief Operating Officer, Stylo Plc

Webb, Martin (Mr)
Director of Trading Support and Procurement,
J Sainsbury Plc

Webb, Steve (Mr)
Corporate Development Director, Safeway Plc

Webster, David (Mr)
Chairman, Safeway Plc
DOB: 1945
Marital Status: Married with three children

Welby, Michaela (Ms)
Financial Director, Habitat UK Limited

Weller, Sara (Ms)
Deputy Managing Director, J Sainsbury Plc
Tel: 020 7695 6443

Wellesley-Wood, Mark (Mr)
Chairman, Unwins Wine Group Ltd

Wells, Mark (Mr)
General Manager, Games Workshop Ltd, Games
Workshop Group Plc

Wemms, Michael (Mr)
Chairman, House of Fraser Plc

Wenham, Alan (Mr)
Customer Services Director, Woolworths Plc

Wenkert, Michaela (Ms)
Head of Footwear, Hobbs Limited

West, Christopher (Mr)
Finance Director, Grattan Plc
Tel: 01274 624425   **Fax:** 01274 625594
Personal Email: chris.west@grattan.co.uk
DOB: 07/03/62
Marital Status: Married
Memberships:
ICAEW
Personal Leisure Interests: Cricket; golf; sports;
children

West, Jim E (Mr)
Sales and Marketing Director, Goldsmiths Group
Plc

West, Sue (Ms)
Retail Director, Selfridges & Co

Westwood, John (Mr)
Non-Executive Director, Matalan plc

Wetherspoon, Gordon (Mr)
Group Property Director, Somerfield Stores Ltd

Wetz, Phillip (Mr)
Joint Managing Director, Unwins Wine Group Ltd

Wetz, Simon (Mr)
Joint Managing Director, Unwins Wine Group Ltd

Whaley, Jeremy (Mr)
Managing Director, Pilot Clothing

Wharton, Nick B E (Mr)
IT and Business Development Director, Halfords
Limited

Wharton, Sue (Ms)
Trading Director, W H Smith Retail Ltd

Wheelwright, Allan (Mr)
Personnel Director, William Jackson & Son Ltd

Whelan, David (Mr)
Executive Chairman, JJB Sports Plc
DOB: 1938

Whitaker, Alec (Mr)
Property Director, Edinburgh Woollen Mill Ltd
Tel: 01387 382827   **Fax:** 01387 382831
Personal Email: whitaker@ewm.co.uk
DOB: 13/01/60

Whitbread, Robin (Mr)
Managing Director, Kwik Save, Somerfield Stores
Ltd

Should you be in this directory? See the form at the back for new entries and amendments

White, Alan (Mr)
Chief Executive, N Brown
DOB: 1956
Marital Status: Married with two children
Personal Leisure Interests: Squash; tennis; football

White, David (Mr)
Trading Director, A F Blakemore & Son Ltd

White, Graham (Mr)
Chief Executive, Londis (Holdings) Ltd
Personal Email: graham.white@londis.co.uk
DOB: 24/03/47
Marital Status: Married
Memberships:
Marketing Society
Personal Leisure Interests: Rugby

White, Jim (Mr)
Human Resources Director, Safeway Plc

White, Joe (Mr)
Marketing Director, Homeform Group Ltd

White, Martin (Mr)
Director of Supply Chain, J Sainsbury Plc

White, Paul (Mr)
Commercial Director, PRG Powerhouse Retail Ltd

White, Peter (Mr)
Retail News Manager, News Shops Ltd

White, Tracy (Ms)
Commercial Director, Bay Trading, Alexon Group Plc

Whitehead, Martin (Mr)
Operations Manager, Bhs Plc

Whiting, Bill (Mr)
Chief Executive, B & Q Plc

Whittle, Allan (Mr)
Joint Managing Director, Bargain Booze Limited

Whittle, David (Mr)
Direct Sales Director, Maplin Electronics Ltd

Whittle, David (Mr)
Merchandise Director, Thermawear Limited (t/a Damart)

Wilburn, Paul (Mr)
Finance Director, Maplin Electronics Ltd

Wilkinson, Brent F (Mr)
Chief Executive Officer, Robert Dyas Holdings Ltd
Tel: 01372 361444   **Fax:** 01372 361968
Personal Email: brent@rdyas.freeserve.co.uk

DOB: 23/04/50
Marital Status: Married

Wilkinson, Julian (Mr)
Director, all:sports Retail Ltd
Tel: 0161 406 1521   **Fax:** 0161 494 8419
Personal Email: jwilkinson@allsportsretail.co.uk
DOB: 17/06/63
Marital Status: Married with three children
Memberships:
Associate Member of the Royal Institute of Chartered Surveyors; Member of the Property Managers Association; Member of the British Council for Out of Town Retail
Personal Leisure Interests: Football; swimming

Wilkinson, Nick (Mr)
Marketing Services, Wilkinson Hardware Stores Limited

Wilkinson, Steve (Mr)
Joint Managing Director, Operations, TM Retail Ltd

Wilkinson, Tony (Mr)
Chairman, Wilkinson Hardware Stores Limited

Williams, Andrew (Mr)
IT Director, Remainders Ltd

Williams, Bill (Mr)
Managing Director, Somerfield, Somerfield Stores Ltd

Williams, David (Mr)
Non-Executive Director, Moss Pharmacy Ltd

Williams, David (Mr)
Chief Executive, Thresher Group

Williams, Karen (Ms)
Marketing Operations Manager, Vision Express UK Ltd

Williams, Mandy (Ms)
Director of Operations, Brown & Jackson

Williams, Mike (Mr)
Property Director, Timpson Ltd

Williams, Neil (Mr)
Chief Operating Director, French Connection
DOB: 1965

Williams, Peter (Mr)
Chairman, Londis (Holdings) Ltd

Williams, Peter (Mr)
Chief Executive, Selfridges & Co
Tel: 020 7318 3200   **Fax:** 020 7355 1141

Should you be in this directory? See the form at the back for new entries and amendments

DOB: 18/12/53
Marital Status: Married with two children
Memberships:
Institute of Chartered Accountants in England and Wales
Personal Leisure Interests: Tennis; skiing; cinema; supporting Southampton Football Club

Williams, Stephen (Mr)
Finance Director, Ethel Austin Ltd

Williams, Stuart (Mr)
Chairman, Topps Tiles Plc

Williamson, Colin (Mr)
Marketing Director, Mackays Stores Ltd

Williamson, Simon (Mr)
Managing Director, Asprey & Garrard Ltd

Willis, Paul (Mr)
Retail Director, Focus, Focus Wickes

Willis, Peter (Mr)
Business Development Manager, National Co-operative Chemists Ltd

Wilson, Bob (Mr)
Manufacturing and Purchasing Director, MFI Furniture Centres Limited

Wilson, David (Mr)
Company Secretary, Safeway Plc
DOB: 1961
Memberships:
Fellow of the Institute of Chartered Secretaries and Administrators

Wilson, Geoff (Mr)
Deputy Chairman and Group Finance Director, Focus Wickes
DOB: 5/12/54
Personal Leisure Interests: Football; golf; travel

Wilson, Joanne (Miss)
Customer Service Manager, Internacionale Limited

Wilson, Neil (Mr)
Finance Director, The Officers Club Ltd

Wimpenny, Marc (Mr)
Retail Operations Director, The Officers Club Ltd

Winstanley, Mark (Mr)
Creative Director, Laura Ashley

Witcher, Geoff (Mr)
Finance Director, Trago Mills

Witts, Kevin (Mr)
Group Finance Director, Adams Childrenswear

Wolfenden, Alex (Mr)
Property Manager, Tulchan Group

Wolfson, Simon (Mr)
Chief Executive, Next Plc
DOB: 1967

Wolstenholme, Bill (Mr)
Managing Director, Benson Beds, Rosebys Ltd

Wood, Fiona (Mrs)
Finance Director and Company Secretary, Heal's Plc
Tel: 020 7896 7436   **Fax:** 020 7896 7435
Personal Email: fwood@heals.co.uk
DOB: 19/02/62
Quals/Educ: BSc Hons at Edinburgh University (1979–83); ACA Chartered Accountant (1983–86)
Employment History:
Auditor at Deloitte Haskins and Sells (1983–87); Audit Manager at PricewaterhouseCoopers (1987–89); Financial Controller at Our Price Music Ltd (1989–95); Finance Director at Waterstones Booksellers Ltd (1995–2000); Finance Director at Heal's Plc (2002–)
Awards: Duke of Edinburgh Gold Award
Memberships:
Institute of Chartered Accountants in England and Wales; The Roehampton Club
Personal Leisure Interests: Spending time with family; squash; swimming; theatre; opera; reading; gardening
Other Biographical Details:
Brought up in Africa and the West Indies; has two children

Woodhead, Carol (Ms)
Distribution Director, Grattan Plc

Woodhouse, Chris (Mr)
Deputy Chairman, Halfords Limited

Woodhouse, Lorraine (Ms)
Head of Investor Relations, Kingfisher Plc

Woods, Peter (Mr)
Finance Director, USC Group Plc

Wooley, Caspar (Mr)
Head of Business Development, John Lewis Plc

Woolf, Jane (Ms)
Head of Buying, Oasis Stores Plc
Tel: 020 7452 1103   **Fax:** 020 7452 1001
Personal Email: janewoo@oasis-stores.demon.co.uk

Should you be in this directory? See the form at the back for new entries and amendments

DOB: 01/05/58
Marital Status: Married

Woolford, Adrian (Mr)
Marketing Director, Hamleys Plc

Wordley, Mark (Mr)
Director, HPJ UK Ltd

Worth, Key
Head of Human Resources and Training, Jaeger Ltd

Wright, Adrian (Mr)
Chief Executive, Moss Bros Group Plc

Wright, Liz (Ms)
Property Director, Majestic Wine Warehouses Ltd
Personal Email: lwright@majestic.co.uk
Marital Status: Married

Wright, Simon (Mr)
Chief Executive Officer, Virgin Retail Group Limited

Wrigley, Phil (Mr)
Managing Director, Operations, New Look Retailers Ltd

Wyles, John (Mr)
Sales and Operations Director, Bewise Ltd

Yates, John (Mr)
Company Secretary, Stylo Plc

Yates, Tim (Mr)
Group Property Director, The Big Food Group Plc
DOB: 1957
Personal Leisure Interests: Hockey; football; travelling; music

Young, Alexander (Mr)
Non-Executive Officer, L Rowland & Co (Retail) Ltd

Young, Mark (Mr)
Company Secretary, Selfridges & Co

Youngs, Peter (Mr)
Global Finance Director, The Body Shop International Plc

Yusuf, Yasmin (Ms)
Creative Director, Clothing, Marks & Spencer Plc

Zaina, Robert (Mr)
Finance Director, Dollond & Aitchison Group Plc

Ziff, Michael (Mr)
Chairman and Chief Executive, Stylo Plc
Fax: 01274 616111
DOB: 06/20/53

Zuppinger, Jamie (Mr)
European Resources Manager, Claire's Accessories
Tel: 0121 2507937   **Fax:** 07970 082066
Personal Email: jamie.zuppinger@claires.co.uk

Should you be in this directory? See the form at the back for new entries and amendments

94

E-TAILERS

Companies marked * are retailers as well as e-tailers.

Adams, George (Mr)
Commercial and Marketing Director, B & Q Plc *

Agar-Hutty, S
IT Director, Argos Retail Group *

Aldis, Peter (Mr)
Managing Director, Holland & Barrett Retail Ltd *

Alexander, Ian David (Mr)
Finance Director, John Lewis Plc *

Alldritt, Nigel (Mr)
Financial Director, Majestic Wine Warehouses Ltd *

Allen, John (Mr)
Managing Director, Screwfix Direct

Anderson, Toby (Mr)
Head of Online Marketing, Sainsbury's Supermarkets Ltd *

Antony, Martyn (Mr)
Acting Head of Retail Operations, T-Mobile (UK) *

Apthorp, John (Mr)
Chairman, Majestic Wine Warehouses Ltd *

Arford, G (Mr)
Head of IT, Comet Direct

Ashton, Richard John (Mr)
Group Finance and Systems Director, Argos Retail Group *
Tel: 01908 600001   **Fax:** 01908 600126
Personal Email: richard.ashton@argos.co.uk
DOB: 31/05/66
Quals/Educ: BSc Hons Economics and Accountancy at Loughborough University (1985–88)
Employment History:
Various positions at PricewaterhouseCoopers (1988–94); various positions at GE Capital (1994–2001); Group Finance Director at Argos Ltd (2001–03)
Memberships:
Institute of Chartered Accountants in England and Wales
Personal Leisure Interests: Rugby; athletics

Baker, Richard (Mr)
Chief Executive, Boots Group Plc *

Ball, Colin (Mr)
Group Commercial Services Director and E-Commerce, Focus DIY Ltd *
Tel: 01270 507276   **Fax:** 01270 250504
Marital Status: Married

Bamford, Peter (Mr)
Chief Marketing Officer, Vodafone Ltd *

Barrow, Steve (Mr)
Finance Director, Screwfix Direct

Barry, Tom (Mr)
Deputy Managing Director, Operations, Comet Direct

Bartup, Phil (Mr)
Business Systems Manager, Debenhams Plc *

Batchellor, Lance (Mr)
Marketing Director, Vodafone Ltd *

Bateman, Paul (Mr)
Group Operations Director, Boots Group Plc *

Bennett, Tony (Mr)
Financial Director, Confetti.co.uk

Benson, Graham (Mr)
Information Systems Director, Screwfix Direct

Beynon, Lee (Mr)
Operations Director, Buy Electrical Direct

Bezos, Jeff (Mr)
Chief Executive, Amazon.co.uk

Bignall, Sue (Ms)
Marketing Director, Capital Sound & Vision

Binnington, Mark (Mr)
Marketing Director, Boden

Bish-Jones, Trevor (Mr)
Chief Executive, Woolworths Plc *

Blackwell, Phillip (Mr)
Chief Executive, Blackwell's UK *

Blackwood, Walter (Mr)
Distribution Director, Grattan Plc *

Blank, Victor (Sir)
Chairman, Argos Retail Group *

Boden, Johnnie (Mr)
Managing Director, Boden

Bodycote, Charlie (Mr)
Technical Director, Figleaves.com

Bowden, Tony (Mr)
Director, BlackStar

Bowles, Glenn (Mr)
Retail Managing Director, Asda Stores Ltd *

Should you be in this directory? See the form at the back for new entries and amendments

Bradley, Hugh (Mr)
Communications Director, Debenhams Plc *

Brazil, Eugene (Mr)
Managing Director, Argos Home Shopping, Argos Retail Group *

Brioch, A (Mr)
Managing Director, BOL.COM

Broadbridge, Bob (Mr)
Managing Director, W H Smith Direct *

Browett, John
Chief Executive, Tesco.com *

Budge, Paul (Mr)
Finance Director, Arcadia Group Ltd *

Bussey, Ed (Mr)
Business Development Director, Figleaves.com

Butler, Richard (Mr)
Human Resources Director, Screwfix Direct

Cannon, Rosy (Ms)
Home Shopping Manager, Asda Stores Ltd *

Carroll, Brian (Mr)
Finance Director, Waitrose Ltd *

Caudwell, John (Mr)
Chairman and Chief Executive, Phones 4u *

Caunce, Steve (Mr)
Finance Director, Phones 4u *

Clare, John (Mr)
Chief Executive, DSG Retail Ltd *

Clark, Murray (Mr)
Head of Retail Finance, T-Mobile (UK) *

Clarke, John (Mr)
Head of Direct Businesses, Waitrose Ltd *

Clement, David
Marketing Director, Tesco.com *

Clifford-King, Martin (Mr)
Group Financial Director, MFI Furniture Centres Limited *
Fax: 01708 558612
DOB: 31/12/63

Collier, Richard (Mr)
Group Property Director, Carphone Warehouse Plc *

Collins, Darryl (Mr)
Joint Managing Director, BlackStar

Collins, John (Sir)
Chairman, DSG Retail Ltd *

Collins, Simon (Mr)
IT Manager, Shoe-Shop.com

Cooper, Mike (Mr)
Managing Director, Iceland, The Big Food Group Plc *

Corbett, Gerald (Mr)
Chairman, Woolworths Plc *

Cross, Jeremy (Mr)
Head of Merchandising, Asda Stores Ltd *
Personal Email: jdcross@asda.co.uk

Crowe, Emma (Ms)
Director, Thinknatural.com

Darroch, Jeremy (Mr)
Finance Director, DSG Retail Ltd *

Davies, Tim (Mr)
Strategy Director, Debenhams Plc *

Davis, Peter (Sir)
Group Chief Executive, Sainsbury's Supermarkets Ltd *

Day, Gill (Mr)
Finance Director, Holland & Barrett Retail Ltd *

Daynes, Mark (Mr)
Managing Director, Littlewoods All-Inclusive, Littlewoods Home Shopping Ltd

de Bourcier, Peter (Mr)
Joint Director, Play.com

de Mellow, Steve (Mr)
Marketing Director, Majestic Wine Warehouses Ltd *

De Nunzio, Tony (Mr)
President and Chief Operating Officer, Asda Stores Ltd *

Derby, Gavin (Mr)
Chief Executive, UK, Vodafone Ltd *

Digregorio, Gina (Ms)
International Marketing Manager, Arcadia Group Ltd *

Dodd, Howard (Mr)
Chief Financial Officer, Boots Group Plc *

Downie, David (Mr)
Operations Director, Asda Stores Ltd *

Should you be in this directory? See the form at the back for new entries and amendments

Duley, Jacques (Mr)
Managing Director, Oddbins UK Ltd *

Dunn, Orla (Ms)
Marketing Manager, BOL.COM

Dunstone, Charles (Mr)
Chief Executive Officer, Carphone Warehouse Plc *
Personal Email: dunstonec@cpw.co.uk

Edwards, Ian (Mr)
Deputy Managing Director, Business Support,
Comet Direct

Esom, Steven (Mr)
Managing Director, Waitrose Ltd *

Evans, Alan (Mr)
Managing Director, Direct, Littlewoods Home
Shopping Ltd

Evans, Paul (Mr)
Managing Director, Buy Electrical Direct

Evans, Trudie (Ms)
Finance Director, Buy Electrical Direct

Felwick, David (Mr)
Deputy Chairman, John Lewis Plc *

Fletcher, Neil (Mr)
IT Manager, Holland & Barrett Retail Ltd *

Foster-Brown, Tania (Miss)
Public Relations and Special Events Director,
Arcadia Group Ltd *

Fraser, Ian (Mr)
**Director of Sales and Distrubution, Personal and
Small Business**, Orange Plc *

Fryatt, Andrew (Mr)
Managing Director, T-Mobile (UK) *

Geary, Phil (Mr)
Marketing Director, Holland & Barrett Retail Ltd *
Personal Email: pgeary@nbty.com

Geddes, Paul (Mr)
Marketing Director, Argos Retail Group *

Geitner, Thomas (Mr)
Chief Technical Officer, Vodafone Ltd *

Gent, Christopher (Sir)
Life President, Vodafone Ltd *

Genthialan, Laurent (Mr)
Finance Director, Oddbins UK Ltd *

Gilbert, David (Mr)
Chief Operating Officer, Central Operations, DSG
Retail Ltd *

Giles, Alan James (Mr)
Chief Executive, HMV UK Ltd

Gissing, John (Mr)
Finance Director, Ocado Ltd

Glover, Jeremy (Mr)
Director, BlackStar

Golding, Richard (Mr)
Joint Director, Play.com

Goodwin, Tony (Mr)
Marketing Director, Audiostreet.com, Streets
Online

Goodwin, Tony (Mr)
**Commercial and Marketing Manager, Streets
Online**, Woolworths Plc *

Goring, Mike (Mr)
Group Operations Director, Arcadia Group Ltd *

Gormley, Rowan (Mr)
Managing Director, Virgin Wines Online Ltd

Grabiner, Anthony (Lord)
Chairman, Arcadia Group Ltd *

Grabiner, Ian (Mr)
Chief Operating Officer, Arcadia Group Ltd *

Granville, Julian (Mr)
Chairman, Boden

Green, Peter (Mr)
Managing Director, Phones 4u *

Green, Philip (Mr)
Owner, Arcadia Group Ltd *

Hallett, David (Mr)
Operations Director, Littlewoods Home Shopping Ltd

Hamburger, Paul (Mr)
Marketing Director, Phones 4u *

Hamid, David (Mr)
Chief Operating Officer, Retail Operations, DSG
Retail Ltd *

Hampson, Stuart (Sir)
Executive Chairman, John Lewis Plc *

Hancock, John (Mr)
Chief Executive, MFI Furniture Centres Limited *
DOB: 1949

Should you be in this directory? See the form at the back for new entries and amendments

97

Harber, Andrew (Mr)
E-Commerce Director, Streets Online, Woolworths Plc *

Harper, Andrew (Mr)
Managing Director, Audiostreet.com, Streets Online

Hawker, Michael L (Mr)
Chief Executive: Grattan Plc *; Freemans Plc *

Heavisides, Henry (Mr)
General Manager, La Redoute UK, Redcats UK (Brands) Ltd *

Henderson, Dennis (Mr)
Group Operations Director, Virgin Megastores Online *

Hill, Peter (Mr)
Finance Director, HMV UK Ltd

Hind, John (Mr)
Trading Director, Arcadia Group Ltd *

Hodgson, Chris (Mr)
Head of Trading, Asda Stores Ltd *

Hollger, Thorsten (Mr)
Director, Haburi.com

Holmes, Roger (Mr)
Chief Executive, Marks & Spencer Plc *

Hook, Jonathan (Mr)
Retail Director, Carphone Warehouse Plc *

Horn-Smith, Julian (Mr)
Chief Operating Officer, Vodafone Ltd *

How, Timothy (Mr)
Managing Director, Majestic Wine Warehouses Ltd *

Hullah, Phil (Mr)
Head of Business Development and Supply Chain, John Lewis Plc *

Hydon, Ken (Mr)
Group Financial Director, Vodafone Ltd *

Imrie, Euan (Mr)
Finance Director, Littlewoods Home Shopping Ltd

Jagger, Denise (Ms)
Company Secretary, Asda Stores Ltd *

James, J (Ms)
Customer Service Representative, BOL.COM

Jeffrey, Jo (Ms)
Communications Director, Figleaves.com

Jensen, Luke (Mr)
Managing Director, Thinknatural.com

Johnson, Steve (Mr)
Managing Director, Focus DIY Ltd *

Jones, David (Mr)
Chairman, Next Plc *

Keenan, Peter (Mr)
Assistant Managing Director, Currys

Keens, David (Mr)
Group Finance Director, Next Plc *

Kendrick, Mark (Mr)
Distribution Director, Holland & Barrett Retail Ltd *

King, Justin (Mr)
Food Director, Marks & Spencer Plc *

Kwakman, Kitty (Ms)
Head of E-Commerce, Argos Retail Group *

Lancaster, Alison (Ms)
Head of Merchandising, John Lewis Direct, John Lewis Plc *

Law, Michael (Mr)
Directory Operations Director, Next Plc *

Lethbridge, David (Mr)
Joint Managing Director, Confetti.co.uk
Personal Email: david@confetti.co.uk

Lewis, Ken (Mr)
Commercial Director, Woolworths Plc *

Lewis, Steve (Mr)
Retail Director, Majestic Wine Warehouses Ltd *

Little, Jill (Ms)
Merchandise Director, John Lewis Plc *

Lloyd, Bethan (Ms)
Internet Marketing Manager, Powerhouse Internet

Loughran, Ian (Mr)
Joint Managing Director, BlackStar

MacDonald, Gordon (Mr)
Chief Operating Officer, MFI Furniture Centres Limited *
Tel: 020 8913 5345   **Fax:** 020 8913 5388
Personal Email: gordon.macdonald@mfi.co.uk

MacLaurin of Knebworth, (Lord)
Chairman, Vodafone Ltd *

Should you be in this directory? See the form at the back for new entries and amendments

98

Malas, Denis (Mr)
Head of Strategic Development, Asda Stores Ltd *

Malcom, Simon (Mr)
Head of E-Marketing, Freemans Plc *

Mann, Kirstie (Ms)
Strategic Development, Woolworths Plc *

Marsh, Peter (Mr)
Joint Managing Director, Confetti.co.uk

Mason, Tim
Chairman, Tesco.com *

Mason, Tony (Mr)
Trading Director, Majestic Wine Warehouses Ltd *

Matthews, Roger (Mr)
Group Finance Director, Sainsbury's Supermarkets Ltd *

Mayfield, Charlie (Mr)
Development Director, John Lewis Plc *

Mayhew, Luke (Mr)
Managing Director, John Lewis Plc *

McAulay, Janet (Ms)
Catalogue Director, Freemans Plc *

McCarthy, Colin (Mr)
Operations Director, Screwfix Direct

McDonald, Jerry (Mr)
President, Avon Cosmetics

McDougall, Shiona (Ms)
Marketing Director, Virgin Wines Online Ltd

McGeorge, Alistair (Mr)
Group Chief Executive, Littlewoods Home Shopping Ltd

McKenna, Peter (Mr)
E-Commerce Manager, MFI Furniture Centres Limited *

McNamara, Mike
IT Director, Tesco.com *

Mitchell, Stuart (Mr)
Managing Director, Sainsbury's Supermarkets Ltd *

Morgan, Jim (Mr)
Director, BlackStar

Morley, Octavia (Ms)
Marketing Director, Woolworths Plc *

Murton, Chris (Mr)
Online Services Director, Carphone Warehouse Plc *

Myers, Dominic (Mr)
Managing Director, Blackwell's UK *
Tel: 01865 333115   **Fax:** 01865 333991
Personal Email: dominic.myers@blackwell.co.uk
DOB: 13/08/62
Quals/Educ: MA Hons at Wadham College, Oxford University (1981–84)
Employment History:
Managing Director at Hasbro Interactive International (1999–2001); Head of Marketing at Somerfield (1993–98)

Neil, Michael (Mr)
Marketing Director, Blackwell's UK *

Nicholls, Peter (Mr)
Vice-President, Sales, Avon Cosmetics

Norgrove, David R (Mr)
Clothing, Outlets and International Director, Marks & Spencer Plc *

Norton, Damian (Mr)
Information Systems Director, DSG Retail Ltd *

Omidyar, Pierre (Mr)
Founder and Chairman, eBay UK Ltd

Page, Tony (Mr)
Director of General Merchandise, Asda Stores Ltd *

Palethorpe, Simon (Mr)
Managing Director, John Lewis Direct, John Lewis Plc *

Palmer, Jeremy (Mr)
E-Commerce Director, Majestic Wine Warehouses Ltd *

Parker, Gary (Mr)
Managing Director, Capital Sound & Vision

Parkes, Steve (Mr)
Head of Marketing and E-Commerce, La Redoute UK, Redcats UK (Brands) Ltd *
Tel: 01274 763778
Personal Email: steve.parkes@redcats.co.uk
DOB: 05/02/63

Patel, Hem (Mr)
Buying Director, Screwfix Direct

Paver, Stuart (Mr)
Managing Director, Shoe-Shop.com

Should you be in this directory? See the form at the back for new entries and amendments

99

Perree, Simon (Mr)
Joint Director, Play.com

Pieri, Paolo (Mr)
Financial Director, Virgin Megastores Online *

Pilling, Chris (Mr)
Marketing Director, Asda Stores Ltd *

Pinnington, Lee (Mr)
Head of Home Shopping, The Big Food Group Plc *

Pollard, Bridie (Ms)
Head of Public Relations, Avon Cosmetics

Powell, Simon (Mr)
Head of Customer Relationship Management, Ocado Ltd

Powers-Freeling, Laurel (Ms)
Director and Chief Executive of Financial Services, Marks & Spencer Plc *
Employment History:
Director at Marks & Spencer Plc (2001–)
Additional Directorships:
Non-Executive Director of the Bank of England

Radice, Vittorio (Mr)
Director, Home, Marks & Spencer Plc *
Employment History:
Managing Director and Chief Executive at Selfridges (1998–2003); Director of Home at Marks & Spencer Plc (2003–)
Additional Directorships:
Non-Executive Director of Abbey National Plc; Non-Executive Director of Shoppers Stop India

Reed, Alison (Ms)
Chief Financial Officer, Marks & Spencer Plc *
Employment History:
Chief Financial Officer at Marks & Spencer Plc (2001–)
Additional Directorships:
Non-Executive Director of HSBC Bank Plc; Trustee of Whizz-Kids

Rice, John (Mr)
IT Director, Focus DIY Ltd *

Richardson, Sam (Mr)
Online Marketing Manager, Oddbins UK Ltd *

Rivett, Carolyn (Ms)
Finance Director, W H Smith Direct *

Robertson, Nigel (Mr)
Managing Director, Ocado Ltd

Robinson, Phillip (Mr)
Managing Director, CD Wow!

Rodriques, Kennedy (Mr)
Financial Manager, Orange Plc *

Roe, Andy (Mr)
Customer Service Director, Littlewoods Home Shopping Ltd

Rogers, Chris (Mr)
Finance Director, Woolworths Plc *
Tel: 01923 714495   **Fax:** 01923 714655
DOB: 21/04/60
Marital Status: Married

Ross, David (Mr)
Chief Operating Officer, Carphone Warehouse Plc *

Ross, Michael (Mr)
Chief Executive Officer, Figleaves.com
Tel: 020 8492 2555   **Fax:** 020 8492 2560
Personal Email: michael.ross@figleaves.com
DOB: 08/04/69
Quals/Educ: MA Maths at Trinity College Cambridge (1986–90)

Rowe, Stuart (Mr)
E-Commerce Director, HMV UK Ltd

Rudd, Nigel (Sir)
Chairman, Boots Group Plc *

Rushforth, Angela (Ms)
Marketing Director, Screwfix Direct

Sarin, Arun (Mr)
Chief Executive, Vodafone Ltd *

Shawe, Jan (Ms)
Director of Group Corporate Communications, Sainsbury's Supermarkets Ltd *

Showan, Madan (Mr)
Chairman, EmpireDirect.co.uk

Showan, Posh (Mr)
Marketing Director, EmpireDirect.co.uk

Skelsey, Jim (Mr)
Merchandise Director: Grattan Plc *; Freemans Plc *

Slater, Andrea (Ms)
Vice-President Marketing, Avon Cosmetics

Slater, Penny (Ms)
Senior Manager Online Marketing, Sainsbury's Supermarkets Ltd *

Should you be in this directory? See the form at the back for new entries and amendments

100

Smith, Andy (Mr)
Group Human Resources Director, Boots Group Plc *

Snook, Hans (Mr)
Non-Executive Chairman, Carphone Warehouse Plc *

Spindler, Angela (Mrs)
Planning Development Director, Asda Stores Ltd *

Steiner, Tim (Mr)
Chief Executive, Ocado Ltd

Swan, Clive (Mr)
Chairman, Capital Sound & Vision
Personal Email: clives@csv.co.uk
Quals/Educ: BSc Economics at Kingston (1969–72)

Tatton-Brown, Duncan (Mr)
Finance Director, B & Q Plc *
Personal Email: duncan.tatton-brown@virgin.co.uk
DOB: 15/03/65
Marital Status: Married
Memberships:
ACMA

Taylor, Roger (Mr)
Chief Financial Officer, Carphone Warehouse Plc *

Terras, Duncan (Mr)
Human Resources Director, Focus DIY Ltd *

Terrell, Robin (Mr)
UK Managing Director, Amazon.co.uk

Thomas, Scott (Mr)
Head of E-Commerce, Phones 4u *

Toor, Jaswant (Mr)
Managing Director, EmpireDirect.co.uk

Trujillo, Solomon (Mr)
Chief Executive, Orange Plc *

Tucker, Phil (Mr)
Sales & Marketing Director, Buy Electrical Direct

Vandenberghe, Mark (Mr)
International Director, Arcadia Group Ltd *

Vandendyck, Pat (Ms)
Finance Director, Capital Sound & Vision

Vandevelde, Luc (Mr)
Chairman, Marks & Spencer Plc *

Vickers, Barry (Mr)
Chief Executive Officer, Holland & Barrett Retail Ltd *

Wall, R
Argos Direct Director, Argos Retail Group *

Walsh-Hill, Stephen (Mr)
Finance Director, Blackwell's UK *

Watts, Christine (Ms)
Corporate Affairs Director, Asda Stores Ltd *

West, Christopher (Mr)
Finance Director, Grattan Plc *

Whiting, Bill (Mr)
Chief Executive, B & Q Plc *

Whitman, Meg (Ms)
President and Chief Executive Officer, eBay UK Ltd

Wilkinson, Nick (Mr)
Managing Director, Currys

Williams, Dave (Mr)
Finance Director, Focus DIY Ltd *

Wolfson, Simon (Mr)
Chief Executive, Next Plc *

Should you be in this directory? See the form at the back for new entries and amendments

101

ALPHABETICAL LISTING BY

Company Name

RETAILERS

A F Blakemore & Son Ltd

Head Office and Spar Depot, Long Acres Industrial
Estate, Rosehill, Willenhall, West Midlands
WV13 2JP
Tel: 01902 366066   **Fax:** 01902 602361
Email: afb@afblakemore.com
Website: www.afblakemore.com
Sector: Convenience Store
Executives:
Geoff Hallam, Managing Director
Anthony Pannell, Finance Director
Sarah Trueman, Marketing Manager
David White, Trading Director

A Jones & Sons Ltd

18 Maple Road, Eastbourne, East Sussex BN23 6NZ
Tel: 01323 730 532
Sector: Footwear
Executives:
Ken Bartle, Managing Director
Emma Halford, Marketing Manager
D Johnson, Financial Director
Ian Long, Merchandising & Logistics Manager
Peter Phillips, Chairman

Adams Childrenswear

Attleborough House, Attleborough Industrial Estate,
Townsend Drive, Nuneaton, Warwickshire CV11 6RU
Tel: 024 7635 1000   **Fax:** 024 7634 5583
Website: www.adams.co.uk
Sector: Clothing
Executives:
Amanda Campbell, Head of Strategic Marketing
Ian Cooper, Multi-Channel Director
David Empson, New Brands Director
Christine Evans, Director of Merchandise
Michael Hobbs, Chief Executive
Sue Mackness, Human Resources Director
Dean Murray, Chief Operating Officer
Brian Smith, Head of Property and Central Retail
    Operations
Philip Walker, Managing Director, Product
Kevin Witts, Group Finance Director

Adminstore Ltd

Europa House, Northolt Industrial Estate, Rowdell
Road, Northolt, Middlesex UB5 6AG
Tel: 020 8845 1255   **Fax:** 020 8842 1353
Website: www.europafoods.com
Sector: Convenience Store
Executives:
Raju Hiremath, Finance Director
Jitu M Patel, Managing Director

AJT Trading Ltd

Marathon House, Olympic Business Park, Drybridge
Road, Dundonald, Ayrshire KA2 9AE, Scotland
Tel: 01563 852 200
Sector: Clothing
Executives:
Mike Drury, Head of Finance
Tom Hunter, Chief Executive
Jim McGonigle, Retail Director

Aldi Stores Ltd

Holly Lane, Atherstone, Warwickshire CV9 2SQ
Tel: 01827 711800   **Fax:** 01827 710866
Website: www.aldi.com
Sector: Food and Drink
Executives:
Tony Bains, Buying Director
Paul Foley, Managing Director
Andreas Siegman, Regional Managing Director

Alexon Group Plc

40–48 Guildford Street, Luton, Bedfordshire LU1 2PB
Tel: 01582 723131   **Fax:** 01582 399890
Sector: Clothing
Executives:
Michael Percy Adams, Non-Executive Director
Patrick E Cooper, Chairman
Annie Davies, Design Director, Eastex
Charles Duffy, Retail Operations Director, Bay
    Trading
Richard Hepton, Property Director
Tony Kirton, Merchandise Director
John Osborn, Chief Executive Officer
David Payne, Brand Retail Operations Director
Robin Piggot, Finance Director
Leslie Thompson, Fashion Director
Tracy White, Commercial Director, Bay Trading

Alfred Jones Ltd

Stanley House, 1 Honiton Way, Penketh, Warrington,
Cheshire WA5 2EY
Tel: 01925 726666   **Fax:** 01925 790375
Sector: Food and Drink
Executives:
Tom Calderbank, Managing Director
Ken Gallant, Development Director
E D Harlow, Director and Company Secretary
Johnathon A Jones, Chairman
Rod Tindall, Trading Director
Mark Turner, Operations Director

all:sports Retail Ltd

Unit 3, Horsfield Way, Bredbury, Stockport, Cheshire
SK6 2RT
Tel: 0161 430 8330   **Fax:** 0161 494 1353
Email: cservices@allsports.co.uk
Website: www.allsports.co.uk

Should you be in this directory? See the form at the back for new entries and amendments

Sector: Sports

Executives:

Jeremy Bradburn, Chief Executive and Financial
Director

Phillip Cormosh, Finance Director

Phillip Cornish, IT Director

Mike Donnelly, Merchandising Director

David E Hughes, Chairman

Ron Rome, Sales Director

Mark Tomlinson, Distribution Director

Julian Wilkinson, Director

Allders Department Stores Limited

P.O. Box 359 Centre Tower, The Whitgift Centre,
Croydon CR9 1NN

Tel: 020 8256 7939　　**Fax:** 020 8256 7913

Email: help@allders.com

Website: www.allders.com

Sector: Department Store

Executives:

Harvey Ainley, Finance Director

Mark Cherry, Head of Property

Richard Collins, Director for Retail Properties

Phil Cox, Commercial Director

Terry Green, Chief Executive

Penny Jeffreys, IT Director

Julian Perryman, Controller of E-Commerce

Paul Rattenbury, Head of Retail, Central UK

Steve Sharp, Marketing Director

Colin Terry, Merchandise Director

Allied Carpets Group

Allied House, 76 High Street, Orpington, Kent BR6 0JQ

Tel: 01689 895000　　**Fax:** 01689 895013

Website: www.alliedcarpets.co.uk

Sector: Carpets

Executives:

Andrew Green, Marketing Manager

Claire Herbert, Head of Property

Clive Hutchinson, Chief Executive

Dave Mills, Head of IT

Simon Stuart, IT Manager

Jean Wattel, Finance Director

Alpha Retail

Fairway House, Green Lane, Hounslow, Middlesex
TW4 6BU

Tel: 020 8707 0300　　**Fax:** 020 8707 0301

Website: www.alpha-retail.co.uk

Sector: Airport Retailing

Executives:

Steve Buckley, Managing Director, UK Specialities

Ben Deller, Marketing Manager, World News

Graham Frost, Chairman

David King, Executive Director and Managing
Director of Alpha Retail Shopping

Heather McRae, Finance Director

Paul Possamai, Managing Director of Alpha Inflight
Retail

American Golf Discount Centre Ltd

Europa Boulevard, Gemini Business Park, Westbrook,
Warrington, Cheshire WA5 7YW

Tel: 01925 488400　　**Fax:** 01925 488411

Website: www.americangolf.co.uk

Sector: Sports

Executives:

Howard Bilton, Purchase Director

Mark Bridge, Marketing Director

Johnathan Fellows, Finance Director

Chris McDonald, Retail Operations Director

Tony Norton, Managing Director

Ann Summers Ltd

Gold Group House, Godstone Road, Whyteleafe,
Caterham, Surrey CR3 0GG

Tel: 01883 629629　　**Fax:** 01883 629220

Website: www.annsummers.com

Sector: Clothing

Executives:

John Clarke, Retail Operations Director

Jacqueline Gold, Chief Executive and Managing
Director

Ray Unadkat, Finance Director

Apollo 2000 Ltd

311 Middlemore Road, Handsworth, Birmingham
B21 0AL

Tel: 0121 551 0633　　**Fax:** 0121 551 0633

Sector: Electricals

Executives:

Nick Barrett, Chairman

John Berlyn, Finance Director

David Broughall, Managing Director

Derek Cooper, Purchasing Director

John Graham, Head of Marketing

Paul Morton, Sales Director

Arcadia Group Ltd

Colegrave House, 70 Berners Street, London W1P
3NL

Tel: 020 7636 8040

Email: customer.service@arcadiagroup.co.uk

Website: www.arcadiagroup.co.uk

Sector: Clothing

Executives:

Amir Afkami, Finance Director, Evans

Paul Budge, Finance Director

Clem Constantine, Property and Retail Planning
Director

Tania Foster-Brown, Director of Public Relations and
Special Events

Mike Goring, Group Operations Director

Lord Anthony Grabiner, Chairman

Should you be in this directory? See the form at the back for new entries and amendments

Ian Grabiner, Chief Operating Officer
Philip Green, Owner
John Hind, Trading Director
Trisha Magowan, Brand Director, Evans
Eva Pascoe, Joint Managing Director, Zoom
Heather Powell, Head of Store Design and
    Development
Frances Russell, Brand Director, Burton
David Shepherd, Brand Director, Topman
Jane Shepherdson, Brand Director, Top Shop
Mark Vandenberghe, International Director

Argos Ltd

489–499 Avebury Boulevard, Saxon Gate West,
Milton Keynes MK9 2NW
Tel: 0845 124 0044   **Fax:** 01908 692301
Website: www.argos.co.uk
Sector: Mixed Retailer
Executives:
Paul Geddes, Marketing Director
B Idun, Stores Director
Carol Kavanagh, Human Resources Director
S Melton, Supply Chain Director
Stephen Robinson, Finance Director
Maria Thompson, Commercial Director

Asda Stores Ltd

Asda House, Southbank, Great Wilson Street, Leeds
LS11 5AD
Tel: 0113 243 5435   **Fax:** 0113 241 7261
Website: www.asda.co.uk
Sector: Food and Drink
Executives:
Richard Baker, Deputy Chief Operating Officer
Andy Bond, Trading Director, Non-Food
Glenn Bowles, Retail Managing Director
David Cheesewright, Deputy Trading Director
Tony De Nunzio, President and Chief Operating
    Officer (Wal-Mart UK)
David Gibbons, Distribution Director
Tracey Grailey, General Manager
John Irwin, Customer Sevices Director
Denise Jagger, Company Secretary
Judith McKenna, Chief Financial Officer
Tony Page, Director, General Merchandise
Chris Pilling, Marketing Director
Angela Spindler, Trading and Marketing Director,
    Food
Christine Watts, Corporate Affairs Director

Asprey & Garrard Ltd

167 New Bond Street, London W1Y 0AR
Tel: 020 7493 6767   **Fax:** 020 7491 0384
Website: www.asprey.com; www.asprey-garrard.com
Sector: Jewellery
Executives:
Gianluca Brozetti, Retail Director

Philip Davis, Marketing Director
Lord Bruce Dundas, Chairman and Chief Executive
Sally Hogg, Merchandise Director
Simon Williamson, Managing Director

Austin Reed Group Plc

16–21 Sackville Street, London W1S 3DN
Tel: 020 7534 7777   **Fax:** 020 7287 6749
Website: www.austinreed.co.uk
Sector: Clothing
Executives:
Geoff Gibson, Group Finance Director
Chris Holmes, Brand Director, Austin Reed
Roger Jennings, Chief Executive
David Lowbridge, Managing Director, Country
    Casuals and Austin Reed
Amanda Macloud-Smith, Sales and Operations
    Director, Country Casuals
Hugh Reynolds, Customer Liason Manager
Nicola Reynolds, Marketing Manager
John Robins, Chairman

B & M Retail Ltd

Unit 1G, Squires Gate Industrial Estate, Squires Gate
Lane, Blackpool FY4 3RN
Tel: 01253 349040   **Fax:** 01253 348721
Website: www.bargainmadness.com
Sector: Discounter
Executives:
David Gravells, Chairman
Stuart Greenwood, Chief Executive
Paul Taylor, Buying Director
John Trubshaw, Retail Operations Manager

B & Q Plc

Portswood House, 1 Hampshire Corporate Park,
Chandlers Ford, Eastleigh, Hampshire SO53 3YX
Tel: 023 8025 6256   **Fax:** 023 8025 7480
Website: www.diy.com
Sector: DIY
Executives:
George Adams, Commercial and Marketing Director
I Morrice, Managing Director, Warehouses
Duncan Tatton-Brown, Finance Director
Matt Tyson, Managing Director, Super Centre
Bill Whiting, Chief Executive

Bally UK Sales Ltd

116 New Bond Street, London W1S 1EN
Tel: 020 7408 9877   **Fax:** 020 7408 9888
Website: www.bally.com
Sector: Footwear
Executives:
Marco Franchini, Chief Executive
Michael Nelson, Finance Director
Robert Robinson, Retail Operations Director, UK

Should you be in this directory? See the form at the back for new entries and amendments

Bargain Booze Limited

Unit 1, Weston Road, Crewe, Cheshire CW1 6BP
Tel: 0845 3450001   **Fax:** 01270 614703
Email: sales@bargainbooze.co.uk
Website: www.bargainbooze.co.uk
Sector: Off Licence
Executives:
Robert Mayor, Joint Managing Director
Allan Whittle, Joint Managing Director

Beaverbrooks the Jewellers Ltd

Adele House, Park Road, St Annes on Sea, Lancashire
FY8 1RE
Tel: 0800 1692329   **Fax:** 01253 729008
Email: info@beaverbrooks.co.uk
Website: www.beaverbrooks.co.uk
Sector: Jewellery
Executives:
Mark Adlestone, Joint Managing Director
Andrew Brown, Joint Managing Director
Brian Nicholson, Finance Director

Bells Stores Limited

Wandhill Avenue, Skelton Industrial Estate, Skelton
TS12 2LQ
Tel: 01287 650640   **Fax:** 01287 653970
Website: www.bellsstores.com
Sector: Convenience Store
Executives:
Les Bell, Chairman
Steven Bell, Joint Managing Director
David Graham, Joint Managing Director
Marcus Leek, Financial and IT Director
Chris Suggett, Buying Director
Michael Walker, Retail Operations Director

Benetton Retail 1988 Ltd

5th Floor, Byron House, 7–9 St James' Street, London
SW1A 1EE
Tel: 020 7389 8120   **Fax:** 020 7389 6260
Website: www.benetton-retail.co.uk;
www.benetton.com
Sector: Clothing
Executives:
Guiseppe Andreini, Product Director
Paolo Panizzo, Managing Consultant
Paul Robinson, Director
Adrian Tanner, Finance Director

Bennetts Retail Ltd

Unit 47, White Lodge Business Park, Hall Road,
Norwich NR4 6DG
Tel: 01603 625955   **Fax:** 01603 627270
Email: headoffice@bennetts.co.uk
Website: www.bennettsonline.co.uk
Sector: Electricals

Executives:
Dean Adams, A/V Purchasing and Marketing Director
Graham Eaglesham, Financial Director
Richard Jackson, Managing Director
Mike Jones, Commercial Director
Lawrence Naylor, Purchasing Director, Domestic
Appliances

Bentalls

Wood Street, Kingston upon Thames KT1 1TX
Tel: 020 8546 1001   **Fax:** 020 8549 6163
Website: www.bentalls.co.uk
Sector: Department Store
Executives:
Adam Fenwick, Deputy Chairman
Ray Harris, Customer Services Manager
Belinda Hide, Head of Marketing

Bewise Ltd[1]

Tureck House, Drayton Road, Shirley, West Midlands
B90 4NG
Tel: 0121 705 8286   **Fax:** 0121 704 5264
Email: marketing@bewise.co.uk
Website: www.bewise.com
Sector: Clothing
Executives:
Tony Holmes, Property Controller
Colin Ingram, Finance Director
David Tucker, Director
John Wyles, Sales and Operations Director
[1]See also QS Plc (parent company)

Bhs Plc

Marylebone House, 129–137 Marylebone Road,
London NW1 5QD
Tel: 020 7262 3288   **Fax:** 020 7723 1115
Website: www.bhs.co.uk
Sector: Mixed Retailer
Executives:
Ian Allkins, Commercial Director
Tony Brown, Retail Director
Paul Coakley, Finance Director
Romney Drury, Marketing Director
Philip Green, Owner
Allan Leighton, Chairman
Martin Whitehead, Operations Manager

Birthdays Group Ltd

Dumers Lane, Bury, Greater Manchester BL9 9UR
Tel: 0161 763 7353   **Fax:** 0161 763 7354
Email: info@birthdays.co.uk
Website: www.birthdays.co.uk
Sector: Stationery
Executives:
Ian Macritchie, Chairman
Chris Tapp, Buying and Merchandising Director
Nick Walters, Finance Director

Should you be in this directory? See the form at the back for new entries and amendments

Blackwell's UK

Beaver House, Hythe Bridge Street, Oxford OX1 2ET
Tel: 01865 792792   **Fax:** 01865 791438
Email: blackwell.extra@blackwell.co.uk
Website: www.blackwell.co.uk
Sector: Books

Executives:

Phillip Blackwell, Chief Executive
Harry Metcalf, Commercial Manager
Dominic Myers, Managing Director
Michael Neil, Marketing Director
Matthew Smith, Customer Services Manager
Steven Walsh-Hill, Finance Director

Blockbuster Entertainment Ltd

Harefield Place, The Drive, Ickenham, Uxbridge,
Middlesex UB10 8AQ
Tel: 01895 258866   **Fax:** 01895 272062
Website: www.blockbuster.co.uk;
www.blockbuster.com
Sector: Music and Video

Executives:

Bryan Bevin, Vice-President International
    Operations
Amon Feeney, Finance Director
Steve Foulser, Vice-President
Jean Jenkins, Retail Operations Director
Vernon Salt, Senior Vice-President
Alexander Sparks, Managing Director

Bodycare (Health & Beauty) Limited

Forefield House, Station Road, Bamber Bridge,
Preston PR5 6GS
Tel: 01772 626628   **Fax:** 01772 627115
Sector: Health and Beauty

Executives:

Graham Blackledge, Joint Managing Director
Margaret Blackledge, Joint Managing Director
Roy McFarland, Finance Director

Bon Marché Ltd

Jubliee Way, Grange Moor, Wakefield, West Yorkshire
WF4 4SJ
Tel: 01924 700100   **Fax:** 01924 700225
Website: www.bonmarche.co.uk
Sector: Clothing

Executives:

Steve Alldridge, Finance Director
Andrew McDonald, Marketing and Retail Director
Zoe Milner, Trade Marketing Manager
David Pidgeon, Managing Director
Charlie Pogson, Head of Marketing
Liz Roy, Customer Services Manager
Julie Taylor, Head of Retail
Thiry Thompson, Head of Buying

Boots Group Plc

1 Thane Road West, Nottingham NG2 3AA
Tel: 0115 950 6111   **Fax:** 0115 959 5083
Website: www.boots.com; www.wellbeing.com
Sector: Health and Beauty

Executives:

Richard Baker, Chief Executive
Paul Bateman, Group Operations Director
Howard Dodd, Chief Financial Officer
Michael Oliver, Company Secretary
Sir Nigel Rudd, Chairman
Andy Smith, Group Human Resources Director

Borders UK Ltd

120 Charing Cross Road, London WC2H 0JR
Tel: 020 7379 7313   **Fax:** 020 7836 0373
Website: www.borders.co.uk
Sector: Books

Executives:

Luthfa Begum, Marketing Manager
Louise Collinge, Merchandise and Marketing Director
Phillip Downer, Managing Director
Sara Halton, Financial Director
Matt Taylor, Marketing Manager

Botterills Convenience Stores Ltd

Block 9, South Avenue, Blantyre Industrial Estate,
Blantyre, Glasgow G72 0XB, Scotland
Tel: 01698 824311   **Fax:** 01698 824231
Sector: Convenience Store

Executives:

James Botterill, Managing Director
James Cochrane, Customer Services Manager
Allan Craig, Financial Director
Lizette Craig, Retail Operations Director
Brian Straiton, Operations Manager

Bowie-Castlebank Group Ltd

1 Downside Lane, Glasgow G1 9BZ, Scotland
Tel: 0141 307 9150   **Fax:** 0141 307 5566
Email: info@klick.co.uk
Website: www.klick.co.uk
Sector: Photographic Services

Executives:

Jonathan Bowie, Managing Director
John Doohan, Finance Controller
Mike Galloway, Customer Services Manager
Sandy Kennedy, Business Development Director

Brantano UK Ltd

Interlink Business Park, Bardon, Coalville, Leicester
LE67 1LD
Tel: 01530 516100   **Fax:** 0870 9901602
Website: www.brantano.co.uk
Sector: Footwear

Executives:

Terry Boot, Financial Director

Should you be in this directory? See the form at the back for new entries and amendments

John Hood, Managing Director
Robert Lowden, Buying and Merchandising Director
Judith Tankard, Customer Services Manager

British Heart Foundation, Shops Division

Crown House, Church Road, Claygate, Surrey
KT10 0BF
Tel: 01372 477300   **Fax:** 01372 477491
Email: enquiries@bhfshops.org.uk
Website: www.bhf.org.uk
Sector: Clothing
Executives:
Ken Blair, Chief Executive, Shops Division
Anita Jani, Marketing Executive

Broughton Brothers Ltd

Carter Lane, Shirebrook, Mansfield, Nottinghamshire
NG20 8AH
Tel: 01623 746270   **Fax:** 01623 744304
Sector: Footwear
Executives:
David S Broughton, Managing Director
Chris Coleman, Financial Director
Robert Nightingale, Customer Services Manager

Brown & Jackson

Knowsthorpe Gate, Cross Green Industrial Estate,
Leeds, West Yorkshire LS9 0NP
Tel: 0113 240 6406   **Fax:** 0113 254 9371
Website: www.poundstretcher.co.uk
Sector: Discounter
Executives:
Gary Brown, Joint Finance Director
Margaret Melville, Buying Director
Mike Morrison, Marketing Director
Pat Quiney, Property Director
Hennie Roelofse, Joint Finance Director
Mark Saunders, Merchandising Director
Les Thomas, IT Director
Mandy Williams, Director of Operations

Budgens Stores Ltd

Stonefield Way, Ruislip, Middlesex HA4 0JR
Tel: 020 8422 9511   **Fax:** 020 8423 2263
Website: www.budgens.co.uk
Sector: Convenience Store
Executives:
Rod Alexander, Communications Director
Garry Barr, IT Director
Cliff Goodman, Trading Director
Richard Hare, Legal and Human Resources Director
Martin Hyson, Chief Executive Officer
Norman Kears, Partnership Director
Greg Kopacz, Manufacturing Director
Vince Maloney, Operations Director
Eoin McGettigan, Chairman
James Pye, Property Director

Simon Pyper, Finance Director
Stephanie Rice, Marketing Director
Mike Taylor, Development Director

Burberrys

18–22 Haymarket, London SW1Y 4DQ
Tel: 020 7968 0000   **Fax:** 020 7968 0067
Website: www.burberry.com
Sector: Accessories
Executives:
Joanna Binder, Head of Merchandising
Sir Victor Blank, Chairman, GUS
Peter Blythe, Finance Director
Rose Maria Bravo, Chief Executive
Pamela Cavenagh, Senior Vice-President, Accessories
William Chellingsworth, Store Operations Manager
Pat Doherty, Senior Vice-President, Marketing
Jason Friend, Advertising Manager

C & J Clark International

40 High Street, Street, Somerset BA16 0YA
Tel: 01458 443131   **Fax:** 01458 447547
Website: www.clarks.co.uk
Sector: Footwear
Executives:
Robin Beecham, Financial Director
Peter Bolliger, Chief Executive
Rosemary Carr, Marketing Services Director
Ken Dobinson, Sales Director
Richard Newman, Director of Retail Operations
Roger A Pedder, Chairman
Christopher Pleeth, Property Director
Melissa Potter, Managing Director, UK Division

Cancer Research UK

61 Lincoln's Inn Fields, London WC2A 3PX
Tel: 020 7269 3209
Website: www.cancerresearchuk.org
Sector: Clothing
Executives:
Paul Nurse, Director General
Richard Taylor, Retail Director

Cargo Homeshop

Carpenter House, Thame Park Industrial Estate,
Thame, Oxfordshire OX9 3HD
Tel: 01844 261800   **Fax:** 01844 261241
Website: www.cargohomeshop.com
Sector: Housewares
Executives:
Peter Bielby, Head of Business Development
Steve Smith, Finance Director
Stephen Tague, Chief Executive

Carpetright Plc

Amberley House, New Road, Rainham, Essex RM13 8QN
Tel: 01708 525522   **Fax:** 01708 559361

Should you be in this directory? See the form at the back for new entries and amendments

Email: enquiries@carpetright.co.uk
Website: www.carpetright.co.uk
Sector: Carpets
Executives:
Patricia Dregent, Company Secretary
Lord Harris of Peckham, Chairman and Chief
    Executive
Martin Harris, Director of Buying
John Kitching, Managing Director
Kevin Nicholson, Head of Finance
Darren Shapland, Finance Director

Carpetworld Manchester Ltd

Macclesfield Road, Hazel Grove, Stockport, Cheshire
SK7 6DD
Tel: 0161 456 9171   **Fax:** 0161 456 1462
Email: info@carpetworld.demon.co.uk
Sector: Carpets
Executives:
Sean Brenna, Company Secretary
Mark Pryer, Managing Director and Marketing
    Director

Carphone Warehouse Plc

North Acton Business Park, Wales Farm Road,
London W3 6RS
Tel: 020 8896 5000   **Fax:** 020 8896 5005
Website: www.carphonewarehouse.com
Sector: Electricals
Executives:
Richard Collier, Group Property Director
Charles Dunstone, Chief Executive Officer
Adrian Guthrie, Head of Human Resources
Jonathan Hook, Retail Director
Gordon Nardini, Head of Retail Marketing
Hans Snook, Non-Executive Chairman
Roger Taylor, Chief Financial Officer
Vanessa Tipple, Head of Press Office

Cash Converters UK Ltd

Cash Converters House, 17 Gentlemans Field, Ware
SG12 0EF
Tel: 01920 485696   **Fax:** 01920 485695
Email: uksupportcentre@cashconverters.net
Website: www.cashconverters.co.uk
Sector: Mixed Retailer
Executives:
Caroline Barbour, Office Manager
Mark Lemmon, Director of Operations, South
Richard Pilgrim, Director of Operations, North
Jim Spratley, Finance Director
Julian Urry, Managing Director

Chevron Texaco

1 Westferry Circus, Canary Wharf, London E14 4HA
Tel: 020 7719 3000
Website: www.chevrontexaco.com

Sector: Petrol
Executives:
Roger Ebert, Executive Vice-President
Dave O'Reilly, Chairman and Chief Executive Officer

Choices Video

19–24 Manasty Road, Orton Southgate,
Peterborough, Cambridgeshire PE2 6UP
Tel: 01733 233464
Website: www.choicesvideo.co.uk
Sector: Music and Video
Executives:
Steve Barker, Development Director
Diane Gardner, Managing Director
John Sealey, Finance Director
Anthony Skilt, Commercial Director
Geoff Spink, Sales Director

Church & Co. Footwear Ltd

St James Road, Northampton NN5 5JB
Tel: 01604 751251   **Fax:** 01604 754405
Website: sales@church-footwear.com
Sector: Footwear
Executives:
Johnathon Church, Finance Director
William Church, Production Director
Stephen Etheridge, Chief Executive
Francesco Kliner, Chief Financial Officer
Steven Martin, IT Director
Jane McCann, Retail Operations Director

Claire's Accessories

Unit 4, Bromford Gate, Bromford Lane, Birmingham
B24 8DW
Tel: 0121 682 8000   **Fax:** 0121 682 8049
Website: www.claires.co.uk
Sector: Accessories
Executives:
Mark Dillane, Head of Property Department
Lyle Finlay, Chief Executive
Anthony Greenwood, Finance Director
Melanie Haworth, Buying and Merchandising Director
Ian Ogden, Retail Director
Andrew Wallbridge, Human Resources Director
Jamie Zuppinger, European Resources Manager

Clinton Cards

The Crystal Building, Langston Road, Loughton,
Essex IG10 3TH
Tel: 020 8502 8236   **Fax:** 020 8502 0295
Website: www.clintoncards.co.uk
Sector: Stationery
Executives:
Mike Bugler, Marketing Director
John Coleman, Non-Executive Director
Barry Hartog, Finance Director and Company
    Secretary

Should you be in this directory? See the form at the back for new entries and amendments

Clinton Lewin, Managing Director
Debbie Lewin, Product Development Director
Donald Lewin, Chairman
John Robinson, Operations Director

Co-operative Group (CWS) Limited

P.O. Box 53, New Century House, Corporation Street, Manchester M60 4ES
Tel: 0161 834 1212   **Fax:** 0161 834 4507
Website: www.co-op.co.uk
Sector: Convenience Store
Executives:
Martin Beaumont, Chief Executive
John Bowes, Chief General Manager, Marketing
Keith Darwin, Chairman
Malcolm Hepworth, Chief Operating Officer
Paul Hewitt, Chief Financial Officer
Tony Robertson, Head of Department Stores
Deborah Robinson, Head of Brand Management
Julia Rogers, General Manger, Central Services
David Seaman, Head of Strategic Development
Michelle Vernon, Public Relations Manager

Comet Group Plc

Comet House, Three Rivers Court, Rickmansworth, Hertfordshire WD3 1FX
Tel: 01923 710000   **Fax:** 01923 714420
Email: direct@comet.co.uk
Website: www.comet.co.uk
Sector: Electricals
Executives:
Bob Darke, Business Unit Head
Simon Fox, Managing Director
Hugh Harvey, Deputy Managing Director, Commercial
David Morriss, Head of Property
Alana O'Sullivan, Corporate Communications

Costcutter Supermarkets Group Limited

Harvest Mills, Common Road, Dunnington, York YO19 5RY
Tel: 01904 488663   **Fax:** 01904 486535
Email: sales@costcutter.com
Website: www.costcutter.com
Sector: Convenience Store
Executives:
Angela Barber, Trading and Marketing Director
Sarah Chick, Sales Development Executive
Colin Graves, Managing Director
Ian Graves, Marketing Manager
Nick Ivel, Finance Director
David Thompson, Sales and Development Director

Cotton Traders Ltd

Cotton Traders House, 1–2 Atlantic Street, Broadheath, Altrincham WA14 5GZ
Tel: 0870 333 3449
Sector: Clothing

Executives:
Fran Cotton, Managing Director
Nick Hamblin, Retail Director
Mark Howling, Finance Controller
David Jones, Chairman
Steve Smith, Sales Director

Courts Plc

The Grange, 1 Central Road, Morden, Surrey SM4 5PQ
Tel: 020 8640 3322   **Fax:** 020 8410 9400
Website: www.courtsplc.com
Sector: Furniture
Executives:
Nigel Blake, Plc Director
Andrew Cohen, Director
Bruce Cohen, Chief Executive
Steven Cohen, UK Managing Director
Sarah Ghinn, Corporate Communications
Chris Lee, Company Secretary
Mark Muller, Finance Director
William Powell, Property Director
Malcolm Samuels, Finance Director
Robert Shrager, Chairman
Gary Tubb, Deputy Managing Director

Cromwells Madhouse

Cromwells House, Unit 3 Palace of Industry, Fulton Road, Wembley, Middlesex HA9 OTF
Tel: 020 8903 5888   **Fax:** 020 8795 3077
Email: sales@madhouse.co.uk
Website: www.madhouse.co.uk
Sector: Clothing
Executives:
Melvyn Reiss, Managing Director
Carol Souber, Finance Controller
Peter Souber, Managing Director
Mick Tesseras, Systems Manager
Nick Tesseras, Customer Service Manager
Peter Tesseras, Marketing Director
Paul Ward, General Manager

Debenhams Plc

1 Welbeck Street, London W1G 0AA
Tel: 020 7408 4444   **Fax:** 020 7408 3366
Website: www.debenhams.com
Sector: Department Store
Executives:
Justine Allister, Head of Public Relations
Hugh Bradley, Communications Director
Timothy Davies, Strategy Director
Belinda Earl, Chief Executive
Joanna George, Head of Corporate Communications
Jane Guillaume, Personnel Director
Peter Jarvis, Chairman
Neil Kennedy, Finance and Planning Director
Amanda Metcalfe, Head of Customer Management
Nigel Palmer, Retail Operations Director

Should you be in this directory? See the form at the back for new entries and amendments

Matthew Roberts, Finance Director
Michael Sharp, Trading Director

DFS Furniture Company plc

Bentley Moor Lane, Adwick-le-Street, Doncaster
DN6 7BD
Tel: 01302 330365   **Fax:** 01302 330880
Website: www.dfs.co.uk
Sector: Furniture
Executives:
Ian Francis Bowness, Finance Director
Lord Graham Kirkham, Executive Chairman
Jon Massey, Chief Operating Officer

Diesel

55 Argyle Street, London WC1H 8EF
Tel: 0207 833 2255
Sector: Clothing
Executives:
Daniel Barton, Head of Marketing
Annie Guerard, Finance Director
Panicko Philipou, Managing Director
Renzo Rosso, Group Chairman
Peter Schofield-Lawley, Commercial Director

Disney Consumer Products

3 Queen Caroline Street, Hammersmith, London
W6 9PE
Tel: 020 8222 1000   **Fax:** 020 8222 2795
Sector: Music and Video
Executives:
Christ Davey, Managing Director
Tessa Moore, Vice-President of Marketing
Ben Teicher, Finance Director

Dollond & Aitchison Group Plc

D&A Campus, 50 Rocky Lane, Aston Cross Business
Park, Aston, Birmingham B6 5RQ
Tel: 0121 706 6133   **Fax:** 0121 697 2700
Website: www.danda.co.uk
Sector: Health and Beauty
Executives:
Andy Ferguson, Operations Director
Russell Hardy, Chief Executive
James Hogg, Franchise Director
Robert Zaina, Finance Director

DSG Retail Ltd

Dixons House, Maylands Avenue, Hemel Hempstead,
Hertfordshire HP2 7TG
Tel: 0870 850 3333   **Fax:** 01442 233218
Website: www.dixons.co.uk
Sector: Electricals
Executives:
John Clare, Chief Executive
Sir John Collins, Chairman
Jeremy Darroch, Finance Diretor

David Gilbert, Chief Operating Officer, Central
Operations
David Hamid, Chief Operating Officer, Retail
Operations
Damian Norton, Information Systems Director

Dunelm (Soft Furnishings) Ltd

Fosse Way, Syston, Leicester, Leicestershire LE7 1NF
Tel: 0116 264 4400   **Fax:** 0116 264 4459
Email: enquiries@dunelm-mill.co.uk
Website: www.dunelm-mill.co.uk
Sector: Furniture
Executives:
Will Adderly, Managing Director
Richard Antcliff, Marketing Manager

E H Booth & Co. Ltd

4–6 Fishergate, Preston, Lancashire PR1 3LJ
Tel: 01772 251701   **Fax:** 01772 204316
Email: admin@booth-supermarkets.co.uk
Website: www.booth-supermarkets.co.uk
Sector: Food and Drink
Executives:
David Benson, Director, Buying and Distribution
Edwin Booth, Chairman
Chris Dee, IT and Marketing Director
John Vandermeer, Finance Director

Early Learning Centre

South Marston Park, Swindon, Wiltshire SN3 4TJ
Tel: 01793 831300   **Fax:** 01793 443114
Website: www.elc.co.uk
Sector: Toys
Executives:
Fiona Davis, Brand Marketing Director
Sue Dorkin, Logistics Director
Mike France, Managing Director
John Goddard, Property Director
David Griffiths, Finance Director

Edinburgh Woollen Mill Ltd

Waverley Mills, Langholm, Dumfriesshire
DG13 OEB, Scotland
Tel: 01387 380611   **Fax:** 01387 380920
Website: www.ewm.co.uk
Sector: Clothing
Executives:
Philip Day, Chief Executive
David Houston, Financial Director
Carmel Leigh, Buying and Merchandising Director
Clare Oliver, Marketing Manager
Ed Sansom, IT Director
Alec Whitaker, Property Director

Esso Petroleum Co. Ltd

Exxonmobil House, Ermyn Way, Leatherhead KT22 8UX
Tel: 01372 222000   **Fax:** 01372 222556

Should you be in this directory? See the form at the back for new entries and amendments

Website: www.exxonmobil.co.uk
Sector: Petrol
Executives:
Gordon Munro, Retail Marketing Director
David Richardson, Convenience Retail Manager, UK
   and Ireland
Martin Todd, Retail Director

Etam Plc
Jubilee House, 213 Oxford Street, London W1D 2LF
Tel: 020 7437 5655   **Fax:** 020 7437 5083
Website: www.etamdeveloppement.com;
www.etam.com
Sector: Clothing
Executives:
Dawn Burrows, Customer Services Manager
Heather Cooper, Marketing Director
Jean-Claude Darrouzet, Chief Executive Officer
Cliff Glanfield, Head of Property
Nick Paine, Managing Director
Jane Perks, Retail Operations Director, UK

Ethel Austin Ltd
School Lane, Knowsley Business Park, Liverpool
L34 9GJ
Tel: 0151 546 7621   **Fax:** 0151 549 1380
Sector: Clothing
Executives:
Ray Carroll, Retail Operations Director
Philip E Hoskinson, Chief Executive
P Johnson, Non-Executive Director
J Martin, Chairman
Sue Tennant, Trading Director
Stephen Williams, Finance Director

F Hinds Ltd
24 Park Road, Uxbridge, Middlesex UB8 1NH
Tel: 01895 201000   **Fax:** 01895 201001
Email: customer.service@fhinds.co.uk
Website: www.fhinds.co.uk
Sector: Jewellery
Executives:
Michael Harding, Financial Director
Andrew Hinds, Buying Director
David Hinds, Managing Director
Neil Hinds, Property Director
Roy Hinds, Chairman

Faith Footwear
Faith House, 40/48 Chase Road, Park Royal, London
NW10 6PX
Tel: 020 8930 3400   **Fax:** 020 8930 3480
Website: www.faith.co.uk
Sector: Footwear
Executives:
Jonathan Faith, Managing Director
Samuel Faith, Chairman

Nilesh Karia, Senior Merchandiser
Paul O'Neill, Retail Director
Lionel Stock, Finance Director
Gemma Turner, Senior Buyer

Farmfoods Freezer Centre
7 Greens Road, Blairlinn Industrial Estate,
Cumbernauld G67 2TU, Scotland
Tel: 01236 456789   **Fax:** 01236 724427
Email: customerservices@farmfoods.co.uk
Website: www.farmfoods.co.uk
Sector: Food and Drink
Executives:
Eric Heard, Managing Director
Willy McReady, Property Director
David Robertson, Financial Director

Fenwick Ltd
63 New Bond Street, London W1A 3BS
Tel: 020 7629 9161   **Fax:** 020 7409 1890
Website: www.fenwick.co.uk
Sector: Department Store
Executives:
Jill Anders, Company Secretary
Peter Coates, Group Chief Accountant
John Fenwick, Deputy Chairman
Mark Fenwick, Group Chairman
Alan Smith, Financial Director
Lara Taglioni, Customer Services Manager

Findel Plc
Burley House, Bradford Road, Burley in Wharfedale,
Ilkley, West Yorkshire LS29 7DZ
Tel: 01943 864686   **Fax:** 01943 864986
Email: enquiries@findel.co.uk
Website: www.findel.co.uk
Sector: Mail Order
Executives:
Ivan Bolton, Director and Company Secretary
Keith Chapman, Chairman
Tony Johnson, Chief Executive
John Padovan, Non-Executive Director
Keith Sutcliffe, Customer Services Manager

Focus Wickes
Gawsworth House, Westmere Drive, Crewe, Cheshire
CW1 6XB
Tel: 01270 501555   **Fax:** 01270 250501
Website: www.focusdiy.co.uk
Sector: DIY
Executives:
Bill Archer, Chairman and Chief Executive Officer
Colin Ball, Group Commercial Services Director and
   E-Commerce
Jeremy Bird, Trading Director, Wickes
Richard Bird, Managing Director
Justin Farrington-Smith, Trading Director, Focus

Should you be in this directory? See the form at the back for new entries and amendments

Rob Gladwin, Operations Director
Jill Keen, Marketing Director
David Pearson, Group Commercial Director
John Rice, Group IT Director
Barbara Rimmer, Company Secretary
Duncan Terras, Group Human Resources Director
Paul Willis, Retail Director, Focus
Geoff Wilson, Deputy Chairman and Group Finance
    Director

Fortnum & Mason Plc

181 Piccadilly, London W1A 1ER
Tel: 020 7734 8040   **Fax:** 020 7437 3278
Email: info@fortnumandmason.co.uk
Website: www.fortnumandmason.co.uk
Sector: Department Store
Executives:
Les Collins, Financial Director
Kenneth Forrest, Managing Director
Stuart Gates, Managing Director
Jana Khayat, Chairman
N Moody, Customer Services Manager
Cathy O'Neill, Personnel Administration and Services
    Director

Fraser Hart Ltd

Hertsmere House, Shenley Road, Borehamwood,
Hertfordshire WD6 1TE
Tel: 020 8967 5800
Website: www.fraserhart.co.uk
Sector: Jewellery
Executives:
Lewis Hill, Managing Director
J Kelly, General Manager
Murray McGarvie, Chief Finance Officer

Freemans Plc

139 Clapham Road, London SW99 0HR
Tel: 020 7820 2000   **Fax:** 020 7820 2769
Website: www.freemans.com
Sector: Mail Order
Executives:
Michael L Hawker, Chief Executive
Simon Malcom, Head of E-Marketing
Jim Skelsey, Merchandise Director

French Connection

60–66 Great Portland Street, London W1N 7HX
Tel: 020 7399 7200   **Fax:** 020 7399 7201
Website: www.frenchconnection.com
Sector: Clothing
Executives:
Matthew Griffiths, Marketing Director
Steven Lock, Customer Services Manager
Stephen Marks, Chief Executive
Roy Naismith, Finance Director
Liz Pynor, Retail Director

Liz Stark, Sales Manager, Great Plains
Neil Williams, Chief Operating Director

Frozen Value Ltd

Lotherton Way, East Garforth Trading Estate,
Garforth, Leeds LS25 2JY
Tel: 0113 286 0254   **Fax:** 0113 232 0032
Website: www.frozen-value.co.uk
Sector: Food and Drink
Executives:
Kevin Gunter, Chief Executive
Karen Rees, Finance Director
P Spicer, Director

Furniture Village Plc

258 Bath Road, Slough SL1 4DX
Tel: 01753 897720   **Fax:** 01753 897730
Email: marketing@furniturevillage.co.uk
Website: www.furniturevillage.co.uk
Sector: Furniture
Executives:
Jack Clark, Finance Director
Peter Harrison, Managing Director
Jim Hodkinson, Chairman
David Imrie, Trading Director

Furnitureland Holdings Ltd

9th Floor, Yeoman House, 57–63 Croydon Road,
London SE20 7TP
Tel: 020 8768 7100   **Fax:** 020 8768 7130
Email: h.o@furnitureland.co.uk
Website: www.furnitureland.co.uk
Sector: Furniture
Executives:
Andrew Bratt, Property Director
Roger Handley, Marketing Director
Garry Hirth, Finance Director
John Jermine, Chairman
Chris Peddar, Managing Director
Jan Read, Customer Services Manager
David Sills, Buying Director

G 101 Off Sales Ltd

Burnfield Road, Thornliebank, Glasgow G46 7TT,
Scotland
Tel: 0141 636 6999
Sector: Off Licence
Executives:
George King, Managing Director
Alexander Miekle, Finance Director

G T Retail

High Wood Way, Lakeside Park, Barlborough,
Derbyshire S43 4XN
Tel: 01246 224800   **Fax:** 01246 283131
Email: enquiries@gtnews.co.uk
Website: www.gtnews.co.uk

Should you be in this directory? See the form at the back for new entries and amendments

Sector: Convenience Store

Executives:

David Clarke, Finance Director

Robert Morgan, Chairman

Richard Stevens, Purchasing Manager

Mark Titterton, Retail Director

Game Stores Group Ltd

Link House, Ellesfield Avenue, Bracknell, Berkshire RG12 8TB

Tel: 01344 464000　　**Fax:** 01344 464007

Website: www.game.uk.com

Sector: Electricals

Executives:

Mark Gawthorne, Financial Director

Martin Long, Chairman

Anna Macario, Director of Marketing

Lisa Morgan, Commercial Director

Games Workshop Group Plc

Willow Road, Nottingham NG7 2WS

Tel: 0115 916 8000　　**Fax:** 0115 916 8008

Website: www.games-workshop.com

Sector: Electricals

Executives:

Tom Kirby, Chairman and Chief Executive

Michael Sherwin, Group Finance Director

Mark Wells, General Manager, Games Workshop Ltd

Gap

Castlemound Way, Rugby, Warwickshire CV23 0WA

Tel: 01788 818300

Website: www.gap.com; www.gapinc.com

Sector: Clothing

Executives:

Andrew Allman, Senior Manager, Financial Planning and Analysis in Europe

Padraig Drennan, Senior Director, IT and Finance in Europe

Steve Finlan, Managing Director

Garry John, Senior Director, Real Estate and Store Development in Europe

Toby Lenk, Head of Online Sales Division

Paul Pressler, Chief Executive

George (Asda)

George House, Magna Park, Lutterworth, Leicestershire LE17 4XN

Tel: 01455 553090

Website: www.asda.co.uk

Sector: Clothing

Executives:

Phillip Auld, George UK Director

Andy Bond, Managing Director

Kate Bostock, Design Director

Neil Harrington, Finance Director

Gilesports Plc

Fortran Road, St Mellons, Cardiff CF3 0LT, Wales

Tel: 029 2077 4400　　**Fax:** 029 2077 4401

Website: www.gilesports.com

Sector: Clothing

Executives:

Andy Giles, Commercial Director

Howard Giles, Chairman

Gill Johnson, Customer Services Adminstrator

Dan Tranfield, Financial Director

Global Video Ltd

Global House, 96 Caledonia Street, Glasgow G5 0XG, Scotland

Tel: 0141 420 2000　　**Fax:** 0141 420 7140

Email: postoffice@globalvideo.co.uk

Website: www.globalvideo.co.uk

Sector: Music and Video

Executives:

Alick Bisset, Finance Director

Maqbool H Rasul, Managing Director

Z Rasul, Director

Globus Office World Plc

Harding Road, Brinklow, Milton Keynes MK10 0DF

Tel: 01908 286200　　**Fax:** 01908 286225

Website: www.office-world.co.uk

Sector: Office Supplies

Executives:

Ian Clarkson, Property Manager

Andy Etherington, Chief Executive Officer

Steven Jenkins, Customer Service Manager

Malcolm Northover, Chief Financial Officer

Goldsmiths Group Plc

Goldsmiths House, 2 Elland Road, Braunstone, Leicester LE3 1TT

Tel: 0116 2322000　　**Fax:** 0116 2322200

Website: www.goldsmiths.co.uk

Sector: Jewellery

Executives:

Robin Philpott, Merchandise and Distribution Director

Jurek Piasecki, Chairman and Chief Executive

Steve C Sargent, Financial Director

Jim E West, Sales and Marketing Director

Grattan Plc

Anchor House, Ingleby Road, Bradford, West Yorkshire BD99 2XG

Tel: 01274 575511　　**Fax:** 01274 625591

Website: www.grattan.co.uk

Sector: Mail Order

Executives:

Ian Andrew, Company Secretary

Norman Finnigan, Human Resources and Customer Services Director

Should you be in this directory? See the form at the back for new entries and amendments

Michael L Hawker, Chief Executive
Simon Malcolm, Head of E-Marketing
Janet McAulay, Publications Catalogue Director
Michael Otto, Chairman
Jim Skelsey, Merchandise Director
Christopher West, Finance Director
Carol Woodhead, Distribution Director

Greggs Plc

Fernwood House, Clayton Road, Jesmond, Newcastle upon Tyne NE2 1TL
Tel: 0191 281 7721   **Fax:** 0191 281 1444
Website: www.greggs.co.uk
Sector: Food and Drink
Executives:
Tony Barcroft, General Manager of Bakers Oven
Michael Darrington, Managing Director
Derek Netherton, Director
Malcolm Simpson, Financial Director

GUS

Universal House, Devonshire Street, Manchester M60 1XA
Tel: 020 7495 0070   **Fax:** 020 7495 1567
Website: www.gusplc.co.uk
Sector: Mail Order
Executives:
Sir Victor Blank, Chairman
Terry Duddy, Chief Executive, Argos Retail Group
John Peace, Chief Executive
Sir Alan Rudge, Non-Executive Director
Oliver Stocken, Non-Executive Director
David Tyler, Finance Director

Habitat UK Limited

42–46 Princelet Street, London E1 5LP
Tel: 0870 411 5500   **Fax:** 0870 411 5200
Website: www.habitat.net
Sector: Housewares
Executives:
Sally Brandon, Customer Services Manager
Tom Dixon, Head of Design
Mark Hislop, Retail Operations Director
Richard Millar, Head of Marketing and UK Retailing
Jens Nordahl, Managing Director
Anne-Marie Schwab, Group Marketing Manager
Michaela Welby, Financial Director

Halfords Limited

Icknield Street Drive, Washford West, Redditch B98 0DE
Tel: 01527 517601   **Fax:** 01527 513201
Email: customer.services@halfords.co.uk
Website: www.halfords.com
Sector: Automotive
Executives:
Nick Carter, Finance and Property Director

David Hamid, Chief Executive
Ian Mcleod, Director of Trading
Andy N Smith, Personnel Director
Rob Templeman, Chairman
Andy J Torrance, Operations Director
Nick B E Wharton, IT and Business Development Director
Chris Woodhouse, Deputy Chairman

Hamleys Plc

2 Fouberts Place, Regent Street, London W1F 7PA
Tel: 020 7479 7317   **Fax:** 020 7479 7319
Website: www.hamleys.com
Sector: Toys
Executives:
Chris Burford, Finance Manager
Ian Parker, Finance Director
John Watkinson, Chief Executive
Adrian Woolford, Marketing Director

Hargreaves Sports

Solent 27, Walton Road, Farlington, Portsmouth PO6 1SX
Tel: 023 9232 1200   **Fax:** 023 9237 1212
Email: enquiries@hargreaves-sports.co.uk
Website: www.hargreaves-sports.co.uk
Sector: Sports
Executives:
Martin Hargreaves, Chairman
Robin Hargreaves, Managing Director

Harrods Limited

87–135 Brompton Road, Knightsbridge, London SW1X 7XL
Tel: 020 7730 1234   **Fax:** 020 7581 0470
Email: customer.services@harrods.com
Website: www.harrods.com
Sector: Department Store
Executives:
Mohammed Al Fayed, Chairman
Raj Assanand, Managing Director
Steve Davie, Finance Director
J Healy, Store Operations Manager
Richard Simonin, Chief Executive Officer

Harvey Nichols Group Plc

Head Office, 67 Brompton Rd, London SW3 1DB
Tel: 020 7584 0011   **Fax:** 020 7823 2128
Website: www.harveynichols.com
Sector: Department Store
Executives:
Julia Bowe, Marketing Director
Dominic Ford, Food and Beverage Director
Patrick Hanly, Commercial Director
Clive Morton, Finance Director
Anne Pitcher, Director, Womenswear

Should you be in this directory? See the form at the back for new entries and amendments

Dickson Poon, Chairman
Joseph Wan, Managing Director

Harveys Furnishing Group

Amberley House, New Road, Rainham, Essex
RM13 8QW
Tel: 01708 521177　　**Fax:** 01708 521514
Website: www.harveysuk.com
Sector: Furniture
Executives:
Alan Hickford, Buying Director
Pat Kelly, Deputy Managing Director
Michael Rosendale, Chairman and Chief Executive
Carolyn Simons, Group Managing Director

Heal's Plc

The Heal's Building, 196 Tottenham Court Road,
London W1T 7LQ
Tel: 020 7896 7555　　**Fax:** 020 7436 5129
Email: enquiries@heals.co.uk
Website: www.heals.co.uk
Sector: Furniture
Executives:
Graham Dean, Retail Operations and Logistics
　Director
Colin Pilgrim, Chief Executive Officer
Liz Steer, Merchandising Director
Fiona Wood, Finance Director and Company
　Secretary

Hennes & Mauritz

2nd Floor, Holdon House, 57 Rathbone Place,
London W1T 1HE
Tel: 020 7323 2211　　**Fax:** 020 7323 9289
Website: www.hm.com
Sector: Clothing
Executives:
Richard Din, Managing Director
Colin Elliott, Finance Director
Kent Gustavesson, Operational Director
Mazz Imani, Customer Service Manager
Stefan Persson, Chairman

Heron Frozen Foods Ltd

Walcott Street, Hessle Road, Hull, East Yorkshire
HU3 4AU
Tel: 01482 323091　　**Fax:** 01482 217317
Sector: Food and Drink
Executives:
Andrew Heuck, Sales and Marketing Director
David Heuck, Finance Director

HMV Group Plc

Shelley House, 2–4 York Road, Maidenhead,
Berkshire SL6 1SR
Tel: 01628 818300　　**Fax:** 01628 818301
Email: enquiries@hmvgroup.com

Website: www.hmvgroup.com
Sector: Music and Video
Executives:
Neil Bright, Group Financial Director
Roy Brown, Deputy Chairman
Jackie Bullock, Head of Business Development
Lesley Cox, Non-Executive Director
Alan James Giles, Chief Executive Officer
Peter Hill, Finance Director
David Kappler, Non-Executive Director
Steve Knott, Managing Director, HMV Europe
Mike Lymath, Human Resources Director
Mark McCafferty, Non-Executive Director
Brian McLaughlin, Chief Operating Officer, HMV
　Media
Eric Nicoli, Chairman
Stuart Rowe, E-Commerce Director
Steve Tadler, Non-Executive Director

Hobbs Limited

122 Gloucester Avenue, London　NW1 8HX
Tel: 020 7449 2000
Sector: Footwear
Executives:
Rohia Karit, Finance Director
Nick Samuel, Chief Executive & Joint Managing
　Director
Nick Standish, Head of Merchandising
Michaela Wenkert, Head of Footwear

Holland & Barrett Retail Ltd

Samuel Ryder House, Townsend Drive, Attleborough
Fields, Nuneaton, Warwickshire　CV11 6XW
Tel: 024 7624 4400　　**Fax:** 024 7632 0094
Email: customerservices@hollandandbarrett.com
Website: www.hollandandbarrett.com
Sector: Health and Beauty
Executives:
Peter Aldis, Managing Director
Gill Day, Finance Director
Neil Fletcher, IT Manager
Phil Geary, Marketing Director
Mark Kendrick, Distribution Director
Christopher Lawton, Direct Marketing Manager
Douglas Sinclair, Property Director
Barry Vickers, Chief Executive Officer

Homebase Ltd

Beddington House, Railway Approach, Wallington,
Surrey　SM6 0HB
Tel: 020 8784 7200　　**Fax:** 020 8784 7755
Website: www.homebase.co.uk
Sector: DIY
Executives:
Neil Fuller, Finance Director
Peter Jones, Operations Director
Paul Loft, Managing Director

Should you be in this directory? See the form at the back for new entries and amendments

Leigh Martin, Trading Director
Penny Teale, Trading Director

Homeform Group Ltd

Cornbrook, 2 Brindley Road, Old Trafford,
Manchester M16 9HQ
Tel: 0161 877 7638   **Fax:** 0161 877 7591
Website: www.homeformgroup.co.uk
Sector: Furniture

Executives:

Phill Hill, Managing Director
Ashley Lewis, Finance Director
Andrew Stanway, Chief Executive
Andrew Thomas, Chairman
Joe White, Marketing Director

House of Fraser Plc

1 Howick Place, London SW1P 1BH
Tel: 020 7963 2000
Website: www.houseoffraser.co.uk
Sector: Department Store

Executives:

David Adams, Deputy Chief Executive and Group
    Finance Director
Chrissie Bacon, Financial Controller
John Coleman, Chief Executive
John Edgar, Trading and Marketing Finance
    Manager
Meg Gilmore, Director of Marketing
Ann Gordon, Trading Director
Liz Gray, Human Resources Director
Robert Hardy, Director of Property
Peter Hearsay, Company Secretary
Steve Hibbert, Operations Director
June Lawlor, Buying and Merchandising Director
Colin Porter, Supply Chain Director
Jane Storer, Buying and Merchandising Director
Tony Sweet, Food Hall Director
Richard Wayment, Retail Sales Director
Michael Wemms, Chairman

HPJ UK Ltd

P.O. Box 40, Congleton, Cheshire CW12 2LQ
Tel: 0870 606 4755   **Fax:** 01260 280184
Email: enquiries@hpj.co.uk
Website: www.hpj.co.uk
Sector: Jewellery

Executives:

Kevin Cook, Director
Gwen Shearer, Customer Service Manager
Mark Wordley, Director

Hughes Electricals

Mobbs Way, Lowestoft, Suffolk NR32 3AL
Tel: 01502 569126   **Fax:** 01502 561815
Website: www.hughesdirect.co.uk
Sector: Electricals

Executives:

Robert Hughes, Managing Director
Robert Soucier, Marketing Director

IKEA Ltd

255 North Circular Road, Neasden, London NW10 0JQ
Tel: 020 8233 2300   **Fax:** 020 8451 2813
Website: www.ikea.com; www.ikea.co.uk
Sector: Furniture

Executives:

Scott Cordrey, UK Property Manager
Andres Dahlvig, Group President
Anders Danielsson, Marketing Director
Peter Hogsted, Managing Director
Andrew North, UK Customer Service Manager
Jean-Louis Ouellette, Finance and Operations
    Director

Internacionale Limited

331 Charles Street, Glasgow G21 2RD, Scotland
Tel: 0141 552 2020   **Fax:** 0141 552 8700
Website: www.eunaturale.co.uk
Sector: Clothing

Executives:

Ken Ceirnduff, Joint Managing Director
Gerard Gavin, Marketing Manager
David Milton, Finance Director
Norrie Stewart, Joint Managing Director
Joanne Wilson, Customer Service Manager

J E Beale Plc

The Granville Chambers, 21 Richmond Hill,
Bournemouth, Dorset BH2 6BJ
Tel: 01202 203484   **Fax:** 01202 317286
Email: headoffice@beals.co.uk
Website: www.beales.co.uk
Sector: Department Store

Executives:

Nigel Beale, Chairman
John Hobdey, Merchandise Systems Executive
Caroline Howard, Marketing Director
Ken Owst, Finance Director
Tim Rathbone, Merchandise Director

J H Leeke & Sons Ltd

Mwyndy Business Park, Pontyclun, Rhondda Cynon
Taff CF72 8PN, Wales
Tel: 01443 667600   **Fax:** 01443 667718
Website: www.leekes.co.uk
Sector: DIY

Executives:

Paul Beddoe, Marketing Director
Diane Cook, Director
Mike Fowler, Finance Director
Terry Jones, Group Design Director
Anne-Marie Leeke, Chairperson
Emma Leeke, Director of Commercial Operations

Should you be in this directory? See the form at the back for new entries and amendments

Gerald Leeke, Managing Director
Stephen J Leeke, Vale Complex Managing Director
Stuart Leeke, Director and Company Secretary
Peter Martin, Group Director, Human Resources
Stephanie Metson, Marketing Manager
Judy Thomas, Garden Centre Manager

J Sainsbury Plc

Sainsbury's Business Centre, 33 Holborn, London
EC1N 2HT
Tel: 020 7695 6000   **Fax:** 020 7695 7610
Website: www.j-sainsbury.co.uk;
www.sainsburys.co.uk
Sector: Food and Drink
Executives:
John Adshead, Group Human Resources and
    Information Systems Director
Beverly Bittner, Director of Strategy and New Business
Sir George Bull, Non-Executive Chairman
Keith Butler-Wheelhouse, Non-Executive Director
Sir Peter Davis, Group Chief Executive ·
June De Moller, Non-Executive Director
Jamie Dundas, Non-Executive Director
Keith Evans, Director of Non-Foods
Adam Fowle, Director of Retail Operations
Andrew Ground, Director of Consumer Marketing
Justin King, Chief Executive Officer[2]
Robin Lassiter, Director of Central Retail Operations
Lord Levene of Portsoken, Non-Executive Director
Bridget Macaskill, Non-Executive Director
Roger Matthews, Group Finance Director
Stuart Mitchell, Managing Director of Sainsburys
    Supermarkets Ltd
Stephen Nelson, Trading Director
Lord Sainsbury of Preston Candover KG, Life
    President
Jeremy Schwarz, Director of Brand Marketing
Jan Shawe, Director of Group Corporate
    Communications
Jeremy Townsend, Director of Strategy and Planning
Martin Webb, Director of Trading Support and
    Procurement
Sara Weller, Deputy Managing Director
Martin White, Director of Supply Chain
[2]From March 2004

Jack Loggin Ltd

Ashgate Road, Chesterfield, Derbyshire S40 4AQ
Tel: 01246 279631   **Fax:** 01246 239044
Sector: Petrol
Executives:
David Jacques, Chairman
Peter Jacques, Managing Director

Jacques Vert Plc

Halldene Way, Seaham Grange Industrial Estate,
Seaham, County Durham SR7 OPZ

Tel: 0191 521 3555   **Fax:** 0191 521 9100
Website: www.jacques-vert.co.uk
Sector: Clothing
Executives:
Paul Allen, Chief Executive
Paul Gerrard, Logistics Manager
Mike Halliday, Merchandising Director
Donna McLean, Operations Manager

Jaeger Ltd

57 Broadwick Street, London W1F 9QS
Tel: 020 7200 4000   **Fax:** 020 7200 4001
Website: www.jaeger.co.uk
Sector: Clothing
Executives:
Peter Leverett, Estates Manager
Andrew Mackenzie, Group Chief Executive
Andrew Morris, Customer Service Manager
Andrea Ward, Marketing Manager
Key Worth, Head of Human Resources and Training

James Beattie PLC

71–78 Victoria Street, Wolverhampton, West
Midlands WV1 3PQ
Tel: 01902 422311   **Fax:** 01902 643355
Website: www.beatties.co.uk
Sector: Department Store
Executives:
John Craddock, Marketing and Merchandise Director
Christopher Jones, Managing Director
William Kelly, Finance Director
Malcolm Phillips, Planning and Development
    Director

Jane Norman

153 Oxford Street, London W1R 1TB
Tel: 020 7437 0132
Sector: Clothing
Executives:
Norman Freed, Managing Director
Saj Shah, Chief Executive
Natasha Ward, Personnel Manager

Jenners Limited

48 Princes Street, Edinburgh EH2 2YJ, Scotland
Tel: 0131 225 2442   **Fax:** 0131 260 2218
Website: www.jenners.com
Sector: Department Store
Executives:
Elizabeth Barcley, Director and Company Secretary
Kenneth Grant, Buying and Marketing Director
Andrew Douglas Miller, Deputy Chairman and
    Development Director
Robert Douglas Miller, Chairman
Lititia Shields, Customer Service Manager

Should you be in this directory? See the form at the back for new entries and amendments

Jessops

98 Scudamore Road, Leicester LE3 1TZ
Tel: 0116 232 6000   **Fax:** 0116 232 0060
Website: www.jessops.com
Sector: Electricals
Executives:
John Crabtree, Finance Director
Derek Hine, Chief Executive
Julia Scott, Purchasing Director

Jigsaw

159 Mortlake Road, Kew, Surrey TW9 4AW
Tel: 020 8392 5678   **Fax:** 020 8878 9456
Website: www.jigsaw-online.com
Sector: Clothing
Executives:
Charlie Atterton, Financial Director
John Robinson, Managing Director and Chairman

JJB Sports Plc

Martland Park, Challenge Way, Wigan WN5 0LD
Tel: 01942 221400   **Fax:** 01942 629809
Website: www.jjb.co.uk
Sector: Sports
Executives:
David Beever, Non-Executive Director
Barry Dunn, Property Director
David Greenwood, Finance Director and Company
    Secretary
Mark Heaton, Merchandising Director
Winston Higham, Marketing Director
Thomas Knight, Chief Executive
David Whelan, Executive Chairman

John David Group Plc

Edinburgh House, Castlebrook Business Park,
Pilsworth, Bury, Lancashire BL9 8RR
Tel: 0161 767 1000
Email: jdsports@dial.pipex.com
Website: www.jdsports.co.uk
Sector: Sports
Executives:
Peter Atkinson, Operations Director
Roger Best, Managing Director
Malcolm Blackhurst, Financial Director
Barry Brown, Chief Executive
Andrew Helm, Marketing Director
Nigel Keen, Property Director
David Makin, Buying and Merchandising Director
Richard Percival, Director

John Lewis Plc

171 Victoria Street, London SW1E 5NN
Tel: 020 7828 1000   **Fax:** 020 7592 6566
Email: enquiries@johnlewis.co.uk
Website: www.johnlewis.co.uk
Sector: Department Store

Executives:
Ian David Alexander, Finance Director
Paul Burden, Communications Director
John Cushen, General Manager, Supply Chain
David Felwick, Deputy Chairman
Sir Stuart Hampson, Executive Chairman
Ann Humphries, Director of Retail Development
Tracey Killen, Personnel Director
Howard King, Property Director
Patrick Lewis, Supply Chain Director
Jill Little, Merchandise Director
Charlie Mayfield, Development Director
Luke Mayhew, Managing Director
Simon Palethorpe, Managing Director, John Lewis
    Direct
Gareth Thomas, Director of Retail Operations
Caspar Wooley, Head of Business Development

Joplings Ltd

John Street, Sunderland, Tyne and Wear SR1 1DP
Tel: 0191 510 2105   **Fax:** 0191 510 5500
Website: www.joplings.co.uk
Sector: Department Store
Executives:
John C Jefferson, Finance Director
David Montgomery, Merchandising Manager, Fashion
    and Household
Wendy Simmons, Marketing Manager

Joseph

50 Carnwath Road, London SW6 3JX
Tel: 020 7736 2522   **Fax:** 020 7736 1644
Sector: Clothing
Executives:
Karen Davidson, Financial Director
Marc Foreftier, Administrative Director
Thierry Letrilliart, Managing Director

Karen Millen

Unit D11, Maidstone Business Centre, St Peter Street,
Maidstone ME16 0ST
Tel: 01622 664032   **Fax:** 01622 664031
Email: enquiries@karenmillen.co.uk
Website: www.karenmillen.co.uk
Sector: Clothing
Executives:
Sandy Goldsbrough, Merchandise Director
Sanjay Sharma, Finance Director
Kevin Stanford, Chief Executive Officer
Michelle Swift, Manager of Customer Services

KESA Electricals Plc

22–24 Ely Place, London EC1N 6TE
Tel: 020 7269 1400   **Fax:** 020 7269 1405
Website: www.kesaelectricals.com
Sector: Electricals

Should you be in this directory? See the form at the back for new entries and amendments

Executives:
Jean Nöel Labroue, Chief Executive
David Newlands, Chairman
Martin Reavley, Finance Director

Kingfisher Plc

3 Sheldon Square, Paddington, London W2 6PX
Tel: 020 7372 8008   **Fax:** 020 7644 1001
Website: www.kingfisher.co.uk;
   www.kingfisher.com
Sector: Mixed Retailer
Executives:
Phil Bentley, Non-Executive Director
Ian Cheshire, Chief Executive of International
   Development
Michael Hepher, Non-Executive Director
Helen Jones, Company Secretary
Hammut Kramer, Non-Executive Director
Jean Noël Labroue, Chief Executive, KESA
Francis Mackay, Chairman
Jeremy Maxwell, Director of Strategy
Gerry M Murphy, Chief Executive Officer
John Nelson, Deputy Chairman
Margaret Salmon, Non-Executive Director
Lorraine Woodhouse, Head of Investor Relations

Kookai

123D Kensington High Street, London W8 5SF
Tel: 020 7937 4411   **Fax:** 020 7937 1198
Website: www.kookai.co.uk
Sector: Clothing
Executives:
Sir Phillip Carter, Chairman
Anita Cashmore, Financial Director
Sue Fox, Retail Director
Rina Loizou, Merchandise Director
Rita O'Sullivan, Retail Operations Director
Michael Rahamin, Managing Director
Patrick Rayner, Property Manager

Kurt Geiger

75 Bermondsey Street, London SE1 3XF
Tel: 020 7546 1888   **Fax:** 020 7546 1880
Website: www.kurtgeiger.co.uk
Sector: Footwear
Executives:
Neil Clifford, Chief Executive
Rebecca Farrar-Hockley, Buying Director
Crispin Mardon, Managing Director

Kuwait Petroleum Ltd

Burgan House, The Causeway, Staines, Middlesex
TW18 3PA
Tel: 01784 467788   **Fax:** 01784 467600
Website: www.q8.com
Sector: Petrol

Executives:
Mark Goldsmith, Retail Director
Gerrit Ruitinga, Managing Director

L Rowland & Co (Retail) Ltd

Rivington Road, Whitehorse Industrial Estate,
Runcorn, Cheshire WA7 3DJ
Tel: 01928 754100   **Fax:** 01928 755041
Website: www.myp-i-n.co.uk
Sector: Health and Beauty
Executives:
Kevin Hudson, Finance Director
Smith, Managing Director
Alexander Young, Non-Executive Officer

La Senza

Ryman House, Swallowfield Way, Hayes, Middlesex
UB3 1DQ
Tel: 020 8569 3000
Sector: Clothing
Executives:
Rachel Brian, Merchandise Director
Malcolm Cooke, Group Managing Director
Theo Paphitis, Chairman
Chris Smith, Property Manager

Lakeland Limited

Alexandra Buildings, Station Precinct, Windermere,
Cumbria LA23 1BQ
Tel: 01539 488200   **Fax:** 01539 488300
Website: www.lakelandlimited.com
Sector: Housewares
Executives:
Mark Goodfellow, Retail Operations Manager
Michelle Kershaw, Customer Director
Chris Long, Finance Director
Julian Rayner, Marketing Director
Martin Rayner, Purchasing Director
Sam Rayner, Managing Director

Land of Leather

Unit K1–K2, Northleigh Industrial Estate, Lower
Road, Gravesend DA11 9BL
Tel: 01474 360428
Website: www.landofleather.com
Sector: Furniture
Executives:
Jerry Briant, Managing Director
Brian Neilly, Finance Director

Laura Ashley

27 Bagleys Lane, Fulham, London SW6 2QA
Tel: 020 7880 5100   **Fax:** 020 7880 5200
Website: www.lauraashley.com
Sector: Clothing
Executives:
David Cook, Finance Director

Should you be in this directory? See the form at the back for new entries and amendments

Iain Nairn, Retail Operations Director
Rebecca Navarednam, Joint Chief Executive
Ainum Mohd Saaid, Joint Chief Executive
David Selby, Head of Mail Order and E-Commerce
Mark Winstanley, Creative Director

Le Riches Stores Limited

Riches House, P.O. Box 4, Plat Douet Road, St Saviour, Jersey JE4 8NB
Tel: 01534 508400 **Fax:** 01534 758488
Website: www.lerichesgroup.com
Sector: Convenience Store
Executives:
Andrew Bagot, Managing Director
Martin Bralsford, Chief Executive
Lee Delamare, Head of Logistics and Distribution
Donal Duff, Group Director of Finance
John Garton, Head of Marketing
Steve Marie, Property Director
Tom Scott, Chairman

Levi Strauss (UK) Ltd

Swan Valley, Northampton NN4 9BA
Tel: 01604 581501 **Fax:** 01604 599815
Website: www.levi.com
Sector: Clothing
Executives:
Rachel Johnson, Regional Marketing Director
Deborah Miller, UK Franchise Manager

Liberty

214–220 Regent Street, London W1B 5AH
Tel: 020 7734 1234 **Fax:** 020 7734 8323
Website: www.liberty.co.uk
Sector: Department Store
Executives:
Richard Balfour Lynn, Chairman
Jane Davis, Buying Director
Deborah Fitzgerald, Marketing and Communications Director
Clare Johnston, Head of Design
Nick Mather, Finance Director
Iain Renwick, Chief Executive

Lillywhites

24–36 Lower Regent Street, London SW1Y 4QF
Tel: 0870 333 9600 **Fax:** 0870 333 9430
Sector: Sports
Executives:
Andy Cronie, Operations Director
Dave Forsey, Managing Director
Francisco Soares Dos Santos, Chairman

Littlewoods Stores Ltd

Sir John Moores Building, 100 Old Hall Street, Liverpool L70 1AB
Tel: 0151 235 2222

Website: www.littlewoods.com; www.indexshop.com
Sector: Clothing
Executives:
Jennifer Bate, Acting Commercial Director, Littlewoods Stores
Peter Burke, Human Resources Director
Kelvin Coyle, Commercial Director, Index
Jim Grant, Operations Director
Tim James, Managing Director, Index
John Jones, Finance Director
Alastair McGeorge, Group Chief Executive
Susan Murray, Acting Managing Director, Littlewoods Stores
David Simons, Group Chairman

Lloyd Shoe Co Ltd

Berwick House, 8–10 Knoll House, Orpington, Kent BR6 0EL
Tel: 01689 824433 **Fax:** 01689 888789
Email: reception@lloydshoes.co.uk
Sector: Footwear
Executives:
Ian Duley, Financial Director
Brian Hogan, Sales Director
Adam Senior, Head Footwear Buyer
Mark Verona, Managing Director

Lloyds Pharmacy

Sapphire Court, Walsgrave Triangle, Coventry, Warwickshire CV2 2TX
Tel: 024 7643 2400 **Fax:** 024 7643 2401
Website: www.lloydspharmacy.co.uk
Sector: Health and Beauty
Executives:
Mark Green, Marketing Director
John Hood, Finance Director
Michael Ward, Chief Executive

Londis (Holdings) Ltd

Eurogroup House, 67–71 High Street, Hampton Hill TW12 1LZ
Tel: 020 8941 0344 **Fax:** 020 8941 6499
Website: www.londis.co.uk
Sector: Food and Drink
Executives:
Terry Bedford, Sales Director
Denise Buller, Commercial Director
Ross Halliday, Trade Marketing Director
Martyn Harvey, Supply Chain Development Director
Kenton Lawton, Marketing Director
Tony Riddy, Retail Director
John Taylor, Trading Director
Steve Tulley, Development Director
Andrew Wallace, Finance Director
Graham White, Chief Executive
Peter Williams, Chairman

Should you be in this directory? See the form at the back for new entries and amendments

Lyndale Foods Ltd

2 Brooklands Place, Brooklands Road, Sale, Cheshire
M33 3SD
Tel: 0161 972 3400 **Fax:** 0161 972 3434
Website: www.lyndale.co.uk
Sector: Food and Drink
Executives:
Tony Gearty, Chief Executive
Colin Hubbold, Marketing Manager
Michael Quinlan, Finance Director

Mackays Stores Ltd

Caledonia House, Caledonia Street, Paisley PA3 2JP,
Scotland
Tel: 0141 887 9151 **Fax:** 0141 887 8069
Website: www.mackaysstores.co.uk
Sector: Clothing
Executives:
James Bell, Chief Accountant
Neil Bennett, Merchandising Director
John A Heaviside, Production Director
Iain McGeoch, Managing Director
Matthew Richard McKimmie, Financial Director
John O'Hara, IT Director
Sue Swannie, Buying Director
Paul Vann, Chairman
Colin Williamson, Marketing Director

Magnet Ltd

Allington Way, Darlington, County Durham BL1 4XT
Tel: 01325 469441
Website: www.magnet.co.uk
Sector: Furniture
Executives:
Matt Bunnell, Director
Gary Favell, Managing Director
Michael Greenhalgh, Group Marketing Director
Richard Gudgeon, Finance Director

Majestic Wine Warehouses Ltd

Majestic House, Otterspool Way, Watford WD25
8WW
Tel: 01923 298200 **Fax:** 01923 819105
Email: info@majestic.co.uk
Website: www.majestic.co.uk
Sector: Off Licence
Executives:
Nigel Alldritt, Financial Director
John Apthorp, Chairman
Steve de Mellow, Marketing Director
Timothy How, Managing Director
Steve Lewis, Retail Director
Tony Mason, Trading Director
Jeremy Palmer, E-Commerce Director
Liz Wright, Property Director

Maplin Electronics Ltd

Valley Road, Off Station Road, Wombwell, Barnsley,
South Yorkshire S73 OBS
Tel: 01226 751155 **Fax:** 0870 264 6001
Website: www.maplin.co.uk
Sector: Electricals
Executives:
Graham Caldwell, Managing Director
David O'Reilly, Marketing Director
Keith Pacey, Chairman
David Whittle, Direct Sales Director
Paul Wilburn, Finance Director

Marks & Spencer Plc

Michael House, 47–67 Baker Street, London W1U 8EP
Tel: 020 7935 4422 **Fax:** 020 7487 2679
Email: customer.services@marksandspencer.com
Website: www.marksandspencer.com
Sector: Clothing
Executives:
Alice Avis, Group Director of Marketing and E-
  Commerce
Barbara Cussani, Non-Executive Director
Maurice Helfgott, Business Unit Director, Menswear
Roger Holmes, Chief Executive
Flic Howard-Allen, Director of Communications
Jack Keenan, Non-Executive Director
Justin King, Food Director
Steve Longdon, Business Unit Director, Womenswear
Steve McGinlay, Director of Supply Chain and
  Technology
Paul Myners, Non-Executive Director
David R Norgrove, Director, Clothing, Outlets and
  International
Graham Oakley, Group Secretary and Head of
  Corporate Governance
Jack Paterson, Business Unit Director, Beauty and
  Lingerie
Laurel Powers-Freeling, Director and Chief Executive
  of Financial Services
Vittorio Radice, Director, Home
Alison Reed, Chief Financial Officer
Stuart Senior, IT Director
Anthony Thompson, Head of Childrenswear
Jean Tomlin, Director of Human Resources
Luc Vandevelde, Chairman
Yasmin Yusuf, Creative Director, Clothing

Matalan plc

Gillibrands Road, Skelmersdale, Lancashire WN8 9TB
Tel: 01695 552400 **Fax:** 01695 552401
Email: webmaster@matalan.co.uk
Website: www.matalan.co.uk
Sector: Clothing
Executives:
John Berry, Group Company Secretary

Should you be in this directory? See the form at the back for new entries and amendments

Roger Burnley, Supply Chain Director
Andy Clarke, Group Retail Director
Phil Dutton, Group Finance Director
Jamey Hargreaves, Director of Category and Brand
    Marketing
John Hargreaves, Chairman
John King, Chief Executive
Adrian Porteous, Merchandising Director
Graham Seaton, Property Director
David Shipley, Non-Executive Director
Robert Shrager, Non-Executive Director
Euan Sutherland, Retail and Marketing Director
Charles Thompson, Non-Executive Director
John Westwood, Non-Executive Director

Merchant Retail Group Plc

Cypress House, The Gateway Centre, Coronation
Road, Cressex Business Park, High Wycombe,
Buckinghamshire HP12 3SU
Tel: 01494 894000   **Fax:** 01494 894093
Website: www.merchantretail.com
Sector: Department Store

Executives:
Reg Heath, Chairman
Chris Lamont, Finance Director
Philip Newton, Chief Executive
Philip Samuel, Managing Director, Joplings
Jeremy Seigal, Managing Director, The Perfume Shop
Melanie Wadeley, Personnel Director

MFI Furniture Centres Limited

Southon House, 333 The Hyde, Edgware Road,
Colindale, London NW9 6TD
Tel: 020 8200 8000   **Fax:** 020 8200 8636
Website: www.mfi.co.uk
Sector: Furniture

Executives:
Martin Clifford-King, Group Financial Director
Bob Connell, Finance and Warranties Director
Pat Fawson, Corporate Affairs Director
Nick Garratt, Director, Marketing Operations
John Hancock, Chief Executive
Mark Horgan, Executive Director, UK Retail
Matthew Ingle, Managing Director, Howden Joinery
Mike Kane, Director, Retail
Gordon MacDonald, Chief Operating Officer
Jim McManus, Property Director
Steven Round, Commercial Director
Peter Wallis, Non-Executive Director
Bob Wilson, Manufacturing and Purchasing Director

Miller Brothers Group Ltd

Miller House, Ogden Road, Shaw Lane, Doncaster
DN2 4SQ
Tel: 0870 741 9860   **Fax:** 01302 341678
Website: www.millerbros.co.uk
Sector: Electricals

Executives:
Martin A Foster, Managing Director
James R Miller, Marketing Director
Jim N Miller, Chairman and Joint Managing Director
Robert Miller, Joint Managing Director
Simon J Miller, Director
Dominic Pearce, Company Secretary
John Sadd, Business Development Director

MK One

16–18 Victoria Industrial Estate, Wales Farm Road,
London W3 6YN
Tel: 020 8993 6262
Website: www.mkone.co.uk
Sector: Clothing

Executives:
Martin Barlow, Project and Property Manager
John Ferguson, Retail Operations Controller
Elaine Gray, Group Buying and Merchandising
    Director
Philip Green, Chief Executive
Dolly Parkash, General Merchandiser
David Thomson, Finance Director

Mole Valley Farmers

Station Road, South Molton, Devon EX36 3BH
Tel: 01769 573431   **Fax:** 01769 573821
Email: mvf@molevalleyfarmers.com
Website: www.molevalleyfarmers.com
Sector: Food and Drink

Executives:
Shaun Carter, Manager
A Jackson, Chief Executive

Monsoon Accessorize Ltd

Monsoon Building, 179 Harrow Road, London
W2 6NB
Tel: 020 7313 3000   **Fax:** 020 7313 4450
Email: monsoon@monsoon.co.uk
Website: www.accessorize.co.uk;
www.monsoon.co.uk
Sector: Accessories

Executives:
Joanna Baxter, Head of Press and Public Relations
Rose Foster, UK Managing Director
Graham Frost, Deputy Chairman
Nikki Hamwee, Brand Director, Accessorize
Andrew May, Finance Director
G W Searle, Non-Executive Director
Graham Sim, Group Marketing Director
Peter Simon, Chief Executive and Chairman
John Spooner, International Development Director

Morley's Stores Ltd

16 St George's Road, London SW19 4DP
Tel: 020 8946 9191   **Fax:** 020 8944 1939
Sector: Department Store

Should you be in this directory? See the form at the back for new entries and amendments

Executives:
June Ahern, Customer Services
Sandra Corridan, Marketing Director
Bernard Dreesmann, Chairman
David Ordman, Managing Director
Maura Syed, Financial Director

Morning, Noon & Night

17 Panmure Street, Broughty Ferry, Dundee DD5 2ER, Scotland
Tel: 01382 738118   **Fax:** 01382 738253
Sector: Convenience Store
Executives:
F Mackay, Development Director
C Mitchell, Director
George Pirie, Operations Director
Edward Thompson, Chief Executive
Stephen Thompson, Marketing Director

Moss Bros Group Plc

8 St Johns Hill, London SW11 1SA
Tel: 020 7447 7200   **Fax:** 020 7350 0112
Email: postmaster@mossbros.co.uk
Website: www.mossbros.co.uk
Sector: Clothing
Executives:
Andrew Barclay, Marketing Manager
Julie Cook, Retail Operations and Marketing Director
Graham Dibb, Property Director
Keith Hamill, Chairman
Vicky Maker, Customer Services Manager
Philip Mountford, Group Trading Director
Roddy Murray, Financial Director
Adrian Wright, Chief Executive

Moss Pharmacy Ltd

Fern House, 53–55 High Street, Feltham, Middlesex TW13 4HU
Tel: 020 8890 9333
Email: press@mosspharmacy.co.uk
Website: www.mosspharmacy.co.uk
Sector: Health and Beauty
Executives:
Barry Andrews, Executive Chairman
Chris Aylward, Business Development Director
Steve Duncan, Managing Director
Simon Hume, Human Resources Director
Andrew Prosser, Finance Director
Susan Rockhill, Marketing Director
Terry Scicluna, Operations Director
David Williams, Non-Executive Director

Mothercare Plc

Cherry Tree Rd, Watford, Hertfordshire WD24 6SH
Tel: 01923 241000   **Fax:** 01923 240944
Website: www.mothercare.com
Sector: Toys

Executives:
Tony Carr, Retail Operations Director
Stephen Glew, Finance Director
Ben Gordon, Chief Executive
Chris Martin, Chief Executive
Ian Peacock, Chairman
Steve Pomphret, Strategic Development Director
Clive Revett, Company Secretary

Motorworld Ltd

Arden House, Masons Road, Stratford upon Avon, Warwickshire CV37 9YW
Tel: 01789 207800   **Fax:** 01789 262573
Website: www.motor-world.co.uk
Sector: Automotive
Executives:
Dave Hudson, Operations Director
John Mousell, Managing Director
Steve Peach, Purchasing Director

Multiyork Furniture Ltd

Stephenson House, 10 Stephenson Way, Thetford, Norfolk IP24 3RD
Tel: 01842 764761   **Fax:** 01842 766850
Email: info@multiyork.co.uk
Website: www.multiyork.co.uk
Sector: Furniture
Executives:
Terry Hawkins, Merchandise Director
Sarah Herbert, Marketing Director
John Higton, Group Financial Director
Peter Mallinson, Chief Executive
Mike Sinnot, Production Director
David Tawns, Commercial Director
Charles Wade, Chairman

N Brown

53 Dale Street, Manchester M60 6ES
Tel: 0161 238 2000   **Fax:** 0161 238 2020
Website: www.nbrown.co.uk
Sector: Mail Order
Executives:
Sir David Alliance, Chairman
Keith Basnett, Customer Services Director
Mike Bullaf, Merchandise Director
Nigel Green, Marketing Director
John Hinchliffe, Marketing and Strategy Director
Tim Kowalski, Finance Director
Jim Martin, Financial Director
Alan White, Chief Executive

National Co-operative Chemists Ltd

Brook House, Oldham Road, Middleton, Manchester M24 1HF
Tel: 0161 654 4488   **Fax:** 0161 654 4499
Website: www.co-oppharmacy.co.uk
Sector: Health and Beauty

Should you be in this directory? See the form at the back for new entries and amendments

Executives:
John Makepiece, General Manager
David Rogers, Head of Sales and Marketing
Chris Stevens, Head of Finance
Peter Willis, Business Development Manager

Netto Foodstores Ltd
Elmsall Way, South Elmsall, Pontefract WF9 2XX, Wales
Tel: 01977 641212 **Fax:** 01977 645852
Sector: Food and Drink
Executives:
Kevin Barber, Purchasing Director
Dawn Heathcote, Customer Services Manager
Mike Hinchcliff, Marketing Manager
Keith Ross, Financial Director
Claus Waedeled, Managing Director

New Look Retailers Ltd
Mercery Road, Weymouth DT3 5HJ
Tel: 01305 765000 **Fax:** 01305 765001
Website: www.newlook.co.uk
Sector: Clothing
Executives:
Janet Biggs, Director of Trading
John Grieves, Chairman
Paul Hitchcott, Property Director
Will Kernan, Director of Finance and IT
Hashim Ladha, Business Development Director
Robin Lewis, Director of Human Resources
Carl McPhail, Group Operations Director
Alaistair Miller, Finance Director
Alan Osbourne, Retail Operations Director
Tom Singh, Non-Executive Director
Stephen Sunnucks, Chief Executive
Phil Wrigley, Managing Director, Operations

News Shops Ltd
51–53 Queen Street, Wolverhampton WV1 3BU
Tel: 01902 422226 **Fax:** 01902 428757
Sector: CTN
Executives:
Bob Franks, Finance Director
Douglas Graham, Chairman
Paul Siviter, Managing Director
Andrew Tomlinson, News Development Manager
Graham Walton, Finance Systems Manager
Peter White, Retail News Manager

Next Plc
Desford Road, Enderby, Leicester LE19 4AT
Tel: 0845 456 7777 **Fax:** 0116 284 8998
Website: www.next.co.uk
Sector: Clothing
Executives:
Christos Angelides, Group Product Director
David Jones, Chairman

David Keens, Group Finance Director
Michael Law, Directory Operations Director
Sue Myatt, Retail Marketing Director
Jane Shields, Retail Operations Director
Andrew Varley, Group Property Director
Simon Wolfson, Chief Executive

Northern Electric Retail
Unit 5, Retail World, Team Valley Trading Estate, Gateshead NE11 0BD
Tel: 0191 210 7000 **Fax:** 0191 210 7001
Website: www.pluggedin.co.uk
Sector: Electricals
Executives:
Gary Boyd, Finance Director
David Crompton, Managing Director, Retail
P Denham, IT Manager
Phil Jackson, Sales and Marketing Director
Simon Rigby, Chairman and Chief Executive

Notcutts Nurseries
74 Cumberland Street, Woodbridge, Suffolk IP12 4AF
Tel: 01394 383344 **Fax:** 01394 445440
Website: www.notcutts.co.uk
Sector: Garden Centres
Executives:
Chris Moss, Finance Director
Charles Notcutt, Chairman
William Notcutt, Group Managing Director
Sally Reed, Marketing Director

O2
260 Bath Road, Slough, Berkshire SL1 4DX
Tel: 01753 565003
Website: www.o2.co.uk
Sector: Electricals
Executives:
David McGlade, Managing Director
Mark Stansfield, Retail Director

Oasis Stores Plc
69–77 Paul Street, London EC2A 4PN
Tel: 020 7452 1000 **Fax:** 020 7452 1001
Website: www.oasis-stores.com
Sector: Clothing
Executives:
Richard Glanville, Finance Director
Geoff Green, Head of Property
Nadia Jones, Design Director
Derek Lovelock, Chief Executive
Meg Lustman, New Business Director
Jacki Nolan, Retail Director
Sharon O'Connor, Merchandising Director
Hannah Russell, Marketing Director
Jane Woolf, Head of Buying

Should you be in this directory? See the form at the back for new entries and amendments

Oddbins UK Ltd
31–33 Weir Road, Wimbledon SW19 8UG
Tel: 020 8944 4400   **Fax:** 020 8944 4411
Email: customer.services@oddbinsmail.com
Website: www.oddbins.com
Sector: Off Licence
Executives:
Jacques Duley, Managing Director
Laurent Genthialan, Finance Director
Dennis Hanns, Head of Retail

Orange Plc
The Chase, John Tate Road, Foxholes Business Park,
Hertford, Hertfordshire SG13 7NN
Tel: 01992 502000   **Fax:** 0870 373 2001
Website: www.orange.co.uk
Sector: Electricals
Executives:
Ian Fraser, Director of Sales and Distribution,
    Personal and Small Business
Mike Newnham, UK Group Finance Director
Kennedy Rodriques, Financial Manager
Solomon Trujillo, Chief Executive

Ottakar's Plc
Brewery House, 36 Milford Street, Salisbury, Wiltshire
SP1 2AP
Tel: 01722 428500   **Fax:** 01722 428530
Website: www.ottakars.co.uk
Sector: Books
Executives:
Suzanne Bradford, Operations Manager
Philip Dunne, Chairman
Paul Henderson, Marketing Director
James Heneage, Managing Director
Edward Knighton, Finance Director and Company
    Secretary

Pets at Home Ltd
Epsom Avenue, Stanley Green Trading Estate,
Handforth, Cheshire FK9 3RN
Tel: 0161 486 6688   **Fax:** 0161 485 4846
Website: www.petsathome.com
Sector: Pets
Executives:
Michelle Begley, Head of Marketing
Matthew Davis, Finance Director
John Farrell, Development Director
Catriona Marshall, Trading Director
Anthony Preston, Chairman

Phones 4u
Swift House, Liverpool Road, Newcastle-under-Lyme,
Staffordshire ST5 9JJ
Tel: 0870 905 0416   **Fax:** 01270 259396
Website: www.phones4u.co.uk
Sector: Electricals

Executives:
Mark Carberry, Customer Services Director
John Caudwell, Chairman and Chief Executive
Steve Caunce, Finance Director
Peter Green, Managing Director
Paul Hamburger, Marketing Director
Tim Walton, Sales Director

Pilot Clothing
Chilcomb Lane, Chilcomb, Winchester, Hampshire
SO21 1HU
Tel: 01962 764300   **Fax:** 01962 764301
Website: www.pilotuk.com
Sector: Clothing
Executives:
Neil Parker, Head of Retail
Paul Roberts, Head of Finance
Mark Walsh, Purchasing Director
Jeremy Whaley, Managing Director

Ponden Mill Ltd
The Courtyard, Royd Ings Avenue, Keighley, West
Yorkshire BD21 4BZ
Tel: 01535 691629   **Fax:** 01535 616900
Sector: Furniture
Executives:
Barry Brookfield, Chairman
Lynton Chopping, Finance Director
Neil Edwards, Commercial Manager
Leo McKee, Chief Executive
Bob Thomson, Head of Retail and Property

Poundland Ltd
Wellmans Road, Willenhall, West Midlands
WV13 2QT
Tel: 0121 568 7000   **Fax:** 0121 568 7007
Website: www.poundland.co.uk
Sector: Discounter
Executives:
Robert Adams, Financial Director
David Dodd, Chief Executive
Cathy Ferrier, Trading Director
Chris Forman, Merchandising Controller
Nigel Peckham, Retail and Operations Director

PRG Powerhouse Retail Ltd
Power House, 7–8 Talisman Road, Bicester,
Oxfordshire OX26 6HR
Tel: 01869 329329   **Fax:** 01869 322780
Website: www.powerhouse.co.uk
Sector: Electricals
Executives:
Sue Gosling, Marketing Director
Peter Halkett, Chairman and Chief Executive
Jon Long, Director of Property
Paul White, Commercial Director

Should you be in this directory? See the form at the back for new entries and amendments

Primark

P.O. Box 644, 47 Mary Street, Dublin 1, Ireland
Tel: 00 353 1 872 7788   **Fax:** 00 353 1 873 3532
Website: www.primark.co.uk
Sector: Clothing
Executives:
Seamus Halford, Store Operations Director
Breege O'Donahue, Personnel and Advertising
    Director
Patrick Pryor, Financial Director
Arthur Ryan, Chairman and Managing Director

QD Stores Ltd

7–10 Anglia Square, Norwich, Norfolk NR3 1DY
Tel: 01603 275200   **Fax:** 01603 275234
Website: www.qdstores.co.uk
Sector: Department Store
Executives:
Louise Drake, Customer Services Manager
Graham Moxam, Finance Director
Ken Turner, Chief Executive

QS Plc

Harbour House, 121 Gardner Road, Portslade,
Brighton BN41 1QS
Tel: 01273 874444   **Fax:** 01273 874433
Email: qsplc@qsgroup.co.uk
Website: www.qsgroup.co.uk
Sector: Clothing
Executives:
Paul Bacon, Buying Director
Tony Dignum, Chairman
Eric Holes, Group Finance Director
Jane Holme, Property and Operations Manager
Ray Kennedy, Operations Finance Director
Ian McCaskey, IT and Customer Services
    Manager

Redcats UK (Brands) Ltd

18 Canal Road, Bradford, West Yorkshire BD99 4XB
Tel: 01274 729544   **Fax:** 01274 763816
Website: www.redcats.com
Sector: Mail Order
Executives:
Francoise Deve, Catalogue Director
Oliver Gimpel, Marketing Director
Marianne Green, Finance Director
Olivier Izard, Managing Director
Andrew Parker, Property Director
Peter Smith, IT Director

Remainders Ltd

Midpoint Park, Minworth, Sutton Coldfield, West
Midlands B76 1RN
Tel: 0121 313 6000   **Fax:** 0121 313 6001
Website: www.remainders.co.uk
Sector: Discounter

Executives:
Chris Maddox, Managing Director
Joy May, Human Resources Director
Terry Norris, Chairman
Ray Thomas, Property Director
Julian Tucki, Marketing Director
Andrew Williams, IT Director

Richer Sounds Plc

Richer House, 4 Hankey Place, London SE1 4BB
Tel: 020 7940 2222   **Fax:** 020 7940 2211
Website: www.richersounds.com
Sector: Electricals
Executives:
Jez Avens, Deputy Managing Director
Jon Currier, Financial Director
James Johnson-Flint, Director
Julian Richer, Chairman
David Robinson, Group Managing Director
Claudia Vernon, Marketing Director

River Island

Chelsea House, West Gate, London W5 1DR
Tel: 020 8998 8822   **Fax:** 020 8997 3953
Website: www.riverisland.com
Sector: Clothing
Executives:
Colin Bailey, Finance Director
Richard Bradbury, Managing Director
Richard Gee, Property Director
Farida Kaikobad, Buying Director
Bernard Lewis, Retail Director
Clive Lewis, Chief Executive
Julian Lewis, Director
Leonard Lewis, Managing Director

Robert Dyas Holdings Ltd

Cleeve Court, Cleeve Road, Leatherhead, Surrey
KT22 7SD
Tel: 01372 361444   **Fax:** 01372 386785
Email: info@robertdyas.co.uk
Website: www.robertdyas.co.uk
Sector: DIY
Executives:
L P Crookshank, Non-Executive Director
Alan Holliman, Store Development and Property
    Manager
J D Leake, Non-Executive Director
M J Naskey, Non-Executive Director
Roger A Pedder, Non-Executive Chairman
Stewart A Rand, Sales and Marketing Director
John P Rowland, Company Secretary
Malcolm Smart, Financial Director
Graham Taylor, Marketing Manager
Brent F Wilkinson, Chief Executive Officer

Should you be in this directory? See the form at the back for new entries and amendments

Rosebys Ltd

Rosedale House, Bramley Way, Hellaby, Rotherham,
South Yorkshire S66 8QB
Tel: 01709 800800   **Fax:** 01709 800876
Website: www.rosebys.com
Sector: Housewares
Executives:
James Cribb, Finance Director
Mark Dyson, Company Secretary
Sir Gordon Hourston, Chairman
Tony Richards, Deputy Managing Director
Michael Rosenblatt, Chief Executive
Carolyn Simons, Managing Director, Rosebys
Bill Wolstenholme, Managing Director, Benson Beds

Royal Doulton Plc

Sir Henry Doulton House, Forge Lane, Etruria, Stoke-
on-Trent ST1 5NN
Tel: 01782 404040   **Fax:** 01782 404000
Website: www.royaldoulton.com
Sector: Housewares
Executives:
Anne Logue, Customer Service Manager
Geoff Martin, Finance Director
Gary Mylum, Group Director of Marketing
Wayne Nutbeen, Chief Executive
Chris Richards, Operations Director

Roys (Wroxham) Ltd

Wroxham, Norwich NR12 8DB
Tel: 01603 782131   **Fax:** 01603 784256
Website: www.roys.co.uk
Sector: Mixed Retailer
Executives:
Rowland Cogman, Company Secretary
Brian Godfrey, Managing Director
Edward Roy, Finance Director
Paul Roy, Merchandising Director
Peter Roy, Chairman
William Warnes, Food Trading Director

Rubicon

19–22 Rathbone Place, London W1T 1HY
Tel: 0207 580 0515
Sector: Clothing
Executives:
Peter Davies, Chief Executive
Jane Hayman, Marketing Director, Principles
Chris Inman, Group Finance Director
Sally McClymont, Retail Operations Director,
    Principles
Hilary Riva, Managing Director, Womenswear
    Warehouse
Chris Rostron, Finance Director

Russell & Bromley

24–34 Farwig Lane, Bromley BR1 3RB
Tel: 020 8460 1122   **Fax:** 020 8460 4424
Website: www.russellandbromley.co.uk
Sector: Footwear
Executives:
Craig Barrett, Retail Operations Executive
Peter Bromley, Chairman and Joint Managing
    Director
Roger Bromley, Joint Managing Director
John Clayton, Merchandise Manager
Avril Copeland, Executive Finance Director
Brendon Regan, Marketing Manager
Peter Saunders, Customer Service Manager

Safeway Plc

Safeway House, 6 Millington Road, Hayes, Middlesex
UB3 4AY
Tel: 020 8848 8744   **Fax:** 020 8573 1865
Website: www.safeway.co.uk
Sector: Food and Drink
Executives:
Mark Aylwin, Supply Chain Director
Fiona Bailey, Culture Director
Lawrence Christensen, Logistics Director
Carlos Criado-Perez, Chief Executive
John Durkin, Trading Director
Rick Francis, IT Director
Kevin Hawkins, Communications Director
Brian Keating, Information Systems Director
Simon Laffin, Finance Director
Martin Pugh, Marketing Director
Karen Shenstrom, Commercial Director, Meat and
    Fresh Foods
Steve Webb, Corporate Development Director
David Webster, Chairman
Jim White, Human Resources Director
David Wilson, Company Secretary

Savers Health & Beauty Plc

Stead House, Faverdale West, Faverdale Industrial
Estate, Darlington, County Durham DL3 0PS
Tel: 01325 251000   **Fax:** 01325 250999
Website: www.savers-hb.co.uk
Sector: Health and Beauty
Executives:
Kevin Cavern, Managing Director
Pamela Flowers, Human Resources and Customer
    Services Manager
Michael Kendall-Smith, Finance Director
Peter MacNab, Commercial Director

Schuh Ltd

1 Neilson Square, Deans Industrial Estate, Livingston
EH54 8RQ, Scotland
Tel: 01506 468762   **Fax:** 01506 460250
Email: solemate@schuh.co.uk

Should you be in this directory? See the form at the back for new entries and amendments

Website: www.schuh.co.uk
Sector: Footwear
Executives:
Sandy Alexander, Founding Director
Fiona Cochrane, Head of Marketing
Mark Crutchley, Finance Director
Lyn Ferguson, Personnel Director
Cred Linton, Customer Services Manager
Tom Lynch, Retail Operations Director
Gilian Macari, Marketing Manager
Terry Racionzer, Chairman
Colin Temple, Managing Director

ScS Upholstery Plc
45–49 Villiers Street, Sunderland, Tyne and Wear
SR1 1HA
Tel: 0191 514 6000   **Fax:** 0191 510 9048
Website: www.scssofas.co.uk
Sector: Furniture
Executives:
Sacha Beere, Finance Director
Mike Browne, Deputy Chairman
Mark Haughney, Sales Director
David Knight, Chief Executive
Marie Matheson, Human Resources Director
Tony McCann, Senior Non-Executive Director
Pam Middleton, Customer Services Manager
Kevin Royal, Marketing Director

Select Retail Plc
Units 4–6, Shakespeare Industrial Estate, Watford
WD2 5HD
Tel: 01923 226646   **Fax:** 01923 817263
Sector: Clothing
Executives:
Nigel Fisher, Finance Director
Kay McIntyre, Buying Director
Roger Pontin, Managing Director
John Sunderland, Business Development Director

Selfridges & Co
400 Oxford Street, London W1A 1AB
Tel: 0870 837 7377   **Fax:** 020 7491 0569
Website: www.selfridges.com
Sector: Department Store
Executives:
Alun Cathcart, Chairman
Philip Clarke, Finance Director
Sue West, Retail Director
Peter Williams, Chief Executive
Mark Young, Company Secretary

Shell Retail UK
P.O. Box 403, Staines, Middlesex TW18 3ZB
Tel: 01784 897700   **Fax:** 01784 897899
Website: www.shell.com
Sector: Petrol

Executives:
Simon Grimsdale, Retail Operations Manager
Mick McMahon, Retail Director
Sir Mark Moody-Stewart, Chairman

Shellys Shoes Ltd[3]
Stylo House, Harrogate Road, Apperley Bridge,
Bradford, West Yorkshire BD10 0NW
Tel: 01274 893300   **Fax:** 01274 616111
Website: www.tallandsmall.co.uk
Sector: Footwear
Executives:
Paul Acheson, Sales Director
Gary Grindlay, Supply Chain Director
Judith Milling, Managing Director
[3]See also Stylo Plc (parent company)

Shoe Studio Group Ltd
Woburn House, 20–24 Tavistock Square, London
WC1H 9HZ
Tel: 020 7380 3800   **Fax:** 020 7388 6905
Website: www.theshoestudio.com
Sector: Footwear
Executives:
Stefan Cassar, Finance Director
Nigel Davis, Managing Director
Don McCarthy, Chairman and Chief Executive Officer

Shoe Zone Ltd
Haramead Business Centre, Humberstone Road,
Leicester LE1 2LH
Tel: 0116 222 3000   **Fax:** 0116 222 3001
Email: info@shoezone.net
Website: www.shoezone.net
Sector: Footwear
Executives:
Steve Brown, Finance Director
Clare Howes, Buying Director
Wendy Lewis, Marketing Director
Anthony Smith, Chief Executive
Charles Smith, Chief Operating Officer
Michael Smith, Chairman

Shoefayre Ltd
Wigston House, Kirkdale Road, South Wigston,
Leicester LE18 4SU
Tel: 0116 278 5264   **Fax:** 0116 247 7192
Website: www.shoefayre.co.uk
Sector: Footwear
Executives:
Frank Croft, Chairman
Ian Hill, Chief Executive
David Markham, Financial Controller
Sue Merry, Customer Service Manager
Tim J Orton, Company Secretary
David Sheffield, Merchandise and Retail Controller

Should you be in this directory? See the form at the back for new entries and amendments

Shop Direct Group Ltd
Arndale House, Market Street, Manchester M60 6EQ
Tel: 0161 615 1615
Website: www.shopdg.com
Sector: Mail Order
Executives:
Simon Dalby, Managing Director, Agency
Linda Green, Managing Director, Direct
Mike Hancox, Chief Operating Officer

Shoprite Group Plc
Centre House, Little Switzerland, Douglas, Isle of Man
IM2 4RE
Tel: 01624 683333   **Fax:** 01624 683344
Email: enquiries@manxshoprite.com
Sector: Convenience Store
Executives:
Deryck Nicholson, Executive Chairman
Ian Nicholson, Managing Director
Martin Poole, Finance Director

Signet Group Plc
Zenith House, The Hyde, London NW9 6EW
Tel: 0870 909 0301   **Fax:** 020 8242 8588
Website: www.signetgroupplc.co.uk
Sector: Jewellery
Executives:
Rob Anderson, Chief Executive, UK
Walker Boyd, Group Financial Director
Terry Burman, Group Chief Executive
James McAdam, Chairman
Bill Pudney, Operations Director
Simon Taylor, Property Director

Slater Menswear
165 Howard Street, Glasgow, Lanarkshire G1 4HF,
Scotland
Tel: 0141 552 7171   **Fax:** 0141 553 1720
Website: www.slatermenswear.com
Sector: Clothing
Executives:
George Ferguson, Operations Director
Joe Ferry, Customer Services Manager
Charles McKenna, Sales Director
Paul Rose, Financial Director
Paul Slater, Managing Director

Somerfield Stores Ltd
Somerfield House, Whitchurch Lane, Bristol BS14 0TJ
Tel: 0117 935 9359   **Fax:** 0117 978 0629
Website: www.somerfield.co.uk
Sector: Food and Drink
Executives:
Steven Back, Group Finance Director
Keith Jackson, New Business Development Director
Kieron Mayes, Format Director
Jill McComas, Marketing Director

Andy Monk, IT Director
Martin Oakes, Director, Logistics and New Business
    Development
Mike Osmond, Retail Director, Kwik Save
Gill Tomey, Customer Service Manager
John von Sprecklesen, Executive Chairman
Gordon Wetherspoon, Group Property Director
Robin Whitbread, Managing Director, Kwik Save
Bill Williams, Managing Director, Somerfield

Spar (UK) Limited
Hygeia Building, 66–68 College Road, Harrow HA1
1BE
Tel: 020 8426 3700   **Fax:** 020 8426 3701
Website: www.spar.co.uk
Sector: Convenience Store
Executives:
Steve Blackmore, Head of Retail
Susan Darbershire, Marketing Director
Richard Hill, Finance Director
Mark Keeley, Buying Director
Chris Lewis, Buying Director
Joey Marwood, Managing Director
Morton Middleditch, Chairman
Peter Miller, Group Trading Director

Speciality Retail Group Plc
SRG House, Chester Road, Borehamwood WD6 1LT
Tel: 020 8327 3000   **Fax:** 020 8327 3001
Email: reception@srghouse.co.uk
Website: www.suitsyou.co.uk; www.youngs-
higher.co.uk
Sector: Clothing
Executives:
Alex Brick, Marketing and Property Director
Brian Brick, Managing Director
Jonathan Freedman, Finance Director
Stephen Hartley, Operations Controller

Specsavers Optical Group
La Villiaze, St Andrews, Guernsey, Channel Islands
GY6 8YP
Tel: 01481 236000   **Fax:** 01481 235555
Website: www.specsavers.net
Sector: Health and Beauty
Executives:
Michael Khan, IT Director
Hugo Lord, Director
Andrew Molle, Marketing Director
Robert Moorhead, Finance Director
Doug Perkins, Managing Director

Sports World International Ltd
Unit C, Chiltern Industrial Park, Boscombe Road,
Dunstable, Bedfordshire LU5 4LT
Tel: 0870 333 9400   **Fax:** 0870 333 9401
Website: www.sports-soccer.co.uk

Should you be in this directory? See the form at the back for new entries and amendments

Sector: Sports
Executives:
Michael Ashley, Proprietor
Sean Nevitt, Purchasing Director

Staples UK Ltd
Westfields, London Road, High Wycombe HP11 1HA
Tel: 01494 469200   **Fax:** 01494 469282
Website: www.staples.com
Sector: Stationery
Executives:
John Laidlaw, Marketing Director
Andy Randall, Managing Director
Ron Sargent, Chief Executive
Richard Smalley, Real Estate Controller
Penny Tapin, Customer Service Manager
Michael Walters, Financial Director

Stationery Box Holdings Ltd
Eagle Park Drive, Warrington, Cheshire WA2 8JA
Tel: 01925 422700   **Fax:** 01925 422701
Website: www.stationerybox.co.uk
Sector: Stationery
Executives:
Alastair Budd, Property Controller
Andrew Clark, Retail Operations Director
Steve Dolman, Buying Director
Alan Gaynor, Chief Executive
Neil Mason, Finance Director
Cheryl Mountford, Operations Manager

Stead & Simpson
Fosse Way, Syston, Leicester LE7 1PG
Tel: 0116 269 1300   **Fax:** 0116 264 0331
Email: enquiry@steadandsimpson.co.uk
Website: www.steadandsimpson.org
Sector: Footwear
Executives:
David Alleston, Retail Operations Manager
T Cartright, Customer Services Manager
Peter Foot, Financial Director
Cyril Freedman, Non-Executive Director
David Lockyer, Chief Executive
Phil Milward, Business Development Director
Roger Parr, Merchandise Director
John Shannon, Non-Executive Chairman
Jonathon Smith, Property Director

Stokes Plc
Unit 1–7, Wholesale Fruit Centre, St Philips, Bristol BS2 0YH
Tel: 0117 972 5700   **Fax:** 0117 972 3877
Email: info@stokesplc.com
Website: www.stokesplc.com
Sector: Food and Drink
Executives:
Julian Barczyk, Purchasing Director

Colin Bews, Company Secretary and Accountant
C Nash, Non-Executive Director
Daniel Stokes, Chairman
T Stokes, Non-Executive Director
Louise Stokes-Johnson, Managing Director

Stylo Plc
Stylo House, Harrogate Road, Apperley Bridge, Bradford, West Yorkshire BD10 0NW
Tel: 01274 617761   **Fax:** 01274 612844
Sector: Footwear
Executives:
Peter Gee, Managing Director
Mike Hodge, Executive Director
David Lovell, Non-Executive Deputy Chairman
Roger McLaughan, Sales and Marketing Director, Barratts
Barry Morris, Non-Executive Director
Simon Robson, Director of Buying
Ron Stark, Managing Director, Priceless Shoes
John Weaving, Chief Operating Officer
John Yates, Company Secretary
Michael Ziff, Chairman and Chief Executive

Superdrug Stores
118 Beddington Lane, Croydon CR0 4TB
Tel: 020 8684 7000
Website: www.superdrug.com
Sector: Health and Beauty
Executives:
Debbie Hansell, Commercial Director
Gerard Hazelebach, Managing Director
Graham Naylor, Retail Director
Neil Page, Financial Director

T J Hughes Plc
Hughes House, London Road, Liverpool L63 8JA
Tel: 0151 207 2600   **Fax:** 0151 298 2871
Website: www.tjhughes.co.uk
Sector: Department Store
Executives:
Brian Douglas, Operations Director
George Foster, Chief Executive
Andy Goody, Finance Director

T J Morris Ltd
Axis Business Park, East Lancashire Road, Gillmoss, Liverpool, Merseyside L11 0JA
Tel: 0151 5302920   **Fax:** 0151 5302922
Website: www.tjmorris.co.uk;
www.homebargains.co.uk
Sector: CTN
Executives:
Graham McLaughlin, Head of Finance
J Morris, E-Commerce and Marketing Director
Tom Morris, Managing Director

Should you be in this directory? See the form at the back for new entries and amendments

T-Mobile (UK)
Hatfield Business Park, Hatfield, Hertfordshire AL10 9BW
Tel: 01707 319001   **Fax:** 01707 315000
Website: www.t-mobile.co.uk
Sector: Electricals
Executives:
Martyn Antony, Acting Head of Retail Operations
Murray Clark, Head of Retail Finance
Andrew Fryatt, Managing Director

Tesco Stores Ltd
New Tesco House, Delamare Road, Cheshunt, Hertfordshire EN8 9SL
Tel: 01992 632222   **Fax:** 01992 630794
Email: customer.service@tesco.com
Website: www.tesco.com
Sector: Food and Drink
Executives:
Rowley Ager, Company Secretary
Philip Clarke, IT and Logistics Director
John Gardiner, Non-Executive Director
Andrew Higginson, Finance Director
John Hoerner, Chief Executive, Clothing
Sir Terry Leahy, Chief Executive
Tim Mason, Marketing and E-Commerce Director
David Potts, Retail Director
David Reid, Deputy Chairman

The Big Food Group Plc
Second Avenue, Deeside Industrial Park, Deeside, Flintshire CH5 2NW, Wales
Tel: 01244 830100   **Fax:** 01244 814531
Website: www.thebigfoodgroup.co.uk
Sector: Food and Drink
Executives:
Norman Bell, Group Strategy Director
Nick Canning, Marketing Director
Mike Coupe, Managing Director
George Greener, Non-Executive Chairman
Jon Grey, Group Logistics Director
Bill Grimsey, Chief Executive
Bill Hoskins, Group Finance Director
Karl Martin, Buying Director
Lee Pinnington, Head of Home Shopping
David Price, Non-Executive Director
Ted Smith, Stores Director
Tim Yates, Group Property Director

The Body Shop International Plc
Watersmead, Littlehampton, West Sussex BN17 6LS
Tel: 01903 731500   **Fax:** 01903 726250
Website: www.the-body-shop.com
Sector: Health and Beauty
Executives:
Diane Ashby, Head of Logistics Projects
Adrian Bellamy, Chairman

Tina Cantello, Marketing Director
Caroline Hadfield, Director of Product
Joe Lyons, Marketing Director, UK
Peter Ridler, Managing Director
Peter Saunders, Chief Executive
Peter Youngs, Global Finance Director

The MW Group Ltd
413 Oxford Street, London W1C 2PF
Tel: 020 7409 3377   **Fax:** 020 7409 1080
Website: www.mappin-and-webb.co.uk
Sector: Jewellery
Executives:
Nicholas Evans, Chief Executive

The Officers Club Ltd
Bassington Avenue, Bassington Industrial Estate, Cramlington, Northumberland NE23 8AH
Tel: 01670 591000   **Fax:** 01670 738468
Website: www.theofficersclub.co.uk
Sector: Clothing
Executives:
David Charlton, Chairman
Tim Lowe, Buying and Merchandising Director
Neil Wilson, Finance Director
Marc Wimpenny, Retail Operations Director

The Outdoor Group Ltd
Mansard Close, Westgate, Northampton NN5 5DL
Tel: 01604 441111   **Fax:** 01604 441164
Website: www.blacksleisure.co.uk
Sector: Sports
Executives:
Roy Crossland, Group Chief Executive
Andy Hall, Group Finance Director
Don Trangmar, Non-Executive Director

The Peacock Group Plc
Atlantic House, Tyndall Street, Cardiff CF10 4PS, Wales
Tel: 029 2027 0000   **Fax:** 029 2027 0224
Website: www.peacocks.co.uk
Sector: Clothing
Executives:
Tim Bettley, Buying and Merchandising Director
Keith Bryant, Group Finance Director
Neil Burnes, IT and Logistics Director
Richard Kirk, Chief Executive Officer
John Lovering, Chairman
Chris Miles, Retail Director
Graham Thomas, General Manager, Estates

The Stationers Ltd
Savoy House, Savoy Road, off Weston Road, Crewe, Cheshire CW1 6NA
Tel: 01270 505888   **Fax:** 01270 501515
Website: www.ryman.co.uk

Should you be in this directory? See the form at the back for new entries and amendments

Sector: Stationery

Executives:

Craig Fraser, Operations Director

Mike Kilcourse, Group Marketing Director

Simon Larkin, Finance Director

Karen Oxley, Customer Services Manager

Thermawear Limited (t/a Damart)

Bowling Green Mills, Bingley, West Yorkshire BD16 3ZD

Tel: 01274 568211   **Fax:** 01274 551024

Website: www.damartonline.co.uk

Sector: Clothing

Executives:

John Bottomley, Marketing Director

Graham Hall, Customer Services Manager

Andy Hill, Managing Director

Linda Montgomery, Retail Manager

Rick Parsons, Operations Director

David Whittle, Merchandise Director

Thorntons Plc

Thornton Park, Somercotes, Alfreton, Derbyshire DE55 4XJ

Tel: 0800 454537   **Fax:** 01773 540757

Email: tplccustserve@thorntons.co.uk

Website: www.thorntons.co.uk

Sector: Food and Drink

Executives:

Martin Allen, Finance Director

Peter Burdon, Chief Executive

Philip Douty, Trading Director

Doug W Phillips, Property Manager

Dominic Prendergast, Retail Director

John Thornton, Chairman

Thresher Group

Enjoyment Hall, Bessemer Road, Welwyn Garden City, Hertfordshire AL7 1BL

Tel: 01707 387200   **Fax:** 01707 387416

Website: www.threshergroup.co.uk

Sector: Off Licence

Executives:

Peter Harvey, Director of Commercial Finance

Steve Headington, Retail Operations Director

Philip Loring, Business Planning Director

Sarah McGlenn, New Channels Finance Director

Kevin Styles, Managing Director, Marketing

Mark Turner, Managing Director of Property

Colin Waggett, Finance Director

David Williams, Chief Executive

Tie Rack Ltd

Capital Interchange Way, Brentford, Middlesex TW8 0EX

Tel: 020 8230 2300   **Fax:** 020 8230 2301

Website: www.tie-rack.co.uk

Sector: Accessories

Executives:

Roy Bishko, Co-Chairman

Simone Frangi, Co-Chairman

David Memory, Financial Director

Martin Morgan, Deputy Chairman

Stephen Reeds, Marketing Director

Timberland UK Ltd

River Park Avenue, Staines TW18 3EN

Tel: 01784 496000   **Fax:** 01784 496002

Email: timberlanduk@euro.timberland.com

Website: www.timberland.com

Sector: Footwear

Executives:

Joanne Higgins, Customer Services Manager

Boo Hodges, Womenswear Director

Mark Jones, Retail Speciality Manager

Pat Mitchensen, Marketing Director

Richard O'Rourke, European Managing Director

Jeff Swartz, Chief Executive

Ian Watson, Managing Director

Time Group Ltd

Time Technology Park, Burnley, Lancashire BB12 7TG

Tel: 01282 770044   **Fax:** 01282 770607

Website: www.timegroup.co.uk

Sector: Electricals

Executives:

Kieran Crowley, Finance Director

Bill Davis, Non-Executive Chairman

John Free, Head of Retail

David Hotson, Customer Services Manager

Brian Lynn, Chief Executive

Tariq Mohammed, Marketing Director

Tahir Mohsan, Managing Director

Timpson Ltd

Timpson House, Claverton Road, Wythenshawe, Manchester M23 9TT

Tel: 0161 946 6200   **Fax:** 0161 946 0135

Email: info@timpson.co.uk

Website: www.timpson.co.uk

Sector: Housewares

Executives:

Patrick Farmer, Non-Executive Director

Christopher Green, Deputy Chairman

James Timpson, Managing Director

John Timpson, Chairman and Chief Executive Officer

Martin Tragen, Finance Director

Mike Williams, Property Director

TK Maxx

50 Clarendon Road, Watford WD17 1TX

Tel: 01923 473000   **Fax:** 01923 473500

Website: www.tkmaxx.com

Should you be in this directory? See the form at the back for new entries and amendments

Sector: Clothing

Executives:
Roger Bannister, Senior Buyer
Gordon Bullock, Chief Executive Officer
Deborah Dolce, Marketing Director
Bill Downing, IT Director
David Hendry, Finance Director
J Marriott, Human Resources Director
Dean Penny, Customer Service Manager
Alan Porte, Distribution Director
Alex Smith, Managing Director
Paul Sweetenham, Buying Director, Men's, Children's, and Shoes
Patrick Turnball, Property Development and Construction Director

TM Retail Ltd
TM House, Ashwells Road, Brentwood, Essex CM15 9ST
Tel: 01277 372916   **Fax:** 01277 372151
Sector: CTN

Executives:
Paul Baxter, Marketing Director
Paul Bennett, Property Director
Russel Cox, Group Financial Director
Kevin Hart, Joint Managing Director, Operations
Martin Kiss, Buying Controller
James Lancaster, Chief Executive
Jonathan Miller, Finance Director
David Saunders, Managing Director
Steve Wilkinson, Joint Managing Director, Operations

Topps Tiles Plc
Rushworth House, Wilmslow Road, Handforth, Wilmslow, Cheshire SK9 3HJ
Tel: 01625 446700   **Fax:** 01625 446800
Website: www.toppstiles.co.uk
Sector: DIY

Executives:
Barry Bester, Executive Chairman
Andrew Liggett, Finance Director
Nick Ounstead, Chief Executive
Stuart Williams, Chairman

Total UK Ltd
40 Clarendon Road, Watford, Hertfordshire WD1 71TQ
Tel: 01923 694000   **Fax:** 01923 694400
Website: www.total.co.uk
Sector: Petrol

Executives:
Malcolm Jones, Managing Director and Chairman

Toys R Us Limited
Geoffrey House, Vanwall Business Park, Vanwall Road, Maidenhead SL6 4UB
Tel: 01628 414141   **Fax:** 01628 414095

Website: www.toysrus.co.uk
Sector: Toys

Executives:
Mike Coogan, Marketing Director
Julia Cooper, Divisional Director, Merchandise
Frank Muzika, Finance, Admin and Logistics Director
David Rurka, Chairman and Managing Director
Phil Shayer, Merchandise Director

Trago Mills
Trago Mills Trading Estate, Twowatersfoot, Liskeard, Cornwall PL14 6HY
Tel: 01579 348877   **Fax:** 01579 346666
Website: www.trago.co.uk
Sector: DIY

Executives:
Tim Philips, Marketing Manager
Bruce Robertson, Chairman
Malcolm Sandbach, Managing Director
Geoff Witcher, Finance Director

Tulchan Group
Bridge Mill, Cowan Bridge, Carnforth, Lancashire LA6 2HS
Tel: 01524 271071   **Fax:** 01524 272058
Website: www.sockshops.com
Sector: Clothing

Executives:
Jeanette Binks, Customer Services Manager
Andrew Fortune, Financial Director
Kirsty Martindale, National Sales Manager
James Pow, Chairman and Chief Executive Officer
Lisa Thornton, Marketing Co-ordinator
Alex Wolfenden, Property Manager

United News Shops
The Maltings, Gelderd Place, Leeds LS12 6HL
Tel: 0113 2430222   **Fax:** 0113 2446330
Sector: CTN

Executives:
Stephen Doughty, Finance Director
Stephen Fearnley, Chairman
Julian Gott, Property Director
Roger Swift, Managing Director

Unwins Wine Group Ltd
Birchwood House, Victoria Road, Dartford, Kent DA1 5AJ
Tel: 01322 272711   **Fax:** 01322 294469
Email: info@unwins.co.uk
Website: www.unwins.co.uk
Sector: Off Licence

Executives:
David Armstrong, Purchasing and Marketing Director
Alex Benge, Property Director
Tim Gerhrad, Finance Director
Ian McLernon, Marketing Director

Should you be in this directory? See the form at the back for new entries and amendments

Mark Wellesley-Wood, Chairman
Phillip Wetz, Joint Managing Director
Simon Wetz, Joint Managing Director

USC Group Plc

4 Maxwell Square, Brucefield Industrial Park,
Livingston, Lothian EH54 9BL, Scotland
Tel: 01506 409000   **Fax:** 01506 409049
Website: www.usc.co.uk
Sector: Clothing
Executives:
Stephen Craig, Marketing Director
David Douglas, Director
Angus Morrison, Managing Director
Peter Woods, Finance Director

Virgin Retail Group Limited

The School House, 50 Brook Green, Hammersmith,
London W6 7RR
Tel: 020 8752 9000   **Fax:** 020 8752 9001
Website: www.virginmega.co.uk
Sector: Mixed Retailer
Executives:
Dennis Henderson, Group Operations Director
Steve Kincade, Commercial Director
Kerry Lee, Head of Retail Marketing
Paolo Pieri, Financial Director
Simon Wright, Chief Executive Officer

Vision Express UK Ltd

Abbeyfield Road, Lenton, Nottingham NG7 2SP
Tel: 0115 9865225   **Fax:** 0115 9850974
Website: www.visionexpress.com
Sector: Health and Beauty
Executives:
Michelle Alldis, Head of Customer Services
Marcel Cèzar, Chairman
Galleran Dejardin, Financial Director
Bernard Nuesser, Marketing Director
Karen Williams, Marketing Operations Manager

Vodafone Ltd

Vodafone House, The Connection, Newbury,
Berkshire RG14 2FN
Tel: 01635 33251
Website: www.vodafone.co.uk
Sector: Electricals
Executives:
Peter Bamford, Chief Marketing Officer
Lance Batchellor, Marketing Director
Thomas Geitner, Chief Technical Officer
Sir Christopher Gent, Life President
Julian Horn-Smith, Chief Operating Officer
Ken Hydon, Group Finance Director
Emma Kenny, Corporate Marketing Director
Lord MacLaurin of Knebworth, Chairman
Arun Sarin, Chief Executive

W Boyes & Company

Havers Hill, Eastfield YO11 3DT
Tel: 01723 582181   **Fax:** 01723 584841
Sector: Department Store
Executives:
Andrew Boyes, Joint Managing Director
Timothy Boyes, Joint Managing Director
R Faley, Finance Director
Ernie Gee, Director

W H Smith Retail Ltd

Greenbridge Road, Swindon, Wiltshire SN3 3LD
Tel: 01793 616161
Email: information@whsmith.co.uk
Website: www.whsmith.co.uk
Sector: Stationery
Executives:
Richard Handover, Chairman
Beverley Hodson, Managing Director
Nigel Leahy, Marketing Director
Simon Marinker, Property Director
Mark McMenemy, High Street Finance Director
Muriel Stirling, UK Brand Director
Richard Street, Stores Director
Kate Swann, Chief Executive Officer
John Warren, Group Finance Director
Sue Wharton, Trading Director

Waitrose Ltd

Doncastle Road, Southern Industrial Area, Bracknell,
Berkshire RG12 8YA
Tel: 01344 424680   **Fax:** 01344 824488
Website: www.waitrose.com
Sector: Food and Drink
Executives:
Nigel Burton, Development and Services Director
Brian Carroll, Finance Director
John Clarke, Head of Direct Businesses
Steven Esom, Managing Director
Kevin Garrett, Customer Services Manager
Howard King, Property Director
Angela Megson, Buying Director
Mark Price, Marketing Director
Geoffrey Salt, Distribution Director

Walmsley Furnishing Plc

12 Starkie Street, Preston, Lancashire PR1 3LU
Tel: 01772 519000   **Fax:** 01772 519030
Sector: Furniture
Executives:
Doreen Lilly, Customer Services Manager
David Ormsby, Managing Director
Philip Walmsley, Chairman

Warren James Ltd

7 Mersey Way, Stockport, Cheshire SK1 1PN
Tel: 0161 477 1814   **Fax:** 0161 429 7317

Should you be in this directory? See the form at the back for new entries and amendments

Website: www.warrenjames.com
Sector: Jewellery
Executives:
John Coulter, Director
Ann Jones, Director

Waterford Wedgwood Retail Ltd

Barlaston, Stoke-on-Trent, Staffordshire ST12 9ES
Tel: 01782 204141
Email: customercare@wedgewood.com
Website: www.wedgewood.com
Sector: Housewares
Executives:
Richard Barnes, Group Finance Director
Chris Beardsley, Business Development Director
Colin Gay, Retail Director, Europe
Jim Harding, Managing Director of UK Sales
Sharon Leibe, Customer Services Manager
Tony O'Reilly, Chief Executive Officer

Waterstone's Booksellers Ltd

Capital Interchange Way, Brentford, Middlesex
TW8 0EX
Tel: 020 8742 3800   **Fax:** 020 8742 0215
Website: www.waterstones.co.uk
Sector: Books
Executives:
Seaun Carney, Finance Director
Martin Carr, Operations Director
Sarah Dormer, Human Resources Director
Brian McLaughlin, Chairman and Managing Director
Lesley Miles, Marketing Director
David Pogrund, IT Director
David Roach, Product Director

WCF Retail

Old Jam Works, Station Road, Wigton, Cumbria CA7
9AX
Tel: 01697 341001   **Fax:** 01697 341020
Sector: Garden Centres
Executives:
Norman Brayton, Marketing Director
Trevor Smith, Finance Director
Eddie Tutt, Operations and IT Director

Whittard of Chelsea Plc

Unit 3 Union Court, 22 Union Road, London SW4
6JP
Tel: 020 7819 6400   **Fax:** 020 7627 8850
Email: info@whittard.co.uk
Website: www.whittard.co.uk;
     www.whittard.com
Sector: Food and Drink
Executives:
Sarah Brass, Head of Marketing
Kegan Copas, Internet Manager
Brian Hay, Operations Director

William Hobhouse, Non-Executive Chairman
Richard Rose, Chief Executive
Caroline Taylor, Head of International Mail Order

Wilkinson Hardware Stores Limited

P.O. Box 20, Roebuck Way, Manton Wood, Worksop,
Nottinghamshire S80 3YY
Tel: 01909 505505   **Fax:** 01909 505777
Email: communications@wilko.co.uk
Website: www.wilko.co.uk
Sector: DIY
Executives:
Dave Bosworth, Customer Services Manager
Gordon Brown, Managing Director
Gillian Reddish, Communications Manager
Paul Testo, Finance Director
David Thornley, Property Director
Nick Wilkinson, Marketing Services
Tony Wilkinson, Chairman

William Jackson & Son Ltd

40 Derringham Street, Hull HU3 1EW
Tel: 01482 224131   **Fax:** 01482 215256
Website: www.wjs.co.uk
Sector: Food and Drink
Executives:
Nick Dawson, Financial Director
Patrick Farnsworth, Joint Managing Director
Sue Gaston, Customer Services Manager
Chris Oughtred, Chairman and Joint Managing
     Director
Phillip Sims, Sales Director
Allan Wheelwright, Personnel Director

Wine Cellar Ltd

PO Box 476, Loushers Lane, Warrington, Cheshire
WA4 6RR
Tel: 01925 454545   **Fax:** 01925 454546
Website: www.winecellar.co.uk
Sector: Mixed Retailer
Executives:
Dave Allen, Financial Controller
Paul Gaskell, Managing Director
Warren Leath, Operations Manager
John Thompson, Operations Manager
David Walker, IT Manager

Wm Morrison Supermarkets Plc

Hilmore House, Thornton Road, Bradford BD8 9AX
Tel: 01274 494166   **Fax:** 01274 498281
Website: www.morereasons.co.uk
Sector: Food and Drink
Executives:
Martin Ackroyd, Finance Director
Chris Blundell, Business Development Director
George Buttle, Deputy Managing Director
Chris Evenson, Development Director

Should you be in this directory? See the form at the back for new entries and amendments

Martyn Jones, Senior Trading Director
Marie Melnyk, Joint Managing Director
Sir Ken Morrison, Chairman
Roger Owen, Property Director
Andrew Pleasance, Head of Home and Leisure
Robert Stott, Joint Managing Director

Woolworths Plc

Woolworth House, 242–246 Marylebone Road,
London NW1 6JL
Tel: 020 7262 1222   **Fax:** 020 7706 5416
Website: www.woolworths.co.uk
Sector: Mixed Retailer
Executives:
Neil Ashworth, Supply Chain Director
Gill Barr, Business Development Director
Trevor Bish-Jones, Chief Executive
Gerald Corbett, Chairman
Jo Hall, Commercial Director

Octavia Morley, Marketing Director
Tim Owrid, Head of Distribution Operations
Chris Rogers, Finance Director
Denise Shane, Head of Home Business Unit
Alan Wenham, Customer Services Director

Wyevale Garden Centres Plc

Kings Acre Road, Hereford HR4 0SE
Tel: 01432 276568   **Fax:** 01432 263289
Website: www.wyevale.co.uk
Sector: Garden Centres
Executives:
Brian A Evans, Chairman
Robert J Hewitt, Chief Executive
Stephen Murfin, Finance Director and Company
  Secretary
Glyn J Price, Group Buying Director
S Walker, Customer Services Manager

Should you be in this directory? See the form at the back for new entries and amendments

E-TAILERS

For a more complete listing of executives of companies marked *, please see their entry under *Retailers* above.

Amazon.co.uk
1–9 The Grove, Slough, Berkshire SL1 1QP
Tel: 020 8636 9200
Sector: Mixed Retailer
Executives:
Jeff Bezos, Chief Executive
Robin Terrell, UK Managing Director

Arcadia Group Ltd *
Colegrave House, 70 Berners Street, London W1P 3NL
Tel: 020 7636 8040
Website: www.arcadiagroup.co.uk
Sector: Clothing
Executives:
Paul Budge, Finance Director
Gina Digregorio, International Marketing Manager
Tania Foster-Brown, Public Relations and Special Events Director
Mike Goring, Group Operations Director
Lord Anthony Grabiner, Chairman
Ian Grabiner, Chief Operating Officer
Philip Green, Owner
John Hind, Trading Director
Mark Vandenberghe, International Director

Argos Retail Group *
489–499 Avebury Boulevard, Saxon Gate West, Milton Keynes MK9 2NW
Tel: 0845 124 0044   **Fax:** 01908 692301
Website: www.argos.co.uk
Sector: Mixed Retailer
Executives:
S Agar-Hutty, IT Director
Richard John Ashton, Group Finance and Systems Director
Sir Victor Blank, Chairman
Eugene Brazil, Managing Director, Argos Home Shopping
Paul Geddes, Marketing Director
Kitty Kwakman, Head of E-Commerce
R Wall, Argos Direct Director

Asda Stores Ltd *
Asda House, Southbank, Great Wilson Street, Leeds LS11 5AD
Tel: 0113 243 5435   **Fax:** 0113 241 7261
Website: www.asda.co.uk
Sector: Food and Drink
Executives:
Glenn Bowles, Retail Managing Director
Rosy Cannon, Home Shopping Manager

Jeremy Cross, Head of Merchandising
Tony De Nunzio, President and Chief Operating Officer
Denise Jagger, Company Secretary
Denis Malas, Head of Strategic Development
Tony Page, Director of General Merchandise
Chris Pilling, Marketing Director
Angela Spindler, Planning Development Director
Christine Watts, Corporate Affairs Director

Avon Cosmetics
Nunn Mills Road, Northampton NN1 5PA
Tel: 01604 232425   **Fax:** 01604 232444
Website: www.avon.uk.com
Sector: Health and Beauty
Executives:
Jerry McDonald, President
Peter Nicholls, Vice-President, Sales
Bridie Pollard, Head of Public Relations
Andrea Slater, Vice-President Marketing

B & Q Plc *
Portswood House, 1 Hampshire Corporate Park, Chandlers Ford, Eastleigh, Hampshire SO53 3YX
Tel: 023 8025 6256   **Fax:** 023 8025 7480
Website: www.diy.com
Sector: DIY
Executives:
George Adams, Commercial and Marketing Director
Duncan Tatton-Brown, Finance Director
Bill Whiting, Chief Executive

BlackStar
42 The Cutts, Dunmurry, Belfast BT17 9HN, Northern Ireland
Tel: 028 9043 0430   **Fax:** 028 9043 0460
Email: info@blackstar.co.uk
Website: www.blackstar.co.uk
Sector: Entertainment
Executives:
Tony Bowden, Director
Darryl Collins, Joint Managing Director
Jeremy Glover, Director
Ian Loughran, Joint Managing Director
Jim Morgan, Director

Blackwell's UK *
Beaver House, Hythe Bridge Street, Oxford OX1 2ET
Tel: 01865 792792   **Fax:** 01865 791438
Email: blackwell.extra@blackwell.co.uk
Website: www.blackwell.co.uk
Sector: Books
Executives:
Phillip Blackwell, Chief Executive
Dominic Myers, Managing Director
Michael Neil, Marketing Director
Stephen Walsh-Hill, Finance Director

Should you be in this directory? See the form at the back for new entries and amendments

Boden

Elliott House, Victoria Road, London NW10 6NY

Tel: 020 8453 1535 **Fax:** 020 8453 1536

Website: www.boden.co.uk

Sector: Clothing

Executives:

Mark Binnington, Marketing Director

Johnnie Boden, Managing Director

Julian Granville, Chairman

BOL.COM

Greater London House, Hampstead Road, London NW1 7TZ

Tel: 0870 607 0205

Sector: Books

Executives:

A Brioch, Managing Director

Orla Dunn, Marketing Manager

J James, Customer Service Representative

Boots Group Plc *

1 Thane Road West, Nottingham NG2 3AA

Tel: 0115 950 6111

Website: www.boots.com; www.wellbeing.com

Sector: Health and Beauty

Executives:

Richard Baker, Chief Executive

Paul Bateman, Group Operations Director

Howard Dodd, Chief Financial Officer

Sir Nigel Rudd, Chairman

Andy Smith, Group Human Resources Director

Buy Electrical Direct

Pentre Road, St Clears, Carmarthenshire SA33 4AA, Wales

Tel: 0870 787 7867 **Fax:** 01994 231244

Email: sales@be-direct.co.uk

Website: www.be direct.co.uk

Sector: Electricals

Executives:

Lee Beynon, Operations Director

Paul Evans, Managing Director

Trudie Evans, Finance Director

Phil Tucker, Sales & Marketing Director

Capital Sound & Vision

Capital House, Link 10, Napier Way, Crawley, West Sussex RH10 2RA

Tel: 01293 543555

Email: abc@unbeatable.co.uk

Website: www.unbeatable.co.uk

Sector: Music and Video

Executives:

Sue Bignall, Marketing Director

Gary Parker, Managing Director

Clive Swan, Chairman

Pat Vandendyck, Finance Director

Carphone Warehouse Plc *

North Acton Business Park, Wales Farm Road, London W3 6RS

Tel: 020 8896 5000 **Fax:** 020 8896 5005

Website: www.carphonewarehouse.com

Sector: Electricals

Executives:

Richard Collier, Group Property Director

Charles Dunstone, Chief Executive Officer

Jonathan Hook, Retail Director

Chris Murton, Online Services Director

David Ross, Chief Operating Officer

Hans Snook, Non-Executive Chairman

Roger Taylor, Chief Financial Officer

CD Wow!

Suite 2a, Gregories Court, Gregories Road, Beaconsfield, Buckinghamshire HP9 1HQ

Tel: 0870 350 0899 **Fax:** 0870 350 0925

Email: help@cd-wow.com

Website: www.cd-wow.com

Sector: Music and Video

Executives:

Phillip Robinson, Managing Director

Comet Direct

Comet House, Three Rivers Court, Rickmansworth, Hertfordshire WD3 1FX

Tel: 01923 710000 **Fax:** 01923 714420

Email: direct@comet.co.uk

Website: www.comet.co.uk

Sector: Electricals

Executives:

G Arford, Head of IT

Tom Barry, Deputy Managing Director, Operations

Ian Edwards, Deputy Managing Director, Business Support

Confetti.co.uk

10 Greenland Street, London NW1 0ND

Tel: 020 7428 8300 **Fax:** 020 7428 8301

Email: customercare@confetti.co.uk

Website: www.confetti.co.uk

Sector: Stationery

Executives:

Tony Bennett, Financial Director

David Lethbridge, Joint Managing Director

Peter Marsh, Joint Managing Director

Currys

Maylands Avenue, Hemel Hempsted, Hertfordshire HP2 7TG

Tel: 0870 850 3333 **Fax:** 01442 233218

Website: www.currys.co.uk

Sector: Electricals

Should you be in this directory? See the form at the back for new entries and amendments

Executives:
Peter Keenan, Assistant Managing Director
Nick Wilkinson, Managing Director

Debenhams Plc *
1 Welbeck Street, London W1G 0AA
Tel: 020 7408 4444   **Fax:** 020 7408 3366
Website: www.debenhams.com
Sector: Department Store
Executives:
Phil Bartup, Business Systems Manager
Hugh Bradley, Communications Director
Tim Davies, Strategy Director

DSG Retail Ltd *
Dixons House, Maylands Avenue, Hemel Hempstead,
Hertfordshire HP2 7TG
Tel: 0870 850 3333   **Fax:** 01442 233218
Website: www.dixons.co.uk
Sector: Electricals
Executives:
John Clare, Chief Executive
Sir John Collins, Chairman
Jeremy Darroch, Finance Director
David Gilbert, Chief Operating Officer, Central
    Operations
David Hamid, Chief Operating Officer, Retail
    Operations
Damian Norton, Information Systems Director

eBay UK Ltd
Bishops Park House, 25–29 Fulham High Street,
London SW6 3JH
Website: www.ebay.co.uk
Sector: Internet shopping
Executives:
Pierre Omidyar, Founder and Chairman
Meg Whitman, President and Chief Executive
    Officer

EmpireDirect.co.uk
The Clock Buildings, Roundhay Road, Leeds LS8 2SH
Tel: 0113 235 1770
Website: www.empiredirect.co.uk
Sector: Electricals
Executives:
Madan Showan, Chairman
Posh Showan, Marketing Director
Jaswant Toor, Managing Director

Figleaves.com
2nd Floor Reco House, 928 High Road, London N12
9RA
Tel: 020 8492 1300   **Fax:** 020 8492 2560
Email: michael.ross@figleaves.com
Website: www.figleaves.com
Sector: Clothing

Executives:
Charlie Bodycote, Technical Director
Ed Bussey, Business Development Director
Jo Jeffrey, Communications Director
Michael Ross, Chief Executive Officer

Focus DIY Ltd *
Gawsworth House, Westmere Drive, Crewe, Cheshire
CW1 6XB
Tel: 01270 501555   **Fax:** 01270 250501
Website: www.focusdiy.co.uk
Sector: DIY
Executives:
Colin Ball, Group Commercial Services Director and
    E-Commerce
Steve Johnson, Managing Director
John Rice, IT Director
Duncan Terras, Human Resources Director
Dave Williams, Finance Director

Freemans Plc *
139 Clapham Road, London SW99 0HR
Tel: 020 7820 2000   **Fax:** 020 7820 2769
Website: www.freemans.com
Sector: Mail Order
Executives:
Michael Hawker, Chief Executive
Simon Malcom, Head of E-Marketing
Janet McAulay, Catalogue Director
Jim Skelsey, Merchandise Director

Grattan Plc *
Anchor House, Ingleby Road, Bradford, West
Yorkshire BD99 2XG
Tel: 01274 575511   **Fax:** 01274 625591
Website: www.grattan.co.uk
Sector: Mail Order
Executives:
Walter Blackwood, Distribution Director
Michael L Hawker, Chief Executive
Jim Skelsey, Merchandise Director
Christopher West, Finance Director

Haburi.com
The Virtual Factory Outlet, Bredgade 65, DK-1260
Copenhagen, Denmark
Tel: 00 49 7131 390 9789
Email: help-uk@haburi.com
Website: www.haburi.com
Sector: Clothing
Executives:
Thorsten Hollger, Director

HMV UK Ltd
Film House, 142 Wardour Street, London W1F 8LN
Tel: 020 7432 2000
Website: www.hmv.co.uk

Should you be in this directory? See the form at the back for new entries and amendments

Sector: Music and Video

Executives:

Alan James Giles, Chief Executive

Peter Hill, Finance Director

Stuart Rowe, E-Commerce Director

Holland & Barrett Retail Ltd *

Samuel Ryder House, Townsend Drive, Attleborough Fields, Nuneaton, Warwickshire CV11 6XW

Tel: 0870 606 6605   **Fax:** 01283 560000

Email: customerservices@hollandandbarrett.com

Website: www.hollandandbarrett.com

Sector: Health and Beauty

Executives:

Peter Aldis, Managing Director

Gill Day, Finance Director

Neil Fletcher, IT Manager

Phil Geary, Marketing Director

Mark Kendrick, Distribution Director

Barry Vickers, Chief Executive Officer

John Lewis Plc *

171 Victoria Street, London SW1E 5NN

Tel: 020 7828 1000   **Fax:** 020 7592 6566

Email: enquiries@johnlewis.co.uk

Website: www.johnlewis.co.uk; www.waitrose.com

Sector: Department Store

Executives:

Ian David Alexander, Finance Director

David Felwick, Deputy Chairman

Sir Stuart Hampson, Executive Chairman

Phil Hullah, Head of Business Development and Supply Chain

Alison Lancaster, Head of Merchandising, John Lewis Direct

Jill Little, Merchandise Director

Charlie Mayfield, Development Director

Luke Mayhew, Managing Director

Simon Palethorpe, Managing Director, John Lewis Direct

Littlewoods Home Shopping Ltd

Sir John Moores Building, 100 Old Hall Street, Liverpool L70 1AB

Tel: 0151 235 2222

Website: www.littlewoods-online.com

Sector: Mail Order

Executives:

Mark Daynes, Managing Director, Littlewoods All-Inclusive

Alan Evans, Managing Director, Direct

David Hallett, Operations Director

Euan Imrie, Finance Director

Alistair McGeorge, Group Chief Executive

Andy Roe, Customer Service Director

Majestic Wine Warehouses Ltd *

Majestic House, Otterspool Way, Watford WD25 8WW

Tel: 01923 928200   **Fax:** 01923 819105

Email: info@majestic.co.uk

Website: www.majestic.co.uk

Sector: Food and Drink

Executives:

Nigel Alldritt, Financial Director

John Apthorp, Chairman

Steve de Mellow, Marketing Director

Timothy How, Managing Director

Steve Lewis, Retail Director

Tony Mason, Trading Director

Jeremy Palmer, E-Commerce Director

Marks & Spencer Plc *

Michael House, 47–67 Baker Street, London W1U 8EP

Tel: 020 7935 4422   **Fax:** 020 7487 2679

Email: customer.services@marksandspencer.com

Website: www.marksandspencer.com

Sector: Clothing

Executives:

Roger Holmes, Chief Executive

Justin King, Food Director

David R Norgrove, Clothing, Outlets and International Director

Laurel Powers-Freeling, Director and Chief Executive of Financial Services

Vittorio Radice, Director, Home

Alison Reed, Chief Financial Officer

Luc Vandevelde, Chairman

MFI Furniture Centres Limited *

Southon House, 333 The Hyde, Edgeware Road, Colindale, London NW9 6TD

Tel: 020 8200 8000   **Fax:** 020 8200 8636

Website: www.mfi.co.uk

Sector: Furniture

Executives:

Martin Clifford-King, Group Financial Director

John Hancock, Chief Executive

Gordon MacDonald, Chief Operating Officer

Peter McKenna, E-Commerce Manager

Next Plc *

Desford Road, Enderby, Leicester LE19 4AT

Tel: 0845 4567777   **Fax:** 0116 2848998

Website: www.next.co.uk

Sector: Clothing

Executives:

David Jones, Chairman

David Keens, Group Finance Director

Michael Law, Directory Operations Director

Simon Wolfson, Chief Executive

Should you be in this directory? See the form at the back for new entries and amendments

143

Ocado Ltd
Gypsy Moth Avenue, Hatfield Business Park, Hatfield,
Hertfordshire AL10 9BD
Tel: 01707 227800   **Fax:** 01727 227999
Email: ocado@ocado.com
Website: www.ocado.com
Sector: Food and Drink
Executives:
John Gissing, Finance Director
Simon Powell, Head of Customer Relationship
    Management
Nigel Robertson, Managing Director
Tim Steiner, Chief Executive

Oddbins UK Ltd *
31–33 Weir Road, Wimbledon, London
SW19 8UG
Tel: 020 8944 4400   **Fax:** 020 8944 4411
Email: customer.service@oddbins.com
Website: www.oddbins.com
Sector: Food and Drink
Executives:
Jacques Duley, Managing Director
Laurent Genthialan, Finance Director
Sam Richardson, Online Marketing Manager

Orange Plc *
The Chase, John Tate Road, Foxholes Business Park,
Hertford, Hertfordshire SG13 7NN
Tel: 01992 502000   **Fax:** 0870 373 2001
Website: www.orange.co.uk
Sector: Electricals
Executives:
Ian Fraser, Director of Sales and Distribution,
    Personal and Small Business
Kennedy Rodriques, Financial Manager
Solomon Trujillo, Chief Executive

Phones 4u *
Swift House, Liverpool Road, Newcastle-under-Lyme,
Staffordshire ST5 9JJ
Tel: 0870 905 0416   **Fax:** 01270 259396
Website: www.phones4u.co.uk
Sector: Electricals
Executives:
John Caudwell, Chairman and Chief Executive
Steve Caunce, Finance Director
Peter Green, Managing Director
Paul Hamburger, Marketing Director
Scott Thomas, Head of E-Commerce

Play.com
P.O. Box 192, Jersey JE4 8RP
Tel: 0845 800 1020   **Fax:** 01534 631580
Email: info@play.com
Website: www.play.com
Sector: Internet shopping

Executives:
Peter de Bourcier, Joint Director
Richard Golding, Joint Director
Simon Perree, Joint Director

Powerhouse Internet
Talbot Close, Walsall WS2 7PE
Tel: 0845 601 2080   **Fax:** 01992 707956
Email: e-sales@powerhouse.co.uk
Website: www.powerhouse.co.uk
Sector: Electricals
Executives:
Bethan Lloyd, Internet Marketing Manager

Redcats UK (Brands) Ltd *
18 Canal Road, Bradford, West Yorkshire
BD99 4XB
Tel: 01274 729544   **Fax:** 01274 763855
Website: www.redoute.co.uk
Sector: Mail Order
Executives:
Henry Heavisides, General Manager, La Redoute UK
Steve Parkes, Head of Marketing and E-Commerce, La
    Redoute UK

Sainsbury's Supermarkets Ltd *
Sainsbury's Business Centre, 33 Holborn, London
EC1N 2HT
Tel: 020 7695 6000   **Fax:** 020 7695 7610
Website: www.sainsburystoyou.co.uk
Sector: Food and Drink
Executives:
Toby Anderson, Head of Online Marketing
Sir Peter Davis, Group Chief Executive
Roger Matthews, Group Finance Director
Stuart Mitchell, Managing Director
Jan Shawe, Director of Group Corporate
    Communications
Penny Slater, Senior Manager Online Marketing

Screwfix Direct
Mead Avenue, Houndstone Business Park, Yeovil,
Somerset BA22 8RT
Tel: 01935 414100   **Fax:** 0800 056 2256
Email: online@screwfix.com
Website: www.screwfix.com
Sector: DIY
Executives:
John Allen, Managing Director
Steve Barrow, Finance Director
Graham Benson, Information Systems Director
Richard Butler, Human Resources Director
Colin McCarthy, Operations Director
Hem Patel, Buying Director
Angela Rushforth, Marketing Director

Should you be in this directory? See the form at the back for new entries and amendments

Shoe-Shop.com

The Kinloch Building, Northminster Business Park,
Upper Poppleton, York, North Yorkshire Y026 6QU
Tel: 0870 011 7227   **Fax:** 01904 528791
Email: helpdesk@shoe-shop.com
Website: www.shoe-shop.com
Sector: Footwear

Executives:
Simon Collins, IT Manager
Stuart Paver, Managing Director

Streets Online

243 Blythe Road, Hayes, Middlesex UB3 1DN
Tel: 0845 6018330   **Fax:** 020 8582 8600
Website: www.streetsonline.co.uk
Sector: Music and Video

Executives:
Tony Goodwin, Marketing Director, Audiostreet.com
Andrew Harper, Managing Director, Audiostreet.com

T-Mobile (UK) *

Hatfield Business Park, Hatfield, Hertfordshire
AL10 9BW
Tel: 0845 412 5000
Website: www.t-mobile.co.uk
Sector: Electricals

Executives:
Martyn Antony, Acting Head of Retail Operations
Murray Clark, Head of Retail Finance
Andrew Fryatt, Managing Director

Tesco.com *

New Tesco House, Delamare Rd, Cheshunt,
Hertfordshire EN8 9SL
Tel: 01992 632222   **Fax:** 01992 630794
Email: customer.service@tesco.co.uk
Website: www.tesco.com
Sector: Food and Drink

Executives:
John Browett, Chief Executive
David Clement, Marketing Director
Tim Mason, Chairman
Mike McNamara, IT Director

The Big Food Group Plc *

Second Avenue, Deeside Industrial Park, Deeside,
Flintshire CH5 2NW, Wales
Tel: 01244 830100   **Fax:** 01244 283220
Website: www.thebigfoodgroup.co.uk;
www.iceland.co.uk
Sector: Food and Drink

Executives:
Mike Cooper, Managing Director, Iceland
Lee Pinnington, Head of Home Shopping

Thinknatural.com

Unit 10, Lindsay Square, Livingstone EH54 OBR,
Scotland
Tel: 0845 601 1948   **Fax:** 01442 866977
Website: www.thinknatural.com
Sector: Health and Beauty

Executives:
Emma Crowe, Director
Luke Jensen, Managing Director

Virgin Megastores Online *

The School House, 50 Brook Green, Hammersmith,
London W6 7RR
Tel: 020 7299 0444
Email: customerservices@virginmega.co.uk
Website: www.virginmegastores.co.uk
Sector: Music and Video

Executives:
Dennis Henderson, Group Operations Director
Paolo Pieri, Financial Director

Virgin Wines Online Ltd

St James' Mill, Whitefriars, Norwich, Norfolk NR3 1TN
Tel: 0870 164 9593   **Fax:** 01603 619277
Email: help@virginwines.com
Website: www.virginwines.com
Sector: Food and Drink

Executives:
Rowan Gormley, Managing Director
Shiona McDougall, Marketing Director

Vodafone Ltd *

Vodafone House, The Connection, Newbury,
Berkshire RG14 2FN
Tel: 01635 33251
Website: www.vodafone.co.uk
Sector: Electricals

Executives:
Peter Bamford, Chief Marketing Officer
Lance Batchellor, Marketing Director
Gavin Derby, Chief Executive, UK
Thomas Geitner, Chief Technical Officer
Sir Christopher Gent, Life President
Julian Horn-Smith, Chief Operating Officer
Ken Hydon, Group Financial Director
Lord MacLaurin of Knebworth, Chairman
Arun Sarin, Chief Executive

W H Smith Direct *

1 Ashville Road, Cowley, Oxford OX4 6TS
Tel: 01865 771772   **Fax:** 01865 771766
Email: support@whsmithonline.co.uk
Website: www.whsmith.co.uk
Sector: Stationery

Executives:
Bob Broadbridge, Managing Director
Carolyn Rivett, Finance Director

Should you be in this directory? See the form at the back for new entries and amendments

Waitrose Ltd *

Doncastle Road, Southern Industrial Area, Bracknell,
Berkshire RG12 8YA

Tel: 01344 424680   **Fax:** 01344 824488

Website: www.waitrose.com

Sector: Food and Drink

Executives:

Brian Carroll, Finance Director

John Clarke, Head of Direct Businesses

Steven Esom, Managing Director

Woolworths Plc *

Woolworth House, 242–246 Marylebone Road,
London NW1 6JL

Tel: 020 7262 1222   **Fax:** 020 7706 5416

Website: www.woolworths.co.uk

Sector: Mixed Retailer

Executives:

Trevor Bish-Jones, Chief Executive

Gerald Corbett, Chairman

Tony Goodwin, Commercial and Marketing Manager,
    Streets Online

Andrew Harber, E-Commerce Director, Streets Online

Ken Lewis, Commercial Director

Kirstie Mann, Strategic Development

Octavia Morley, Marketing Director

Chris Rogers, Finance Director

Should you be in this directory? See the form at the back for new entries and amendments

146

ALPHABETICAL LISTING BY

Retail Sector

Note: Some companies are marked * to identify an e-tailer from the corresponding retail company (i.e. where they have the same name).

ACCESSORIES

Baxter, Joanna	Head of Press and Public Relations	Monsoon Accessorize Ltd
Binder, Joanna	Head of Merchandising	Burberrys
Bishko, Roy	Co-Chairman	Tie Rack Ltd
Blank, Sir Victor	Chairman, GUS	Burberrys
Blythe, Peter	Finance Director	Burberrys
Bravo, Rose Maria	Chief Executive	Burberrys
Cavenagh, Pamela	Senior Vice-President, Accessories	Burberrys
Chellingsworth, William	Store Operations Manager	Burberrys
Dillane, Mark	Head of Property Department	Claire's Accessories
Doherty, Pat	Senior Vice-President, Marketing	Burberrys
Finlay, Lyle	Chief Executive	Claire's Accessories
Foster, Rose	UK Managing Director	Monsoon Accessorize Ltd
Frangi, Simone	Co-Chairman	Tie Rack Ltd
Friend, Jason	Advertising Manager	Burberrys
Frost, Graham	Deputy Chairman	Monsoon Accessorize Ltd
Greenwood, Anthony	Finance Director	Claire's Accessories
Hamwee, Nikki	Brand Director, Accessorize	Monsoon Accessorize Ltd
Haworth, Melanie	Buying and Merchandising Director	Claire's Accessories
May, Andrew	Finance Director	Monsoon Accessorize Ltd
Memory, David	Financial Director	Tie Rack Ltd
Morgan, Martin	Deputy Chairman	Tie Rack Ltd
Ogden, Ian	Retail Director	Claire's Accessories
Reeds, Stephen	Marketing Director	Tie Rack Ltd
Searle, G W	Non-Executive Director	Monsoon Accessorize Ltd
Sim, Graham	Group Marketing Director	Monsoon Accessorize Ltd
Simon, Peter	Chief Executive and Chairman	Monsoon Accessorize Ltd
Spooner, John	International Development Director	Monsoon Accessorize Ltd
Wallbridge, Andrew	Human Resources Director	Claire's Accessories
Zuppinger, Jamie	European Resources Manager	Claire's Accessories

AIRPORT RETAILING

Buckley, Steve	Managing Director, UK Specialities	Alpha Retail
Deller, Ben	Marketing Manager, World News	Alpha Retail
Frost, Graham	Chairman	Alpha Retail
King, David	Executive Director and Managing Director of Alpha Retail Shopping	Alpha Retail
McRae, Heather	Finance Director	Alpha Retail
Possamai, Paul	Managing Director of Alpha Inflight Retail	Alpha Retail

AUTOMOTIVE

Carter, Nick	Finance and Property Director	Halfords Limited
Hamid, David	Chief Executive	Halfords Limited
Hudson, Dave	Operations Director	Motorworld Ltd
Mcleod, Ian	Director of Trading	Halfords Limited
Mousell, John	Managing Director	Motorworld Ltd
Peach, Steve	Purchasing Director	Motorworld Ltd
Smith, Andy N	Personnel Director	Halfords Limited
Templeman, Rob	Chairman	Halfords Limited
Torrance, Andy J	Operations Director	Halfords Limited
Wharton, Nick B E	IT and Business Development Director	Halfords Limited
Woodhouse, Chris	Deputy Chairman	Halfords Limited

Should you be in this directory? See the form at the back for new entries and amendments

BOOKS

Begum, Luthfa	Marketing Manager	Borders UK Ltd
Blackwell, Phillip	Chief Executive	Blackwell's UK
Bradford, Suzanne	Operations Manager	Ottakar's Plc
Brioch, A	Managing Director	BOL.COM
Carney, Seaun	Finance Director	Waterstone's Booksellers Ltd
Carr, Martin	Operations Director	Waterstone's Booksellers Ltd
Collinge, Louise	Merchandise and Marketing Director	Borders UK Ltd
Dormer, Sarah	Human Resources Director	Waterstone's Booksellers Ltd
Downer, Phillip	Managing Director	Borders UK Ltd
Dunn, Orla	Marketing Manager	BOL.COM
Dunne, Philip	Chairman	Ottakar's Plc
Halton, Sara	Financial Director	Borders UK Ltd
Henderson, Paul	Marketing Director	Ottakar's Plc
Heneage, James	Managing Director	Ottakar's Plc
James, J	Customer Service Representative	BOL.COM
Knighton, Edward	Finance Director and Company Secretary	Ottakar's Plc
McLaughlin, Brian	Chairman and Managing Director	Waterstone's Booksellers Ltd
Metcalf, Harry	Commercial Manager	Blackwell's UK
Miles, Lesley	Marketing Director	Waterstone's Booksellers Ltd
Myers, Dominic	Managing Director	Blackwell's UK
Neil, Michael	Marketing Director	Blackwell's UK
Pogrund, David	IT Director	Waterstone's Booksellers Ltd
Roach, David	Product Director	Waterstone's Booksellers Ltd
Smith, Matthew	Customer Services Manager	Blackwell's UK
Taylor, Matt	Marketing Manager	Borders UK Ltd
Walsh-Hill, Steven	Finance Director	Blackwell's UK

CARPETS

Brenna, Sean	Company Secretary	Carpetworld Manchester Ltd
Dregent, Patricia	Company Secretary	Carpetright Plc
Green, Andrew	Marketing Manager	Allied Carpets Group
Harris, Martin	Director of Buying	Carpetright Plc
Harris of Peckham, Lord	Chairman and Chief Executive	Carpetright Plc
Herbert, Claire	Head of Property	Allied Carpets Group
Hutchinson, Clive	Chief Executive	Allied Carpets Group
Kitching, John	Managing Director	Carpetright Plc
Mills, Dave	Head of IT	Allied Carpets Group
Nicholson, Kevin	Head of Finance	Carpetright Plc
Pryer, Mark	Managing Director and Marketing Director	Carpetworld Manchester Ltd
Shapland, Darren	Finance Director	Carpetright Plc
Stuart, Simon	IT Manager	Allied Carpets Group
Wattel, Jean	Finance Director	Allied Carpets Group

CLOTHING

Adams, Michael Percy	Non-Executive Director	Alexon Group Plc
Afkami, Amir	Finance Director, Evans	Arcadia Group Ltd
Alldridge, Steve	Finance Director	Bon Marché Ltd
Allen, Paul	Chief Executive	Jacques Vert Plc
Allman, Andrew	Senior Manager, Financial Planning and Analysis in Europe	Gap
Andreini, Guiseppe	Product Director	Benetton Retail 1988 Ltd
Angelides, Christos	Group Product Director	Next Plc
Atterton, Charlie	Financial Director	Jigsaw
Auld, Phillip	George UK Director	George (Asda)

Should you be in this directory? See the form at the back for new entries and amendments

Avis, Alice	Group Director of Marketing and E-Commerce	Marks & Spencer Plc
Bacon, Paul	Buying Director	QS Plc
Bailey, Colin	Finance Director	River Island
Bannister, Roger	Senior Buyer	TK Maxx
Barclay, Andrew	Marketing Manager	Moss Bros Group Plc
Barlow, Martin	Project and Property Manager	MK One
Barton, Daniel	Head of Marketing	Diesel
Bate, Jennifer	Acting Commercial Director, Littlewoods Stores	Littlewoods Stores Ltd
Bell, James	Chief Accountant	Mackays Stores Ltd
Bennett, Neil	Merchandising Director	Mackays Stores Ltd
Berry, John	Group Company Secretary	Matalan plc
Bettley, Tim	Buying and Merchandising Director	The Peacock Group Plc
Biggs, Janet	Director of Trading	New Look Retailers Ltd
Binks, Jeanette	Customer Services Manager	Tulchan Group
Binnington, Mark	Marketing Director	Boden
Blair, Ken	Chief Executive, Shops Division	British Heart Foundation, Shops Division
Boden, Johnnie	Managing Director	Boden
Bodycote, Charlie	Technical Director	Figleaves.com
Bond, Andy	Managing Director	George (Asda)
Bostock, Kate	Design Director	George (Asda)
Bottomley, John	Marketing Director	Thermawear Limited (t/a Damart)
Bradbury, Richard	Managing Director	River Island
Brian, Rachel	Merchandise Director	La Senza
Brick, Alex	Marketing and Property Director	Speciality Retail Group Plc
Brick, Brian	Managing Director	Speciality Retail Group Plc
Bryant, Keith	Group Finance Director	The Peacock Group Plc
Budge, Paul	Finance Director	Arcadia Group Ltd
Bullock, Gordon	Chief Executive Officer	TK Maxx
Burke, Peter	Human Resources Director	Littlewoods Stores Ltd
Burnes, Neil	IT and Logistics Director	The Peacock Group Plc
Burnley, Roger	Supply Chain Director	Matalan plc
Burrows, Dawn	Customer Services Manager	Etam Plc
Bussey, Ed	Business Development Director	Figleaves.com
Campbell, Amanda	Head of Strategic Marketing	Adams Childrenswear
Carroll, Ray	Retail Operations Director	Ethel Austin Ltd
Carter, Sir Phillip	Chairman	Kookai
Cashmore, Anita	Financial Director	Kookai
Ceirnduff, Ken	Joint Managing Director	Internacionale Limited
Charlton, David	Chairman	The Officers Club Ltd
Clarke, Andy	Group Retail Director	Matalan plc
Clarke, John	Retail Operations Director	Ann Summers Ltd
Constantine, Clem	Property and Retail Planning Director	Arcadia Group Ltd
Cook, David	Finance Director	Laura Ashley
Cook, Julie	Retail Operations and Marketing Director	Moss Bros Group Plc
Cooke, Malcolm	Group Managing Director	La Senza
Cooper, Heather	Marketing Director	Etam Plc
Cooper, Ian	Multi-Channel Director	Adams Childrenswear
Cooper, Patrick F	Chairman	Alexon Group Plc
Cotton, Fran	Managing Director	Cotton Traders Ltd
Coyle, Kelvin	Commercial Director, Index	Littlewoods Stores Ltd
Craig, Stephen	Marketing Director	USC Group Plc
Cussani, Barbara	Non-Executive Director	Marks & Spencer Plc
Darrouzet, Jean-Claude	Chief Executive Officer	Etam Plc
Davidson, Karen	Financial Director	Joseph

Should you be in this directory? See the form at the back for new entries and amendments

Davies, Annie	Design Director, Eastex	Alexon Group Plc
Davies, Peter	Chief Executive	Rubicon
Day, Philip	Chief Executive	Edinburgh Woollen Mill Ltd
Dibb, Graham	Property Director	Moss Bros Group Plc
Dignum, Tony	Chairman	QS Plc
Digregorio, Gina	International Marketing Manager	Arcadia Group Ltd *
Din, Richard	Managing Director	Hennes & Mauritz
Dolce, Deborah	Marketing Director	TK Maxx
Douglas, David	Director	USC Group Plc
Downing, Bill	IT Director	TK Maxx
Drennan, Padraig	Senior Director, IT and Finance in Europe	Gap
Drury, Mike	Head of Finance	AJT Trading Ltd
Duffy, Charles	Retail Operations Director, Bay Trading	Alexon Group Plc
Dutton, Phil	Group Finance Director	Matalan plc
Elliott, Colin	Finance Director	Hennes & Mauritz
Empson, David	New Brands Director	Adams Childrenswear
Evans, Christine	Director of Merchandise	Adams Childrenswear
Ferguson, George	Operations Director	Slater Menswear
Ferguson, John	Retail Operations Controller	MK One
Ferry, Joe	Customer Services Manager	Slater Menswear
Finlan, Steve	Managing Director	Gap
Fisher, Nigel	Finance Director	Select Retail Plc
Foreftier, Marc	Administrative Director	Joseph
Fortune, Andrew	Financial Director	Tulchan Group
Foster-Brown, Tania	Director of Public Relations and Special Events	Arcadia Group Ltd
Fox, Sue	Retail Director	Kookai
Freed, Norman	Managing Director	Jane Norman
Freedman, Jonathan	Finance Director	Speciality Retail Group Plc
Gavin, Gerard	Marketing Manager	Internacionale Limited
Gee, Richard	Property Director	River Island
Gerrard, Paul	Logistics Manager	Jacques Vert Plc
Gibson, Geoff	Group Finance Director	Austin Reed Group Plc
Giles, Andy	Commercial Director	Gilesports Plc
Giles, Howard	Chairman	Gilesports Plc
Glanfield, Cliff	Head of Property	Etam Plc
Glanville, Richard	Finance Director	Oasis Stores Plc
Gold, Jacqueline	Chief Executive and Managing Director	Ann Summers Ltd
Goldsbrough, Sandy	Merchandise Director	Karen Millen
Goring, Mike	Group Operations Director	Arcadia Group Ltd
Grabiner, Lord Anthony	Chairman	Arcadia Group Ltd
Grabiner, Ian	Chief Operating Officer	Arcadia Group Ltd
Grant, Jim	Operations Director	Littlewoods Stores Ltd
Granville, Julian	Chairman	Boden
Gray, Elaine	Group Buying and Merchandising Director	MK One
Green, Geoff	Head of Property	Oasis Stores Plc
Green, Philip	Chief Executive	MK One
Green, Philip	Owner	Arcadia Group Ltd
Grieves, John	Chairman	New Look Retailers Ltd
Griffiths, Matthew	Marketing Director	French Connection
Guerard, Annie	Finance Director	Diesel
Gustavesson, Kent	Operational Director	Hennes & Mauritz
Halford, Seamus	Store Operations Director	Primark
Hall, Graham	Customer Services Manager	Thermawear Limited (t/a Damart)
Halliday, Mike	Merchandising Director	Jacques Vert Plc
Hamblin, Nick	Retail Director	Cotton Traders Ltd
Hamill, Keith	Chairman	Moss Bros Group Plc

Should you be in this directory? See the form at the back for new entries and amendments

Hargreaves, Jamey	Director of Category and Brand Marketing	Matalan plc
Hargreaves, John	Chairman	Matalan plc
Harrington, Neil	Finance Director	George (Asda)
Hartley, Stephen	Operations Controller	Speciality Retail Group Plc
Hayman, Jane	Marketing Director, Principles	Rubicon
Heaviside, John A	Production Director	Mackays Stores Ltd
Helfgott, Maurice	Business Unit Director, Menswear	Marks & Spencer Plc
Hendry, David	Finance Director	TK Maxx
Hepton, Richard	Property Director	Alexon Group Plc
Hill, Andy	Managing Director	Thermawear Limited (t/a Damart)
Hind, John	Trading Director	Arcadia Group Ltd
Hitchcott, Paul	Property Director	New Look Retailers Ltd
Hobbs, Michael	Chief Executive	Adams Childrenswear
Holes, Eric	Group Finance Director	QS Plc
Hollger, Thorsten	Director	Haburi.com
Holme, Jane	Property and Operations Manager	QS Plc
Holmes, Chris	Brand Director, Austin Reed	Austin Reed Group Plc
Holmes, Roger	Chief Executive	Marks & Spencer Plc
Holmes, Tony	Property Controller	Bewise Ltd
Hoskinson, Philip E	Chief Executive	Ethel Austin Ltd
Houston, David	Financial Director	Edinburgh Woollen Mill Ltd
Howard-Allen, Flic	Director of Communications	Marks & Spencer Plc
Howling, Mark	Finance Controller	Cotton Traders Ltd
Hunter, Tom	Chief Executive	AJT Trading Ltd
Imani, Mazz	Customer Service Manager	Hennes & Mauritz
Ingram, Colin	Finance Director	Bewise Ltd
Inman, Chris	Group Finance Director	Rubicon
James, Tim	Managing Director, Index	Littlewoods Stores Ltd
Jani, Anita	Marketing Executive	British Heart Foundation, Shops Division
Jeffrey, Jo	Communications Director	Figleaves.com
Jennings, Roger	Chief Executive	Austin Reed Group Plc
John, Garry	Senior Director, Real Estate and Store Development in Europe	Gap
Johnson, Gill	Customer Services Adminstrator	Gilesports Plc
Johnson, P	Non-Executive Director	Ethel Austin Ltd
Johnson, Rachel	Regional Marketing Director	Levi Strauss (UK) Ltd
Jones, David	Chairman	Cotton Traders Ltd
Jones, David	Chairman	Next Plc
Jones, John	Finance Director	Littlewoods Stores Ltd
Jones, Nadia	Design Director	Oasis Stores Plc
Kaikobad, Farida	Buying Director	River Island
Keenan, Jack	Non-Executive Director	Marks & Spencer Plc
Keens, David	Group Finance Director	Next Plc
Kennedy, Ray	Operations Finance Director	QS Plc
Kernan, Will	Director of Finance and IT	New Look Retailers Ltd
King, John	Chief Executive	Matalan plc
King, Justin	Food Director	Marks & Spencer Plc
Kirk, Richard	Chief Executive Officer	The Peacock Group Plc
Kirton, Tony	Merchandise Director	Alexon Group Plc
Ladha, Hashim	Business Development Director	New Look Retailers Ltd
Law, Michael	Directory Operations Director	Next Plc
Leigh, Carmel	Buying and Merchandising Director	Edinburgh Woollen Mill Ltd
Lenk, Toby	Head of Online Sales Division	Gap
Letrilliart, Thierry	Managing Director	Joseph
Leverett, Peter	Estates Manager	Jaeger Ltd

Should you be in this directory? See the form at the back for new entries and amendments

Lewis, Bernard	Retail Director	River Island
Lewis, Clive	Chief Executive	River Island
Lewis, Julian	Director	River Island
Lewis, Leonard	Managing Director	River Island
Lewis, Robin	Director of Human Resources	New Look Retailers Ltd
Lock, Steven	Customer Services Manager	French Connection
Loizou, Rina	Merchandise Director	Kookai
Longdon, Steve	Business Unit Director, Womenswear	Marks & Spencer Plc
Lovelock, Derek	Chief Executive	Oasis Stores Plc
Lovering, John	Chairman	The Peacock Group Plc
Lowbridge, David	Managing Director, Country Casuals and Austin Reed	Austin Reed Group Plc
Lowe, Tim	Buying and Merchandising Director	The Officers Club Ltd
Lustman, Meg	New Business Director	Oasis Stores Plc
Mackenzie, Andrew	Group Chief Executive	Jaeger Ltd
Mackness, Sue	Human Resources Director	Adams Childrenswear
Macloud-Smith, Amanda	Sales and Operations Director, Country Casuals	Austin Reed Group Plc
Magowan, Trisha	Brand Director, Evans	Arcadia Group Ltd
Maker, Vicky	Customer Services Manager	Moss Bros Group Plc
Marks, Stephen	Chief Executive	French Connection
Marriott, J	Human Resources Director	TK Maxx
Martin, J	Chairman	Ethel Austin Ltd
Martindale, Kirsty	National Sales Manager	Tulchan Group
McCaskey, Ian	IT and Customer Services Manager	QS Plc
McClymont, Sally	Retail Operations Director, Principles	Rubicon
McDonald, Andrew	Marketing and Retail Director	Bon Marché Ltd
McGeoch, Iain	Managing Director	Mackays Stores Ltd
McGeorge, Alastair	Group Chief Executive	Littlewoods Stores Ltd
McGinlay, Steve	Director of Supply Chain and Technology	Marks & Spencer Plc
McGonigle, Jim	Retail Director	AJT Trading Ltd
McIntyre, Kay	Buying Director	Select Retail Plc
McKenna, Charles	Sales Director	Slater Menswear
McKimmie, Matthew Richard	Financial Director	Mackays Stores Ltd
McLean, Donna	Operations Manager	Jacques Vert Plc
McPhail, Carl	Group Operations Director	New Look Retailers Ltd
Miles, Chris	Retail Director	The Peacock Group Plc
Miller, Alaistair	Finance Director	New Look Retailers Ltd
Miller, Deborah	UK Franchise Manager	Levi Strauss (UK) Ltd
Milner, Zoe	Trade Marketing Manager	Bon Marché Ltd
Milton, David	Finance Director	Internacionale Limited
Montgomery, Linda	Retail Manager	Thermawear Limited (t/a Damart)
Morris, Andrew	Customer Service Manager	Jaeger Ltd
Morrison, Angus	Managing Director	USC Group Plc
Mountford, Philip	Group Trading Director	Moss Bros Group Plc
Murray, Dean	Chief Operating Officer	Adams Childrenswear
Murray, Roddy	Financial Director	Moss Bros Group Plc
Murray, Susan	Acting Managing Director, Littlewoods Stores	Littlewoods Stores Ltd
Myatt, Sue	Retail Marketing Director	Next Plc
Myners, Paul	Non-Executive Director	Marks & Spencer Plc
Nairn, Iain	Retail Operations Director	Laura Ashley
Naismith, Roy	Finance Director	French Connection
Navarednam, Rebecca	Joint Chief Executive	Laura Ashley
Nolan, Jacki	Retail Director	Oasis Stores Plc
Norgrove, David R	Director, Clothing, Outlets and International	Marks & Spencer Plc

Should you be in this directory? See the form at the back for new entries and amendments

Nurse, Paul	Director General	Cancer Research UK
O'Connor, Sharon	Merchandising Director	Oasis Stores Plc
O'Donahue, Breege	Personnel and Advertising Director	Primark
O'Hara, John	IT Director	Mackays Stores Ltd
O'Sullivan, Rita	Retail Operations Director	Kookai
Oakley, Graham	Group Secretary and Head of Corporate Governance	Marks & Spencer Plc
Oliver, Clare	Marketing Manager	Edinburgh Woollen Mill Ltd
Osborn, John	Chief Executive Officer	Alexon Group Plc
Osbourne, Alan	Retail Operations Director	New Look Retailers Ltd
Paine, Nick	Managing Director	Etam Plc
Panizzo, Paolo	Managing Consultant	Benetton Retail 1988 Ltd
Paphitis, Theo	Chairman	La Senza
Parkash, Dolly	General Merchandiser	MK One
Parker, Neil	Head of Retail	Pilot Clothing
Parsons, Rick	Operations Director	Thermawear Limited (t/a Damart)
Pascoe, Eva	Joint Managing Director, Zoom	Arcadia Group Ltd
Paterson, Jack	Business Unit Director, Beauty and Lingerie	Marks & Spencer Plc
Payne, David	Brand Retail Operations Director	Alexon Group Plc
Penny, Dean	Customer Service Manager	TK Maxx
Perks, Jane	Retail Operations Director, UK	Etam Plc
Persson, Stefan	Chairman	Hennes & Mauritz
Philipou, Panicko	Managing Director	Diesel
Pidgeon, David	Managing Director	Bon Marché Ltd
Piggot, Robin	Finance Director	Alexon Group Plc
Pogson, Charlie	Head of Marketing	Bon Marché Ltd
Pontin, Roger	Managing Director	Select Retail Plc
Porte, Alan	Distribution Director	TK Maxx
Porteous, Adrian	Merchandising Director	Matalan plc
Pow, James	Chairman and Chief Executive Officer	Tulchan Group
Powell, Heather	Head of Store Design and Development	Arcadia Group Ltd
Powers-Freeling, Laurel	Director and Chief Executive of Financial Services	Marks & Spencer Plc
Pressler, Paul	Chief Executive	Gap
Pryor, Patrick	Financial Director	Primark
Pynor, Liz	Retail Director	French Connection
Radice, Vittorio	Director, Home	Marks & Spencer Plc
Rahamin, Michael	Managing Director	Kookai
Rayner, Patrick	Property Manager	Kookai
Reed, Alison	Chief Financial Officer	Marks & Spencer Plc
Reiss, Melvyn	Managing Director	Cromwells Madhouse
Reynolds, Hugh	Customer Liason Manager	Austin Reed Group Plc
Reynolds, Nicola	Marketing Manager	Austin Reed Group Plc
Riva, Hilary	Managing Director, Womenswear Warehouse	Rubicon
Roberts, Paul	Head of Finance	Pilot Clothing
Robins, John	Chairman	Austin Reed Group Plc
Robinson, John	Managing Director and Chairman	Jigsaw
Robinson, Paul	Director	Benetton Retail 1988 Ltd
Rose, Paul	Financial Director	Slater Menswear
Ross, Michael	Chief Executive Officer	Figleaves.com
Rosso, Renzo	Group Chairman	Diesel
Rostron, Chris	Finance Director	Rubicon
Roy, Liz	Customer Services Manager	Bon Marché Ltd
Russell, Frances	Brand Director, Burton	Arcadia Group Ltd
Russell, Hannah	Marketing Director	Oasis Stores Plc
Ryan, Arthur	Chairman and Managing Director	Primark

Should you be in this directory? See the form at the back for new entries and amendments

Saaid, Ainum Mohd	Joint Chief Executive	Laura Ashley
Sansom, Ed	IT Director	Edinburgh Woollen Mill Ltd
Schofield-Lawley, Peter	Commercial Director	Diesel
Seaton, Graham	Property Director	Matalan plc
Selby, David	Head of Mail Order and E-Commerce	Laura Ashley
Senior, Stuart	IT Director	Marks & Spencer Plc
Shah, Saj	Chief Executive	Jane Norman
Sharma, Sanjay	Finance Director	Karen Millen
Shepherd, David	Brand Director, Topman	Arcadia Group Ltd
Shepherdson, Jane	Brand Director, Top Shop	Arcadia Group Ltd
Shields, Jane	Retail Operations Director	Next Plc
Shipley, David	Non-Executive Director	Matalan plc
Shrager, Robert	Non-Executive Director	Matalan plc
Simons, David	Group Chairman	Littlewoods Stores Ltd
Singh, Tom	Non-Executive Director	New Look Retailers Ltd
Slater, Paul	Managing Director	Slater Menswear
Smith, Alex	Managing Director	TK Maxx
Smith, Brian	Head of Property and Central Retail Operations	Adams Childrenswear
Smith, Chris	Property Manager	La Senza
Smith, Steve	Sales Director	Cotton Traders Ltd
Souber, Carol	Finance Controller	Cromwells Madhouse
Souber, Peter	Managing Director	Cromwells Madhouse
Stanford, Kevin	Chief Executive Officer	Karen Millen
Stark, Liz	Sales Manager, Great Plains	French Connection
Stewart, Norrie	Joint Managing Director	Internacionale Limited
Sunderland, John	Business Development Director	Select Retail Plc
Sunnucks, Stephen	Chief Executive	New Look Retailers Ltd
Sutherland, Euan	Retail and Marketing Director	Matalan plc
Swannie, Sue	Buying Director	Mackays Stores Ltd
Sweetenham, Paul	Buying Director, Men's, Children's, and Shoes	TK Maxx
Swift, Michelle	Manager of Customer Services	Karen Millen
Tanner, Adrian	Finance Director	Benetton Retail 1988 Ltd
Taylor, Julie	Head of Retail	Bon Marché Ltd
Taylor, Richard	Retail Director	Cancer Research UK
Tennant, Sue	Trading Director	Ethel Austin Ltd
Tesseras, Mick	Systems Manager	Cromwells Madhouse
Tesseras, Nick	Customer Service Manager	Cromwells Madhouse
Tesseras, Peter	Marketing Director	Cromwells Madhouse
Thomas, Graham	General Manager, Estates	The Peacock Group Plc
Thompson, Anthony	Head of Childrenswear	Marks & Spencer Plc
Thompson, Charles	Non-Executive Director	Matalan plc
Thompson, Leslie	Fashion Director	Alexon Group Plc
Thompson, Thiry	Head of Buying	Bon Marché Ltd
Thomson, David	Finance Director	MK One
Thornton, Lisa	Marketing Co-ordinator	Tulchan Group
Tomlin, Jean	Director of Human Resources	Marks & Spencer Plc
Tranfield, Dan	Financial Director	Gilesports Plc
Tucker, David	Director	Bewise Ltd
Turnball, Patrick	Property Development and Construction Director	TK Maxx
Unadkat, Ray	Finance Director	Ann Summers Ltd
Vandenberghe, Mark	International Director	Arcadia Group Ltd
Vandevelde, Luc	Chairman	Marks & Spencer Plc
Vann, Paul	Chairman	Mackays Stores Ltd
Varley, Andrew	Group Property Director	Next Plc

Should you be in this directory? See the form at the back for new entries and amendments

Walker, Philip	Managing Director, Product	Adams Childrenswear
Walsh, Mark	Purchasing Director	Pilot Clothing
Ward, Andrea	Marketing Manager	Jaeger Ltd
Ward, Natasha	Personnel Manager	Jane Norman
Ward, Paul	General Manager	Cromwells Madhouse
Westwood, John	Non-Executive Director	Matalan plc
Whaley, Jeremy	Managing Director	Pilot Clothing
Whitaker, Alec	Property Director	Edinburgh Woollen Mill Ltd
White, Tracy	Commercial Director, Bay Trading	Alexon Group Plc
Whittle, David	Merchandise Director	Thermawear Limited (t/a Damart)
Williams, Neil	Chief Operating Director	French Connection
Williams, Stephen	Finance Director	Ethel Austin Ltd
Williamson, Colin	Marketing Director	Mackays Stores Ltd
Wilson, Joanne	Customer Service Manager	Internacionale Limited
Wilson, Neil	Finance Director	The Officers Club Ltd
Wimpenny, Marc	Retail Operations Director	The Officers Club Ltd
Winstanley, Mark	Creative Director	Laura Ashley
Witts, Kevin	Group Finance Director	Adams Childrenswear
Wolfenden, Alex	Property Manager	Tulchan Group
Wolfson, Simon	Chief Executive	Next Plc
Woods, Peter	Finance Director	USC Group Plc
Woolf, Jane	Head of Buying	Oasis Stores Plc
Worth, Key	Head of Human Resources and Training	Jaeger Ltd
Wright, Adrian	Chief Executive	Moss Bros Group Plc
Wrigley, Phil	Managing Director, Operations	New Look Retailers Ltd
Wyles, John	Sales and Operations Director	Bewise Ltd
Yusuf, Yasmin	Creative Director, Clothing	Marks & Spencer Plc

CONVENIENCE STORE

Alexander, Rod	Communications Director	Budgens Stores Ltd
Bagot, Andrew	Managing Director	Le Riches Stores Limited
Barber, Angela	Trading and Marketing Director	Costcutter Supermarkets Group Limited
Barr, Garry	IT Director	Budgens Stores Ltd
Beaumont, Martin	Chief Executive	Co-operative Group (CWS) Limited
Bell, Les	Chairman	Bells Stores Limited
Bell, Steven	Joint Managing Director	Bells Stores Limited
Blackmore, Steve	Head of Retail	Spar (UK) Limited
Botterill, James	Managing Director	Botterills Convenience Stores Ltd
Bowes, John	Chief General Manager, Marketing	Co-operative Group (CWS) Limited
Bralsford, Martin	Chief Executive	Le Riches Stores Limited
Chick, Sarah	Sales Development Executive	Costcutter Supermarkets Group Limited
Clarke, David	Finance Director	G T Retail
Cochrane, James	Customer Services Manager	Botterills Convenience Stores Ltd
Craig, Allan	Financial Director	Botterills Convenience Stores Ltd
Craig, Lizette	Retail Operations Director	Botterills Convenience Stores Ltd
Darbershire, Susan	Marketing Director	Spar (UK) Limited
Darwin, Keith	Chairman	Co-operative Group (CWS) Limited
Delamare, Lee	Head of Logistics and Distribution	Le Riches Stores Limited
Duff, Donal	Group Director of Finance	Le Riches Stores Limited
Garton, John	Head of Marketing	Le Riches Stores Limited
Goodman, Cliff	Trading Director	Budgens Stores Ltd
Graham, David	Joint Managing Director	Bells Stores Limited
Graves, Colin	Managing Director	Costcutter Supermarkets Group Limited

Should you be in this directory? See the form at the back for new entries and amendments

Graves, Ian	Marketing Manager	Costcutter Supermarkets Group Limited
Hallam, Geoff	Managing Director	A F Blakemore & Son Ltd
Hare, Richard	Legal and Human Resources Director	Budgens Stores Ltd
Hepworth, Malcolm	Chief Operating Officer	Co-operative Group (CWS) Limited
Hewitt, Paul	Chief Financial Officer	Co-operative Group (CWS) Limited
Hill, Richard	Finance Director	Spar (UK) Limited
Hiremath, Raju	Finance Director	Adminstore Ltd
Hyson, Martin	Chief Executive Officer	Budgens Stores Ltd
Ivel, Nick	Finance Director	Costcutter Supermarkets Group Limited
Kears, Norman	Partnership Director	Budgens Stores Ltd
Keeley, Mark	Buying Director	Spar (UK) Limited
Kopacz, Greg	Manufacturing Director	Budgens Stores Ltd
Leek, Marcus	Financial and IT Director	Bells Stores Limited
Lewis, Chris	Buying Director	Spar (UK) Limited
Mackay, F	Development Director	Morning, Noon & Night
Maloney, Vince	Operations Director	Budgens Stores Ltd
Marie, Steve	Property Director	Le Riches Stores Limited
Marwood, Joey	Managing Director	Spar (UK) Limited
McGettigan, Eoin	Chairman	Budgens Stores Ltd
Middleditch, Morton	Chairman	Spar (UK) Limited
Miller, Peter	Group Trading Director	Spar (UK) Limited
Mitchell, C	Director	Morning, Noon & Night
Morgan, Robert	Chairman	G T Retail
Nicholson, Deryck	Executive Chairman	Shoprite Group Plc
Nicholson, Ian	Managing Director	Shoprite Group Plc
Pannell, Anthony	Finance Director	A F Blakemore & Son Ltd
Patel, Jitu M	Managing Director	Adminstore Ltd
Pirie, George	Operations Director	Morning, Noon & Night
Poole, Martin	Finance Director	Shoprite Group Plc
Pye, James	Property Director	Budgens Stores Ltd
Pyper, Simon	Finance Director	Budgens Stores Ltd
Rice, Stephanie	Marketing Director	Budgens Stores Ltd
Robertson, Tony	Head of Department Stores	Co-operative Group (CWS) Limited
Robinson, Deborah	Head of Brand Management	Co-operative Group (CWS) Limited
Rogers, Julia	General Manger, Central Services	Co-operative Group (CWS) Limited
Scott, Tom	Chairman	Le Riches Stores Limited
Seaman, David	Head of Strategic Development	Co-operative Group (CWS) Limited
Stevens, Richard	Purchasing Manager	G T Retail
Straiton, Brian	Operations Manager	Botterills Convenience Stores Ltd
Suggett, Chris	Buying Director	Bells Stores Limited
Taylor, Mike	Development Director	Budgens Stores Ltd
Thompson, David	Sales and Development Director	Costcutter Supermarkets Group Limited
Thompson, Edward	Chief Executive	Morning, Noon & Night
Thompson, Stephen	Marketing Director	Morning, Noon & Night
Titterton, Mark	Retail Director	G T Retail
Trueman, Sarah	Marketing Manager	A F Blakemore & Son Ltd
Vernon, Michelle	Public Relations Manager	Co-operative Group (CWS) Limited
Walker, Michael	Retail Operations Director	Bells Stores Limited
White, David	Trading Director	A F Blakemore & Son Ltd

CTN

Baxter, Paul	Marketing Director	TM Retail Ltd
Bennett, Paul	Property Director	TM Retail Ltd

Should you be in this directory? See the form at the back for new entries and amendments

Cox, Russel	Group Financial Director	TM Retail Ltd
Doughty, Stephen	Finance Director	United News Shops
Fearnley, Stephen	Chairman	United News Shops
Franks, Bob	Finance Director	News Shops Ltd
Gott, Julian	Property Director	United News Shops
Graham, Douglas	Chairman	News Shops Ltd
Hart, Kevin	Joint Managing Director, Operations	TM Retail Ltd
Kiss, Martin	Buying Controller	TM Retail Ltd
Lancaster, James	Chief Executive	TM Retail Ltd
McLaughlin, Graham	Head of Finance	T J Morris Ltd
Miller, Jonathan	Finance Director	TM Retail Ltd
Morris, J	E-Commerce and Marketing Director	T J Morris Ltd
Morris, Tom	Managing Director	T J Morris Ltd
Saunders, David	Managing Director	TM Retail Ltd
Siviter, Paul	Managing Director	News Shops Ltd
Swift, Roger	Managing Director	United News Shops
Tomlinson, Andrew	News Development Manager	News Shops Ltd
Walton, Graham	Finance Systems Manager	News Shops Ltd
White, Peter	Retail News Manager	News Shops Ltd
Wilkinson, Steve	Joint Managing Director, Operations	TM Retail Ltd

DEPARTMENT STORE

Adams, David	Deputy Chief Executive and Group Finance Director	House of Fraser Plc
Ahern, June	Customer Services	Morley's Stores Ltd
Ainley, Harvey	Finance Director	Allders Department Stores Limited
Al Fayed, Mohammed	Chairman	Harrods Limited
Alexander, Ian David	Finance Director	John Lewis Plc
Allister, Justine	Head of Public Relations	Debenhams Plc
Anders, Jill	Company Secretary	Fenwick Ltd
Assanand, Raj	Managing Director	Harrods Limited
Bacon, Chrissie	Financial Controller	House of Fraser Plc
Balfour Lynn, Richard	Chairman	Liberty
Barcley, Elizabeth	Director and Company Secretary	Jenners Limited
Bartup, Phil	Business Systems Manager	Debenhams Plc *
Beale, Nigel	Chairman	J E Beale Plc
Bowe, Julia	Marketing Director	Harvey Nichols Group Plc
Boyes, Andrew	Joint Managing Director	W Boyes & Company
Boyes, Timothy	Joint Managing Director	W Boyes & Company
Bradley, Hugh	Communications Director	Debenhams Plc
Burden, Paul	Communications Director	John Lewis Plc
Cathcart, Alun	Chairman	Selfridges & Co
Cherry, Mark	Head of Property	Allders Department Stores Limited
Clarke, Philip	Finance Director	Selfridges & Co
Coates, Peter	Group Chief Accountant	Fenwick Ltd
Coleman, John	Chief Executive	House of Fraser Plc
Collins, Les	Financial Director	Fortnum & Mason Plc
Collins, Richard	Director for Retail Properties	Allders Department Stores Limited
Corridan, Sandra	Marketing Director	Morley's Stores Ltd
Cox, Phil	Commercial Director	Allders Department Stores Limited
Craddock, John	Marketing and Merchandise Director	James Beattie PLC
Cushen, John	General Manager, Supply Chain	John Lewis Plc
Davie, Steve	Finance Director	Harrods Limited
Davies, Timothy	Strategy Director	Debenhams Plc
Davis, Jane	Buying Director	Liberty
Douglas, Brian	Operations Director	T J Hughes Plc

Should you be in this directory? See the form at the back for new entries and amendments

Drake, Louise	Customer Services Manager	QD Stores Ltd
Dreesmann, Bernard	Chairman	Morley's Stores Ltd
Earl, Belinda	Chief Executive	Debenhams Plc
Edgar, John	Trading and Marketing Finance Manager	House of Fraser Plc
Faley, R	Finance Director	W Boyes & Company
Felwick, David	Deputy Chairman	John Lewis Plc
Fenwick, Adam	Deputy Chairman	Bentalls
Fenwick, John	Deputy Chairman	Fenwick Ltd
Fenwick, Mark	Group Chairman	Fenwick Ltd
Fitzgerald, Deborah	Marketing and Communications Director	Liberty
Ford, Dominic	Food and Beverage Director	Harvey Nichols Group Plc
Forrest, Kenneth	Managing Director	Fortnum & Mason Plc
Foster, George	Chief Executive	T J Hughes Plc
Gates, Stuart	Managing Director	Fortnum & Mason Plc
Gee, Ernie	Director	W Boyes & Company
George, Joanna	Head of Corporate Communications	Debenhams Plc
Gilmore, Meg	Director of Marketing	House of Fraser Plc
Goody, Andy	Finance Director	T J Hughes Plc
Gordon, Ann	Trading Director	House of Fraser Plc
Grant, Kenneth	Buying and Marketing Director	Jenners Limited
Gray, Liz	Human Resources Director	House of Fraser Plc
Green, Terry	Chief Executive	Allders Department Stores Limited
Guillaume, Jane	Personnel Director	Debenhams Plc
Hampson, Sir Stuart	Executive Chairman	John Lewis Plc
Hanly, Patrick	Commercial Director	Harvey Nichols Group Plc
Hardy, Robert	Director of Property	House of Fraser Plc
Harris, Ray	Customer Services Manager	Bentalls
Healy, J	Store Operations Manager	Harrods Limited
Hearsay, Peter	Company Secretary	House of Fraser Plc
Heath, Reg	Chairman	Merchant Retail Group Plc
Hibbert, Steve	Operations Director	House of Fraser Plc
Hide, Belinda	Head of Marketing	Bentalls
Hobdey, John	Merchandise Systems Executive	J E Beale Plc
Howard, Caroline	Marketing Director	J E Beale Plc
Hullah, Phil	Head of Business Development and Supply Chain	John Lewis Plc *
Humphries, Ann	Director of Retail Development	John Lewis Plc
Jarvis, Peter	Chairman	Debenhams Plc
Jefferson, John C	Finance Director	Joplings Ltd
Jeffreys, Penny	IT Director	Allders Department Stores Limited
Johnston, Clare	Head of Design	Liberty
Jones, Christopher	Managing Director	James Beattie PLC
Kelly, William	Finance Director	James Beattie PLC
Kennedy, Neil	Finance and Planning Director	Debenhams Plc
Khayat, Jana	Chairman	Fortnum & Mason Plc
Killen, Tracey	Personnel Director	John Lewis Plc
King, Howard	Property Director	John Lewis Plc
Lamont, Chris	Finance Director	Merchant Retail Group Plc
Lancaster, Alison	Head of Merchandising, John Lewis Direct	John Lewis Plc *
Lawlor, June	Buying and Merchandising Director	House of Fraser Plc
Lewis, Patrick	Supply Chain Director	John Lewis Plc
Little, Jill	Merchandise Director	John Lewis Plc
Mather, Nick	Finance Director	Liberty
Mayfield, Charlie	Development Director	John Lewis Plc
Mayhew, Luke	Managing Director	John Lewis Plc
Mayhew, Luke	Managing Director	John Lewis Plc *

Should you be in this directory? See the form at the back for new entries and amendments

Metcalfe, Amanda	Head of Customer Management	Debenhams Plc
Miller, Andrew Douglas	Deputy Chairman and Development Director	Jenners Limited
Miller, Robert Douglas	Chairman	Jenners Limited
Montgomery, David	Merchandising Manager, Fashion and Household	Joplings Ltd
Moody, N	Customer Services Manager	Fortnum & Mason Plc
Morton, Clive	Finance Director	Harvey Nichols Group Plc
Moxam, Graham	Finance Director	QD Stores Ltd
Newton, Philip	Chief Executive	Merchant Retail Group Plc
O'Neill, Cathy	Personnel Administration and Services Director	Fortnum & Mason Plc
Ordman, David	Managing Director	Morley's Stores Ltd
Owst, Ken	Finance Director	J E Beale Plc
Palethorpe, Simon	Managing Director, John Lewis Direct	John Lewis Plc
Palmer, Nigel	Retail Operations Director	Debenhams Plc
Perryman, Julian	Controller of E-Commerce	Allders Department Stores Limited
Phillips, Malcolm	Planning and Development Director	James Beattie PLC
Pitcher, Anne	Director, Womenswear	Harvey Nichols Group Plc
Poon, Dickson	Chairman	Harvey Nichols Group Plc
Porter, Colin	Supply Chain Director	House of Fraser Plc
Rathbone, Tim	Merchandise Director	J E Beale Plc
Rattenbury, Paul	Head of Retail, Central UK	Allders Department Stores Limited
Renwick, Iain	Chief Executive	Liberty
Roberts, Matthew	Finance Director	Debenhams Plc
Samuel, Philip	Managing Director, Joplings	Merchant Retail Group Plc
Seigal, Jeremy	Managing Director, The Perfume Shop	Merchant Retail Group Plc
Sharp, Michael	Trading Director	Debenhams Plc
Sharp, Steve	Marketing Director	Allders Department Stores Limited
Shields, Lititia	Customer Service Manager	Jenners Limited
Simmons, Wendy	Marketing Manager	Joplings Ltd
Simonin, Richard	Chief Executive Officer	Harrods Limited
Smith, Alan	Financial Director	Fenwick Ltd
Storer, Jane	Buying and Merchandising Director	House of Fraser Plc
Sweet, Tony	Food Hall Director	House of Fraser Plc
Syed, Maura	Financial Director	Morley's Stores Ltd
Taglioni, Lara	Customer Services Manager	Fenwick Ltd
Terry, Colin	Merchandise Director	Allders Department Stores Limited
Thomas, Gareth	Director of Retail Operations	John Lewis Plc
Turner, Ken	Chief Executive	QD Stores Ltd
Wadeley, Melanie	Personnel Director	Merchant Retail Group Plc
Wan, Joseph	Managing Director	Harvey Nichols Group Plc
Wayment, Richard	Retail Sales Director	House of Fraser Plc
Wemms, Michael	Chairman	House of Fraser Plc
West, Sue	Retail Director	Selfridges & Co
Williams, Peter	Chief Executive	Selfridges & Co
Wooley, Caspar	Head of Business Development	John Lewis Plc
Young, Mark	Company Secretary	Selfridges & Co

DISCOUNTER

Adams, Robert	Financial Director	Poundland Ltd
Brown, Gary	Joint Finance Director	Brown & Jackson
Dodd, David	Chief Executive	Poundland Ltd
Ferrier, Cathy	Trading Director	Poundland Ltd
Forman, Chris	Merchandising Controller	Poundland Ltd
Gravells, David	Chairman	B & M Retail Ltd

Should you be in this directory? See the form at the back for new entries and amendments

Greenwood, Stuart	Chief Executive	B & M Retail Ltd
Maddox, Chris	Managing Director	Remainders Ltd
May, Joy	Human Resources Director	Remainders Ltd
Melville, Margaret	Buying Director	Brown & Jackson
Morrison, Mike	Marketing Director	Brown & Jackson
Norris, Terry	Chairman	Remainders Ltd
Peckham, Nigel	Retail and Operations Director	Poundland Ltd
Quiney, Pat	Property Director	Brown & Jackson
Roelofse, Hennie	Joint Finance Director	Brown & Jackson
Saunders, Mark	Merchandising Director	Brown & Jackson
Taylor, Paul	Buying Director	B & M Retail Ltd
Thomas, Les	IT Director	Brown & Jackson
Thomas, Ray	Property Director	Remainders Ltd
Trubshaw, John	Retail Operations Manager	B & M Retail Ltd
Tucki, Julian	Marketing Director	Remainders Ltd
Williams, Andrew	IT Director	Remainders Ltd
Williams, Mandy	Director of Operations	Brown & Jackson

DIY

Adams, George	Commercial and Marketing Director	B & Q Plc
Allen, John	Managing Director	Screwfix Direct
Archer, Bill	Chairman and Chief Executive Officer	Focus Wickes
Ball, Colin	Group Commercial Services Director and E-Commerce	Focus Wickes
Barrow, Steve	Finance Director	Screwfix Direct
Beddoe, Paul	Marketing Director	J H Leeke & Sons Ltd
Benson, Graham	Information Systems Director	Screwfix Direct
Bester, Barry	Executive Chairman	Topps Tiles Plc
Bird, Jeremy	Trading Director, Wickes	Focus Wickes
Bird, Richard	Managing Director	Focus Wickes
Bosworth, Dave	Customer Services Manager	Wilkinson Hardware Stores Limited
Brown, Gordon	Managing Director	Wilkinson Hardware Stores Limited
Butler, Richard	Human Resources Director	Screwfix Direct
Cook, Diane	Director	J H Leeke & Sons Ltd
Crookshank, L P	Non-Executive Director	Robert Dyas Holdings Ltd
Farrington-Smith, Justin	Trading Director, Focus	Focus Wickes
Fowler, Mike	Finance Director	J H Leeke & Sons Ltd
Fuller, Neil	Finance Director	Homebase Ltd
Gladwin, Rob	Operations Director	Focus Wickes
Holliman, Alan	Store Development and Property Manager	Robert Dyas Holdings Ltd
Johnson, Steve	Managing Director	Focus DIY Ltd *
Jones, Peter	Operations Director	Homebase Ltd
Jones, Terry	Group Design Director	J H Leeke & Sons Ltd
Keen, Jill	Marketing Director	Focus Wickes
Leake, J D	Non-Executive Director	Robert Dyas Holdings Ltd
Leeke, Anne-Marie	Chairperson	J H Leeke & Sons Ltd
Leeke, Emma	Director of Commercial Operations	J H Leeke & Sons Ltd
Leeke, Gerald	Managing Director	J H Leeke & Sons Ltd
Leeke, Stephen J	Vale Complex Managing Director	J H Leeke & Sons Ltd
Leeke, Stuart	Director and Company Secretary	J H Leeke & Sons Ltd
Liggett, Andrew	Finance Director	Topps Tiles Plc
Loft, Paul	Managing Director	Homebase Ltd
Martin, Leigh	Trading Director	Homebase Ltd
Martin, Peter	Group Director, Human Resources	J H Leeke & Sons Ltd
McCarthy, Colin	Operations Director	Screwfix Direct
Metson, Stephanie	Marketing Manager	J H Leeke & Sons Ltd

Should you be in this directory? See the form at the back for new entries and amendments

Morrice, I	Managing Director, Warehouses	B & Q Plc
Naskey, M J	Non-Executive Director	Robert Dyas Holdings Ltd
Ounstead, Nick	Chief Executive	Topps Tiles Plc
Patel, Hem	Buying Director	Screwfix Direct
Pearson, David	Group Commercial Director	Focus Wickes
Pedder, Roger A	Non-Executive Chairman	Robert Dyas Holdings Ltd
Philips, Tim	Marketing Manager	Trago Mills
Rand, Stewart A	Sales and Marketing Director	Robert Dyas Holdings Ltd
Reddish, Gillian	Communications Manager	Wilkinson Hardware Stores Limited
Rice, John	Group IT Director	Focus Wickes
Rimmer, Barbara	Company Secretary	Focus Wickes
Robertson, Bruce	Chairman	Trago Mills
Rowland, John P	Company Secretary	Robert Dyas Holdings Ltd
Rushforth, Angela	Marketing Director	Screwfix Direct
Sandbach, Malcolm	Managing Director	Trago Mills
Smart, Malcolm	Financial Director	Robert Dyas Holdings Ltd
Tatton-Brown, Duncan	Finance Director	B & Q Plc
Taylor, Graham	Marketing Manager	Robert Dyas Holdings Ltd
Teale, Penny	Trading Director	Homebase Ltd
Terras, Duncan	Group Human Resources Director	Focus Wickes
Testo, Paul	Finance Director	Wilkinson Hardware Stores Limited
Thomas, Judy	Garden Centre Manager	J H Leeke & Sons Ltd
Thornley, David	Property Director	Wilkinson Hardware Stores Limited
Tyson, Matt	Managing Director, Super Centre	B & Q Plc
Whiting, Bill	Chief Executive	B & Q Plc
Wilkinson, Brent F	Chief Executive Officer	Robert Dyas Holdings Ltd
Wilkinson, Nick	Marketing Services	Wilkinson Hardware Stores Limited
Wilkinson, Tony	Chairman	Wilkinson Hardware Stores Limited
Williams, Dave	Finance Director	Focus DIY Ltd *
Williams, Stuart	Chairman	Topps Tiles Plc
Willis, Paul	Retail Director, Focus	Focus Wickes
Wilson, Geoff	Deputy Chairman and Group Finance Director	Focus Wickes
Witcher, Geoff	Finance Director	Trago Mills

ELECTRICALS

Adams, Dean	A/V Purchasing and Marketing Director	Bennetts Retail Ltd
Antony, Martyn	Acting Head of Retail Operations	T-Mobile (UK)
Arford, G	Head of IT	Comet Direct
Avens, Jez	Deputy Managing Director	Richer Sounds Plc
Bamford, Peter	Chief Marketing Officer	Vodafone Ltd
Barrett, Nick	Chairman	Apollo 2000 Ltd
Barry, Tom	Deputy Managing Director, Operations	Comet Direct
Batchellor, Lance	Marketing Director	Vodafone Ltd
Berlyn, John	Finance Director	Apollo 2000 Ltd
Beynon, Lee	Operations Director	Buy Electrical Direct
Boyd, Gary	Finance Director	Northern Electric Retail
Broughall, David	Managing Director	Apollo 2000 Ltd
Caldwell, Graham	Managing Director	Maplin Electronics Ltd
Carberry, Mark	Customer Services Director	Phones 4u
Caudwell, John	Chairman and Chief Executive	Phones 4u
Caunce, Steve	Finance Director	Phones 4u
Clare, John	Chief Executive	DSG Retail Ltd
Clark, Murray	Head of Retail Finance	T-Mobile (UK)
Collier, Richard	Group Property Director	Carphone Warehouse Plc
Collins, Sir John	Chairman	DSG Retail Ltd

Should you be in this directory? See the form at the back for new entries and amendments

Cooper, Derek	Purchasing Director	Apollo 2000 Ltd
Crabtree, John	Finance Director	Jessops
Crompton, David	Managing Director, Retail	Northern Electric Retail
Crowley, Kieran	Finance Director	Time Group Ltd
Currier, Jon	Financial Director	Richer Sounds Plc
Darke, Bob	Business Unit Head	Comet Group Plc
Darroch, Jeremy	Finance Diretor	DSG Retail Ltd
Davis, Bill	Non-Executive Chairman	Time Group Ltd
Denham, P	IT Manager	Northern Electric Retail
Derby, Gavin	Chief Executive, UK	Vodafone Ltd *
Dunstone, Charles	Chief Executive Officer	Carphone Warehouse Plc
Eaglesham, Graham	Financial Director	Bennetts Retail Ltd
Edwards, Ian	Deputy Managing Director, Business Support	Comet Direct
Evans, Paul	Managing Director	Buy Electrical Direct
Evans, Trudie	Finance Director	Buy Electrical Direct
Foster, Martin A	Managing Director	Miller Brothers Group Ltd
Fox, Simon	Managing Director	Comet Group Plc
Fraser, Ian	Director of Sales and Distribution, Personal and Small Business	Orange Plc
Free, John	Head of Retail	Time Group Ltd
Fryatt, Andrew	Managing Director	T-Mobile (UK)
Gawthorne, Mark	Financial Director	Game Stores Group Ltd
Geitner, Thomas	Chief Technical Officer	Vodafone Ltd
Gent, Sir Christopher	Life President	Vodafone Ltd
Gilbert, David	Chief Operating Officer, Central Operations	DSG Retail Ltd
Gosling, Sue	Marketing Director	PRG Powerhouse Retail Ltd
Graham, John	Head of Marketing	Apollo 2000 Ltd
Green, Peter	Managing Director	Phones 4u
Guthrie, Adrian	Head of Human Resources	Carphone Warehouse Plc
Halkett, Peter	Chairman and Chief Executive	PRG Powerhouse Retail Ltd
Hamburger, Paul	Marketing Director	Phones 4u
Hamid, David	Chief Operating Officer, Retail Operations	DSG Retail Ltd
Harvey, Hugh	Deputy Managing Director, Commercial	Comet Group Plc
Hine, Derek	Chief Executive	Jessops
Hook, Jonathan	Retail Director	Carphone Warehouse Plc
Horn-Smith, Julian	Chief Operating Officer	Vodafone Ltd
Hotson, David	Customer Services Manager	Time Group Ltd
Hughes, Robert	Managing Director	Hughes Electricals
Hydon, Ken	Group Finance Director	Vodafone Ltd
Jackson, Phil	Sales and Marketing Director	Northern Electric Retail
Jackson, Richard	Managing Director	Bennetts Retail Ltd
Johnson-Flint, James	Director	Richer Sounds Plc
Jones, Mike	Commercial Director	Bennetts Retail Ltd
Keenan, Peter	Assistant Managing Director	Currys
Kenny, Emma	Corporate Marketing Director	Vodafone Ltd
Kirby, Tom	Chairman and Chief Executive	Games Workshop Group Plc
Labroue, Jean Nöel	Chief Executive	KESA Electricals Plc
Lloyd, Bethan	Internet Marketing Manager	Powerhouse Internet
Long, Jon	Director of Property	PRG Powerhouse Retail Ltd
Long, Martin	Chairman	Game Stores Group Ltd
Lynn, Brian	Chief Executive	Time Group Ltd
Macario, Anna	Director of Marketing	Game Stores Group Ltd
MacLaurin of Knebworth, Lord	Chairman	Vodafone Ltd
McGlade, David	Managing Director	O2
Miller, James R	Marketing Director	Miller Brothers Group Ltd

Should you be in this directory? See the form at the back for new entries and amendments

164

Miller, Jim N	Chairman and Joint Managing Director	Miller Brothers Group Ltd
Miller, Robert	Joint Managing Director	Miller Brothers Group Ltd
Miller, Simon J	Director	Miller Brothers Group Ltd
Mohammed, Tariq	Marketing Director	Time Group Ltd
Mohsan, Tahir	Managing Director	Time Group Ltd
Morgan, Lisa	Commercial Director	Game Stores Group Ltd
Morriss, David	Head of Property	Comet Group Plc
Morton, Paul	Sales Director	Apollo 2000 Ltd
Murton, Chris	Online Services Director	Carphone Warehouse Plc *
Nardini, Gordon	Head of Retail Marketing	Carphone Warehouse Plc
Naylor, Lawrence	Purchasing Director, Domestic Appliances	Bennetts Retail Ltd
Newlands, David	Chairman	KESA Electricals Plc
Newnham, Mike	UK Group Finance Director	Orange Plc
Norton, Damian	Information Systems Director	DSG Retail Ltd
O'Reilly, David	Marketing Director	Maplin Electronics Ltd
O'Sullivan, Alana	Corporate Communications	Comet Group Plc
Pacey, Keith	Chairman	Maplin Electronics Ltd
Pearce, Dominic	Company Secretary	Miller Brothers Group Ltd
Reavley, Martin	Finance Director	KESA Electricals Plc
Richer, Julian	Chairman	Richer Sounds Plc
Rigby, Simon	Chairman and Chief Executive	Northern Electric Retail
Robinson, David	Group Managing Director	Richer Sounds Plc
Rodriques, Kennedy	Financial Manager	Orange Plc
Ross, David	Chief Operating Officer	Carphone Warehouse Plc *
Sadd, John	Business Development Director	Miller Brothers Group Ltd
Sarin, Arun	Chief Executive	Vodafone Ltd
Scott, Julia	Purchasing Director	Jessops
Sherwin, Michael	Group Finance Director	Games Workshop Group Plc
Showan, Madan	Chairman	EmpireDirect.co.uk
Showan, Posh	Marketing Director	EmpireDirect.co.uk
Snook, Hans	Non-Executive Chairman	Carphone Warehouse Plc
Soucier, Robert	Marketing Director	Hughes Electricals
Stansfield, Mark	Retail Director	O2
Taylor, Roger	Chief Financial Officer	Carphone Warehouse Plc
Thomas, Scott	Head of E-Commerce	Phones 4u *
Tipple, Vanessa	Head of Press Office	Carphone Warehouse Plc
Toor, Jaswant	Managing Director	EmpireDirect.co.uk
Trujillo, Solomon	Chief Executive	Orange Plc
Tucker, Phil	Sales & Marketing Director	Buy Electrical Direct
Vernon, Claudia	Marketing Director	Richer Sounds Plc
Walton, Tim	Sales Director	Phones 4u
Wells, Mark	General Manager, Games Workshop Ltd	Games Workshop Group Plc
White, Paul	Commercial Director	PRG Powerhouse Retail Ltd
Whittle, David	Direct Sales Director	Maplin Electronics Ltd
Wilburn, Paul	Finance Director	Maplin Electronics Ltd
Wilkinson, Nick	Managing Director	Currys

ENTERTAINMENT

Bowden, Tony	Director	BlackStar
Collins, Darryl	Joint Managing Director	BlackStar
Glover, Jeremy	Director	BlackStar
Loughran, Ian	Joint Managing Director	BlackStar
Morgan, Jim	Director	BlackStar

Should you be in this directory? See the form at the back for new entries and amendments

FOOD AND DRINK

Ackroyd, Martin	Finance Director	Wm Morrison Supermarkets Plc
Adshead, John	Group Human Resources and Information Systems Director	J Sainsbury Plc
Ager, Rowley	Company Secretary	Tesco Stores Ltd
Alldritt, Nigel	Financial Director	Majestic Wine Warehouses Ltd *
Allen, Martin	Finance Director	Thorntons Plc
Anderson, Toby	Head of Online Marketing	Sainsbury's Supermarkets Ltd *
Apthorp, John	Chairman	Majestic Wine Warehouses Ltd *
Aylwin, Mark	Supply Chain Director	Safeway Plc
Back, Steven	Group Finance Director	Somerfield Stores Ltd
Bailey, Fiona	Culture Director	Safeway Plc
Bains, Tony	Buying Director	Aldi Stores Ltd
Baker, Richard	Deputy Chief Operating Officer	Asda Stores Ltd
Barber, Kevin	Purchasing Director	Netto Foodstores Ltd
Barcroft, Tony	General Manager of Bakers Oven	Greggs Plc
Barczyk, Julian	Purchasing Director	Stokes Plc
Bedford, Terry	Sales Director	Londis (Holdings) Ltd
Bell, Norman	Group Strategy Director	The Big Food Group Plc
Benson, David	Director, Buying and Distribution	E H Booth & Co. Ltd
Bews, Colin	Company Secretary and Accountant	Stokes Plc
Bittner, Beverly	Director of Strategy and New Business	J Sainsbury Plc
Blundell, Chris	Business Development Director	Wm Morrison Supermarkets Plc
Bond, Andy	Trading Director, Non-Food	Asda Stores Ltd
Booth, Edwin	Chairman	E H Booth & Co. Ltd
Bowles, Glenn	Retail Managing Director	Asda Stores Ltd
Brass, Sarah	Head of Marketing	Whittard of Chelsea Plc
Browett, John	Chief Executive	Tesco.com *
Bull, Sir George	Non-Executive Chairman	J Sainsbury Plc
Buller, Denise	Commercial Director	Londis (Holdings) Ltd
Burdon, Peter	Chief Executive	Thorntons Plc
Burton, Nigel	Development and Services Director	Waitrose Ltd
Butler-Wheelhouse, Keith	Non-Executive Director	J Sainsbury Plc
Buttle, George	Deputy Managing Director	Wm Morrison Supermarkets Plc
Calderbank, Tom	Managing Director	Alfred Jones Ltd
Canning, Nick	Marketing Director	The Big Food Group Plc
Cannon, Rosy	Home Shopping Manager	Asda Stores Ltd *
Carroll, Brian	Finance Director	Waitrose Ltd
Carter, Shaun	Manager	Mole Valley Farmers
Cheesewright, David	Deputy Trading Director	Asda Stores Ltd
Christensen, Lawrence	Logistics Director	Safeway Plc
Clarke, John	Head of Direct Businesses	Waitrose Ltd
Clarke, Philip	IT and Logistics Director	Tesco Stores Ltd
Clement, David	Marketing Director	Tesco.com *
Cooper, Mike	Managing Director, Iceland	The Big Food Group Plc *
Copas, Kegan	Internet Manager	Whittard of Chelsea Plc
Coupe, Mike	Managing Director	The Big Food Group Plc
Criado-Perez, Carlos	Chief Executive	Safeway Plc
Cross, Jeremy	Head of Merchandising	Asda Stores Ltd *
Darrington, Michael	Managing Director	Greggs Plc
Davis, Sir Peter	Group Chief Executive	J Sainsbury Plc
Dawson, Nick	Financial Director	William Jackson & Son Ltd
de Mellow, Steve	Marketing Director	Majestic Wine Warehouses Ltd *
De Moller, June	Non-Executive Director	J Sainsbury Plc
De Nunzio, Tony	President and Chief Operating Officer (Wal-Mart UK)	Asda Stores Ltd

Should you be in this directory? See the form at the back for new entries and amendments

Dee, Chris	IT and Marketing Director	E H Booth & Co. Ltd
Douty, Philip	Trading Director	Thorntons Plc
Downie, David	Operations Director	Asda Stores Ltd *
Duley, Jacques	Managing Director	Oddbins UK Ltd *
Dundas, Jamie	Non-Executive Director	J Sainsbury Plc
Durkin, John	Trading Director	Safeway Plc
Esom, Steven	Managing Director	Waitrose Ltd
Evans, Keith	Director of Non-Foods	J Sainsbury Plc
Evenson, Chris	Development Director	Wm Morrison Supermarkets Plc
Farnsworth, Patrick	Joint Managing Director	William Jackson & Son Ltd
Foley, Paul	Managing Director	Aldi Stores Ltd
Fowle, Adam	Director of Retail Operations	J Sainsbury Plc
Francis, Rick	IT Director	Safeway Plc
Gallant, Ken	Development Director	Alfred Jones Ltd
Gardiner, John	Non-Executive Director	Tesco Stores Ltd
Garrett, Kevin	Customer Services Manager	Waitrose Ltd
Gaston, Sue	Customer Services Manager	William Jackson & Son Ltd
Gearty, Tony	Chief Executive	Lyndale Foods Ltd
Genthialan, Laurent	Finance Director	Oddbins UK Ltd *
Gibbons, David	Distribution Director	Asda Stores Ltd
Gissing, John	Finance Director	Ocado Ltd
Gormley, Rowan	Managing Director	Virgin Wines Online Ltd
Grailey, Tracey	General Manager	Asda Stores Ltd
Greener, George	Non-Executive Chairman	The Big Food Group Plc
Grey, Jon	Group Logistics Director	The Big Food Group Plc
Grimsey, Bill	Chief Executive	The Big Food Group Plc
Ground, Andrew	Director of Consumer Marketing	J Sainsbury Plc
Gunter, Kevin	Chief Executive	Frozen Value Ltd
Halliday, Ross	Trade Marketing Director	Londis (Holdings) Ltd
Harlow, E D	Director and Company Secretary	Alfred Jones Ltd
Harvey, Martyn	Supply Chain Development Director	Londis (Holdings) Ltd
Hawkins, Kevin	Communications Director	Safeway Plc
Hay, Brian	Operations Director	Whittard of Chelsea Plc
Heard, Eric	Managing Director	Farmfoods Freezer Centre
Heathcote, Dawn	Customer Services Manager	Netto Foodstores Ltd
Heuck, Andrew	Sales and Marketing Director	Heron Frozen Foods Ltd
Heuck, David	Finance Director	Heron Frozen Foods Ltd
Higginson, Andrew	Finance Director	Tesco Stores Ltd
Hinchcliff, Mike	Marketing Manager	Netto Foodstores Ltd
Hobhouse, William	Non-Executive Chairman	Whittard of Chelsea Plc
Hoerner, John	Chief Executive, Clothing	Tesco Stores Ltd
Hoskins, Bill	Group Finance Director	The Big Food Group Plc
How, Timothy	Managing Director	Majestic Wine Warehouses Ltd *
Hubbold, Colin	Marketing Manager	Lyndale Foods Ltd
Irwin, John	Customer Sevices Director	Asda Stores Ltd
Jackson, A	Chief Executive	Mole Valley Farmers
Jackson, Keith	New Business Development Director	Somerfield Stores Ltd
Jagger, Denise	Company Secretary	Asda Stores Ltd
Jagger, Denise	Company Secretary	Asda Stores Ltd *
Jones, Johnathon A	Chairman	Alfred Jones Ltd
Jones, Martyn	Senior Trading Director	Wm Morrison Supermarkets Plc
Keating, Brian	Information Systems Director	Safeway Plc
King, Howard	Property Director	Waitrose Ltd
King, Justin	Chief Executive Officer	J Sainsbury Plc
Laffin, Simon	Finance Director	Safeway Plc
Lassiter, Robin	Director of Central Retail Operations	J Sainsbury Plc

Should you be in this directory? See the form at the back for new entries and amendments

Lawton, Kenton	Marketing Director	Londis (Holdings) Ltd
Leahy, Sir Terry	Chief Executive	Tesco Stores Ltd
Levene of Portsoken, Lord	Non-Executive Director	J Sainsbury Plc
Lewis, Steve	Retail Director	Majestic Wine Warehouses Ltd *
Macaskill, Bridget	Non-Executive Director	J Sainsbury Plc
Malas, Denis	Head of Strategic Development	Asda Stores Ltd *
Martin, Karl	Buying Director	The Big Food Group Plc
Mason, Tim	Marketing and E-Commerce Director	Tesco Stores Ltd
Mason, Tim	Chairman	Tesco.com *
Mason, Tony	Trading Director	Majestic Wine Warehouses Ltd *
Matthews, Roger	Group Finance Director	J Sainsbury Plc
Matthews, Roger	Group Finance Director	Sainsbury's Supermarkets Ltd *
Mayes, Kieron	Format Director	Somerfield Stores Ltd
McComas, Jill	Marketing Director	Somerfield Stores Ltd
McDougall, Shiona	Marketing Director	Virgin Wines Online Ltd
McKenna, Judith	Chief Financial Officer	Asda Stores Ltd
McNamara, Mike	IT Director	Tesco.com *
McReady, Willy	Property Director	Farmfoods Freezer Centre
Megson, Angela	Buying Director	Waitrose Ltd
Melnyk, Marie	Joint Managing Director	Wm Morrison Supermarkets Plc
Mitchell, Stuart	Managing Director of Sainsburys Supermarkets Ltd	J Sainsbury Plc
Monk, Andy	IT Director	Somerfield Stores Ltd
Morrison, Sir Ken	Chairman	Wm Morrison Supermarkets Plc
Nash, C	Non-Executive Director	Stokes Plc
Nelson, Stephen	Trading Director	J Sainsbury Plc
Netherton, Derek	Director	Greggs Plc
Oakes, Martin	Director, Logistics and New Business Development	Somerfield Stores Ltd
Osmond, Mike	Retail Director, Kwik Save	Somerfield Stores Ltd
Oughtred, Chris	Chairman and Joint Managing Director	William Jackson & Son Ltd
Owen, Roger	Property Director	Wm Morrison Supermarkets Plc
Page, Tony	Director, General Merchandise	Asda Stores Ltd
Palmer, Jeremy	E-Commerce Director	Majestic Wine Warehouses Ltd *
Phillips, Doug W	Property Manager	Thorntons Plc
Pilling, Chris	Marketing Director	Asda Stores Ltd
Pinnington, Lee	Head of Home Shopping	The Big Food Group Plc
Pleasance, Andrew	Head of Home and Leisure	Wm Morrison Supermarkets Plc
Potts, David	Retail Director	Tesco Stores Ltd
Powell, Simon	Head of Customer Relationship Management	Ocado Ltd
Prendergast, Dominic	Retail Director	Thorntons Plc
Price, David	Non-Executive Director	The Big Food Group Plc
Price, Mark	Marketing Director	Waitrose Ltd
Pugh, Martin	Marketing Director	Safeway Plc
Quinlan, Michael	Finance Director	Lyndale Foods Ltd
Rees, Karen	Finance Director	Frozen Value Ltd
Reid, David	Deputy Chairman	Tesco Stores Ltd
Richardson, Sam	Online Marketing Manager	Oddbins UK Ltd *
Riddy, Tony	Retail Director	Londis (Holdings) Ltd
Robertson, David	Financial Director	Farmfoods Freezer Centre
Robertson, Nigel	Managing Director	Ocado Ltd
Rose, Richard	Chief Executive	Whittard of Chelsea Plc
Ross, Keith	Financial Director	Netto Foodstores Ltd
Sainsbury of Preston Candover KG, Lord	Life President	J Sainsbury Plc
Salt, Geoffrey	Distribution Director	Waitrose Ltd

Should you be in this directory? See the form at the back for new entries and amendments

Schwarz, Jeremy	Director of Brand Marketing	J Sainsbury Plc
Shawe, Jan	Director of Group Corporate Communications	J Sainsbury Plc
Shenstrom, Karen	Commercial Director, Meat and Fresh Foods	Safeway Plc
Siegman, Andreas	Regional Managing Director	Aldi Stores Ltd
Simpson, Malcolm	Financial Director	Greggs Plc
Sims, Phillip	Sales Director	William Jackson & Son Ltd
Slater, Penny	Senior Manager Online Marketing	Sainsbury's Supermarkets Ltd *
Smith, Ted	Stores Director	The Big Food Group Plc
Spicer, P	Director	Frozen Value Ltd
Spindler, Angela	Trading and Marketing Director, Food	Asda Stores Ltd
Steiner, Tim	Chief Executive	Ocado Ltd
Stokes, Daniel	Chairman	Stokes Plc
Stokes, T	Non-Executive Director	Stokes Plc
Stokes-Johnson, Louise	Managing Director	Stokes Plc
Stott, Robert	Joint Managing Director	Wm Morrison Supermarkets Plc
Taylor, Caroline	Head of International Mail Order	Whittard of Chelsea Plc
Taylor, John	Trading Director	Londis (Holdings) Ltd
Thornton, John	Chairman	Thorntons Plc
Tindall, Rod	Trading Director	Alfred Jones Ltd
Tomey, Gill	Customer Service Manager	Somerfield Stores Ltd
Townsend, Jeremy	Director of Strategy and Planning	J Sainsbury Plc
Tulley, Steve	Development Director	Londis (Holdings) Ltd
Turner, Mark	Operations Director	Alfred Jones Ltd
Vandermeer, John	Finance Director	E H Booth & Co. Ltd
von Sprecklesen, John	Executive Chairman	Somerfield Stores Ltd
Waedeled, Claus	Managing Director	Netto Foodstores Ltd
Wallace, Andrew	Finance Director	Londis (Holdings) Ltd
Watts, Christine	Corporate Affairs Director	Asda Stores Ltd
Webb, Martin	Director of Trading Support and Procurement	J Sainsbury Plc
Webb, Steve	Corporate Development Director	Safeway Plc
Webster, David	Chairman	Safeway Plc
Weller, Sara	Deputy Managing Director	J Sainsbury Plc
Wetherspoon, Gordon	Group Property Director	Somerfield Stores Ltd
Wheelwright, Allan	Personnel Director	William Jackson & Son Ltd
Whitbread, Robin	Managing Director, Kwik Save	Somerfield Stores Ltd
White, Graham	Chief Executive	Londis (Holdings) Ltd
White, Jim	Human Resources Director	Safeway Plc
White, Martin	Director of Supply Chain	J Sainsbury Plc
Williams, Bill	Managing Director, Somerfield	Somerfield Stores Ltd
Williams, Peter	Chairman	Londis (Holdings) Ltd
Wilson, David	Company Secretary	Safeway Plc
Yates, Tim	Group Property Director	The Big Food Group Plc

FOOTWEAR

Acheson, Paul	Sales Director	Shellys Shoes Ltd
Alexander, Sandy	Founding Director	Schuh Ltd
Alleston, David	Retail Operations Manager	Stead & Simpson
Barrett, Craig	Retail Operations Executive	Russell & Bromley
Bartle, Ken	Managing Director	A Jones & Sons Ltd
Beecham, Robin	Financial Director	C & J Clark International
Bolliger, Peter	Chief Executive	C & J Clark International
Boot, Terry	Financial Director	Brantano UK Ltd
Bromley, Peter	Chairman and Joint Managing Director	Russell & Bromley
Bromley, Roger	Joint Managing Director	Russell & Bromley
Broughton, David S	Managing Director	Broughton Brothers Ltd

Should you be in this directory? See the form at the back for new entries and amendments

Brown, Steve	Finance Director	Shoe Zone Ltd
Carr, Rosemary	Marketing Services Director	C & J Clark International
Cartright, T	Customer Services Manager	Stead & Simpson
Cassar, Stefan	Finance Director	Shoe Studio Group Ltd
Church, Johnathon	Finance Director	Church & Co. Footwear Ltd
Church, William	Production Director	Church & Co. Footwear Ltd
Clayton, John	Merchandise Manager	Russell & Bromley
Clifford, Neil	Chief Executive	Kurt Geiger
Cochrane, Fiona	Head of Marketing	Schuh Ltd
Coleman, Chris	Financial Director	Broughton Brothers Ltd
Collins, Simon	IT Manager	Shoe-Shop.com
Copeland, Avril	Executive Finance Director	Russell & Bromley
Croft, Frank	Chairman	Shoefayre Ltd
Crutchley, Mark	Finance Director	Schuh Ltd
Davis, Nigel	Managing Director	Shoe Studio Group Ltd
Dobinson, Ken	Sales Director	C & J Clark International
Duley, Ian	Financial Director	Lloyd Shoe Co Ltd
Etheridge, Stephen	Chief Executive	Church & Co. Footwear Ltd
Faith, Jonathan	Managing Director	Faith Footwear
Faith, Samuel	Chairman	Faith Footwear
Farrar-Hockley, Rebecca	Buying Director	Kurt Geiger
Ferguson, Lyn	Personnel Director	Schuh Ltd
Foot, Peter	Financial Director	Stead & Simpson
Franchini, Marco	Chief Executive	Bally UK Sales Ltd
Freedman, Cyril	Non-Executive Director	Stead & Simpson
Gee, Peter	Managing Director	Stylo Plc
Grindlay, Gary	Supply Chain Director	Shellys Shoes Ltd
Halford, Emma	Marketing Manager	A Jones & Sons Ltd
Higgins, Joanne	Customer Services Manager	Timberland UK Ltd
Hill, Ian	Chief Executive	Shoefayre Ltd
Hodge, Mike	Executive Director	Stylo Plc
Hodges, Boo	Womenswear Director	Timberland UK Ltd
Hogan, Brian	Sales Director	Lloyd Shoe Co Ltd
Hood, John	Managing Director	Brantano UK Ltd
Howes, Clare	Buying Director	Shoe Zone Ltd
Johnson, D	Financial Director	A Jones & Sons Ltd
Jones, Mark	Retail Speciality Manager	Timberland UK Ltd
Karia, Rohit	Finance Director	Hobbs Limited
Kliner, Francesco	Chief Financial Officer	Church & Co. Footwear Ltd
Lewis, Wendy	Marketing Director	Shoe Zone Ltd
Linton, Cred	Customer Services Manager	Schuh Ltd
Lockyer, David	Chief Executive	Stead & Simpson
Long, Ian	Merchandising & Logistics Manager	A Jones & Sons Ltd
Lovell, David	Non-Executive Deputy Chairman	Stylo Plc
Lowden, Robert	Buying and Merchandising Director	Brantano UK Ltd
Lynch, Tom	Retail Operations Director	Schuh Ltd
Macari, Gilian	Marketing Manager	Schuh Ltd
Mardon, Crispin	Managing Director	Kurt Geiger
Markham, David	Financial Controller	Shoefayre Ltd
Martin, Steven	IT Director	Church & Co. Footwear Ltd
McCann, Jane	Retail Operations Director	Church & Co. Footwear Ltd
McCarthy, Don	Chairman and Chief Executive Officer	Shoe Studio Group Ltd
McLaughan, Roger	Sales and Marketing Director, Barratts	Stylo Plc
Merry, Sue	Customer Service Manager	Shoefayre Ltd
Milling, Judith	Managing Director	Shellys Shoes Ltd
Milward, Phil	Business Development Director	Stead & Simpson

Should you be in this directory? See the form at the back for new entries and amendments

Mitchensen, Pat	Marketing Director	Timberland UK Ltd
Morris, Barry	Non-Executive Director	Stylo Plc
Nelson, Michael	Finance Director	Bally UK Sales Ltd
Newman, Richard	Director of Retail Operations	C & J Clark International
Nightingale, Robert	Customer Services Manager	Broughton Brothers Ltd
O'Neill, Paul	Retail Director	Faith Footwear
O'Rourke, Richard	European Managing Director	Timberland UK Ltd
Orton, Tim J	Company Secretary	Shoefayre Ltd
Parr, Roger	Merchandise Director	Stead & Simpson
Paver, Stuart	Managing Director	Shoe-Shop.com
Pedder, Roger A	Chairman	C & J Clark International
Phillips, Peter	Chairman	A Jones & Sons Ltd
Pleeth, Christopher	Property Director	C & J Clark International
Potter, Melissa	Managing Director, UK Division	C & J Clark International
Racionzer, Terry	Chairman	Schuh Ltd
Regan, Brendon	Marketing Manager	Russell & Bromley
Robinson, Robert	Retail Operations Director, UK	Bally UK Sales Ltd
Robson, Simon	Director of Buying	Stylo Plc
Samuel, Nick	Chief Executive & Joint Managing Director	Hobbs Limited
Saunders, Peter	Customer Service Manager	Russell & Bromley
Senior, Adam	Head Footwear Buyer	Lloyd Shoe Co Ltd
Shannon, John	Non-Executive Chairman	Stead & Simpson
Sheffield, David	Merchandise and Retail Controller	Shoefayre Ltd
Smith, Anthony	Chief Executive	Shoe Zone Ltd
Smith, Charles	Chief Operating Officer	Shoe Zone Ltd
Smith, Jonathon	Property Director	Stead & Simpson
Smith, Michael	Chairman	Shoe Zone Ltd
Standish, Nick	Head of Merchandising	Hobbs Limited
Stark, Ron	Managing Director, Priceless Shoes	Stylo Plc
Stock, Lionel	Finance Director	Faith Footwear
Swartz, Jeff	Chief Executive	Timberland UK Ltd
Tankard, Judith	Customer Services Manager	Brantano UK Ltd
Temple, Colin	Managing Director	Schuh Ltd
Turner, Gemma	Senior Buyer	Faith Footwear
Verona, Mark	Managing Director	Lloyd Shoe Co Ltd
Watson, Ian	Managing Director	Timberland UK Ltd
Weaving, John	Chief Operating Officer	Stylo Plc
Wenkert, Michaela	Head of Footwear	Hobbs Limited
Yates, John	Company Secretary	Stylo Plc
Ziff, Michael	Chairman and Chief Executive	Stylo Plc

FURNITURE

Adderly, Will	Managing Director	Dunelm (Soft Furnishings) Ltd
Antcliff, Richard	Marketing Manager	Dunelm (Soft Furnishings) Ltd
Beere, Sacha	Finance Director	ScS Upholstery Plc
Blake, Nigel	Plc Director	Courts Plc
Bowness, Ian Francis	Finance Director	DFS Furniture Company plc
Bratt, Andrew	Property Director	Furnitureland Holdings Ltd
Briant, Jerry	Managing Director	Land of Leather
Brookfield, Barry	Chairman	Ponden Mill Ltd
Browne, Mike	Deputy Chairman	ScS Upholstery Plc
Bunnell, Matt	Director	Magnet Ltd
Chopping, Lynton	Finance Director	Ponden Mill Ltd
Clark, Jack	Finance Director	Furniture Village Plc
Clifford-King, Martin	Group Financial Director	MFI Furniture Centres Limited
Cohen, Andrew	Director	Courts Plc

Should you be in this directory? See the form at the back for new entries and amendments

Cohen, Bruce	Chief Executive	Courts Plc
Cohen, Steven	UK Managing Director	Courts Plc
Connell, Bob	Finance and Warranties Director	MFI Furniture Centres Limited
Cordrey, Scott	UK Property Manager	IKEA Ltd
Dahlvig, Andres	Group President	IKEA Ltd
Danielsson, Anders	Marketing Director	IKEA Ltd
Dean, Graham	Retail Operations and Logistics Director	Heal's Plc
Edwards, Neil	Commercial Manager	Ponden Mill Ltd
Favell, Gary	Managing Director	Magnet Ltd
Fawson, Pat	Corporate Affairs Director	MFI Furniture Centres Limited
Garratt, Nick	Director, Marketing Operations	MFI Furniture Centres Limited
Ghinn, Sarah	Corporate Communications	Courts Plc
Greenhalgh, Michael	Group Marketing Director	Magnet Ltd
Gudgeon, Richard	Finance Director	Magnet Ltd
Hancock, John	Chief Executive	MFI Furniture Centres Limited
Handley, Roger	Marketing Director	Furnitureland Holdings Ltd
Harrison, Peter	Managing Director	Furniture Village Plc
Haughney, Mark	Sales Director	ScS Upholstery Plc
Hawkins, Terry	Merchandise Director	Multiyork Furniture Ltd
Herbert, Sarah	Marketing Director	Multiyork Furniture Ltd
Hickford, Alan	Buying Director	Harveys Furnishing Group
Higton, John	Group Financial Director	Multiyork Furniture Ltd
Hill, Phill	Managing Director	Homeform Group Ltd
Hirth, Garry	Finance Director	Furnitureland Holdings Ltd
Hodkinson, Jim	Chairman	Furniture Village Plc
Hogsted, Peter	Managing Director	IKEA Ltd
Horgan, Mark	Executive Director, UK Retail	MFI Furniture Centres Limited
Imrie, David	Trading Director	Furniture Village Plc
Ingle, Matthew	Managing Director, Howden Joinery	MFI Furniture Centres Limited
Jermine, John	Chairman	Furnitureland Holdings Ltd
Kane, Mike	Director, Retail	MFI Furniture Centres Limited
Kelly, Pat	Deputy Managing Director	Harveys Furnishing Group
Kirkham, Lord Graham	Executive Chairman	DFS Furniture Company plc
Knight, David	Chief Executive	ScS Upholstery Plc
Lee, Chris	Company Secretary	Courts Plc
Lewis, Ashley	Finance Director	Homeform Group Ltd
Lilly, Doreen	Customer Services Manager	Walmsley Furnishing Plc
MacDonald, Gordon	Chief Operating Officer	MFI Furniture Centres Limited
Mallinson, Peter	Chief Executive	Multiyork Furniture Ltd
Massey, Jon	Chief Operating Officer	DFS Furniture Company plc
Matheson, Marie	Human Resources Director	ScS Upholstery Plc
McCann, Tony	Senior Non-Executive Director	ScS Upholstery Plc
McKee, Leo	Chief Executive	Ponden Mill Ltd
McKenna, Peter	E-Commerce Manager	MFI Furniture Centres Limited *
McManus, Jim	Property Director	MFI Furniture Centres Limited
Middleton, Pam	Customer Services Manager	ScS Upholstery Plc
Muller, Mark	Finance Director	Courts Plc
Neilly, Brian	Finance Director	Land of Leather
North, Andrew	UK Customer Service Manager	IKEA Ltd
Ormsby, David	Managing Director	Walmsley Furnishing Plc
Ouellette, Jean-Louis	Finance and Operations Director	IKEA Ltd
Peddar, Chris	Managing Director	Furnitureland Holdings Ltd
Pilgrim, Colin	Chief Executive Officer	Heal's Plc
Powell, William	Property Director	Courts Plc
Read, Jan	Customer Services Manager	Furnitureland Holdings Ltd
Rosendale, Michael	Chairman and Chief Executive	Harveys Furnishing Group

Should you be in this directory? See the form at the back for new entries and amendments

Round, Steven	Commercial Director	MFI Furniture Centres Limited
Royal, Kevin	Marketing Director	ScS Upholstery Plc
Samuels, Malcolm	Finance Director	Courts Plc
Shrager, Robert	Chairman	Courts Plc
Sills, David	Buying Director	Furnitureland Holdings Ltd
Simons, Carolyn	Group Managing Director	Harveys Furnishing Group
Sinnot, Mike	Production Director	Multiyork Furniture Ltd
Stanway, Andrew	Chief Executive	Homeform Group Ltd
Steer, Liz	Merchandising Director	Heal's Plc
Tawns, David	Commercial Director	Multiyork Furniture Ltd
Thomas, Andrew	Chairman	Homeform Group Ltd
Thomson, Bob	Head of Retail and Property	Ponden Mill Ltd
Tubb, Gary	Deputy Managing Director	Courts Plc
Wade, Charles	Chairman	Multiyork Furniture Ltd
Wallis, Peter	Non-Executive Director	MFI Furniture Centres Limited
Walmsley, Philip	Chairman	Walmsley Furnishing Plc
White, Joe	Marketing Director	Homeform Group Ltd
Wilson, Bob	Manufacturing and Purchasing Director	MFI Furniture Centres Limited
Wood, Fiona	Finance Director and Company Secretary	Heal's Plc

GARDEN CENTRES

Brayton, Norman	Marketing Director	WCF Retail
Evans, Brian A	Chairman	Wyevale Garden Centres Plc
Hewitt, Robert J	Chief Executive	Wyevale Garden Centres Plc
Moss, Chris	Finance Director	Notcutts Nurseries
Murfin, Stephen	Finance Director and Company Secretary	Wyevale Garden Centres Plc
Notcutt, Charles	Chairman	Notcutts Nurseries
Notcutt, William	Group Managing Director	Notcutts Nurseries
Price, Glyn J	Group Buying Director	Wyevale Garden Centres Plc
Reed, Sally	Marketing Director	Notcutts Nurseries
Smith, Trevor	Finance Director	WCF Retail
Tutt, Eddie	Operations and IT Director	WCF Retail
Walker, S	Customer Services Manager	Wyevale Garden Centres Plc

HEALTH AND BEAUTY

Aldis, Peter	Managing Director	Holland & Barrett Retail Ltd
Alldis, Michelle	Head of Customer Services	Vision Express UK Ltd
Andrews, Barry	Executive Chairman	Moss Pharmacy Ltd
Ashby, Diane	Head of Logistics Projects	The Body Shop International Plc
Aylward, Chris	Business Development Director	Moss Pharmacy Ltd
Baker, Richard	Chief Executive	Boots Group Plc
Bateman, Paul	Group Operations Director	Boots Group Plc
Bellamy, Adrian	Chairman	The Body Shop International Plc
Blackledge, Graham	Joint Managing Director	Bodycare (Health & Beauty) Limited
Blackledge, Margaret	Joint Managing Director	Bodycare (Health & Beauty) Limited
Cantello, Tina	Marketing Director	The Body Shop International Plc
Cavern, Kevin	Managing Director	Savers Health & Beauty Plc
Cèzar, Marcel	Chairman	Vision Express UK Ltd
Crowe, Emma	Director	Thinknatural.com
Day, Gill	Finance Director	Holland & Barrett Retail Ltd
Dejardin, Galleran	Financial Director	Vision Express UK Ltd
Dodd, Howard	Chief Financial Officer	Boots Group Plc
Duncan, Steve	Managing Director	Moss Pharmacy Ltd
Ferguson, Andy	Operations Director	Dollond & Aitchison Group Plc
Fletcher, Neil	IT Manager	Holland & Barrett Retail Ltd

Should you be in this directory? See the form at the back for new entries and amendments

Flowers, Pamela	Human Resources and Customer Services Manager	Savers Health & Beauty Plc
Geary, Phil	Marketing Director	Holland & Barrett Retail Ltd
Green, Mark	Marketing Director	Lloyds Pharmacy
Hadfield, Caroline	Director of Product	The Body Shop International Plc
Hansell, Debbie	Commercial Director	Superdrug Stores
Hardy, Russell	Chief Executive	Dollond & Aitchison Group Plc
Hazelebach, Gerard	Managing Director	Superdrug Stores
Hogg, James	Franchise Director	Dollond & Aitchison Group Plc
Hood, John	Finance Director	Lloyds Pharmacy
Hudson, Kevin	Finance Director	L Rowland & Co (Retail) Ltd
Hume, Simon	Human Resources Director	Moss Pharmacy Ltd
Jensen, Luke	Managing Director	Thinknatural.com
Kendall-Smith, Michael	Finance Director	Savers Health & Beauty Plc
Kendrick, Mark	Distribution Director	Holland & Barrett Retail Ltd
Khan, Michael	IT Director	Specsavers Optical Group
Lawton, Christopher	Direct Marketing Manager	Holland & Barrett Retail Ltd
Lord, Hugo	Director	Specsavers Optical Group
Lyons, Joe	Marketing Director, UK	The Body Shop International Plc
MacNab, Peter	Commercial Director	Savers Health & Beauty Plc
Makepiece, John	General Manager	National Co-operative Chemists Ltd
McDonald, Jerry	President	Avon Cosmetics
McFarland, Roy	Finance Director	Bodycare (Health & Beauty) Limited
Molle, Andrew	Marketing Director	Specsavers Optical Group
Moorhead, Robert	Finance Director	Specsavers Optical Group
Naylor, Graham	Retail Director	Superdrug Stores
Nicholls, Peter	Vice-President, Sales	Avon Cosmetics
Nuesser, Bernard	Marketing Director	Vision Express UK Ltd
Oliver, Michael	Company Secretary	Boots Group Plc
Page, Neil	Financial Director	Superdrug Stores
Perkins, Doug	Managing Director	Specsavers Optical Group
Pollard, Bridie	Head of Public Relations	Avon Cosmetics
Prosser, Andrew	Finance Director	Moss Pharmacy Ltd
Ridler, Peter	Managing Director	The Body Shop International Plc
Rockhill, Susan	Marketing Director	Moss Pharmacy Ltd
Rogers, David	Head of Sales and Marketing	National Co-operative Chemists Ltd
Rudd, Sir Nigel	Chairman	Boots Group Plc
Saunders, Peter	Chief Executive	The Body Shop International Plc
Scicluna, Terry	Operations Director	Moss Pharmacy Ltd
Sinclair, Douglas	Property Director	Holland & Barrett Retail Ltd
Slater, Andrea	Vice-President Marketing	Avon Cosmetics
Smith	Managing Director	L Rowland & Co (Retail) Ltd
Smith, Andy	Group Human Resources Director	Boots Group Plc
Stevens, Chris	Head of Finance	National Co-operative Chemists Ltd
Vickers, Barry	Chief Executive Officer	Holland & Barrett Retail Ltd
Ward, Michael	Chief Executive	Lloyds Pharmacy
Williams, David	Non-Executive Director	Moss Pharmacy Ltd
Williams, Karen	Marketing Operations Manager	Vision Express UK Ltd
Willis, Peter	Business Development Manager	National Co-operative Chemists Ltd
Young, Alexander	Non-Executive Officer	L Rowland & Co (Retail) Ltd
Youngs, Peter	Global Finance Director	The Body Shop International Plc
Zaina, Robert	Finance Director	Dollond & Aitchison Group Plc

HOUSEWARES

Barnes, Richard	Group Finance Director	Waterford Wedgwood Retail Ltd
Beardsley, Chris	Business Development Director	Waterford Wedgwood Retail Ltd

Should you be in this directory? See the form at the back for new entries and amendments

Bielby, Peter	Head of Business Development	Cargo Homeshop
Brandon, Sally	Customer Services Manager	Habitat UK Limited
Cribb, James	Finance Director	Rosebys Ltd
Dixon, Tom	Head of Design	Habitat UK Limited
Dyson, Mark	Company Secretary	Rosebys Ltd
Farmer, Patrick	Non-Executive Director	Timpson Ltd
Gay, Colin	Retail Director, Europe	Waterford Wedgwood Retail Ltd
Goodfellow, Mark	Retail Operations Manager	Lakeland Limited
Green, Christopher	Deputy Chairman	Timpson Ltd
Harding, Jim	Managing Director of UK Sales	Waterford Wedgwood Retail Ltd
Hislop, Mark	Retail Operations Director	Habitat UK Limited
Hourston, Sir Gordon	Chairman	Rosebys Ltd
Kershaw, Michelle	Customer Director	Lakeland Limited
Leibe, Sharon	Customer Services Manager	Waterford Wedgwood Retail Ltd
Logue, Anne	Customer Service Manager	Royal Doulton Plc
Long, Chris	Finance Director	Lakeland Limited
Martin, Geoff	Finance Director	Royal Doulton Plc
Millar, Richard	Head of Marketing and UK Retailing	Habitat UK Limited
Mylum, Gary	Group Director of Marketing	Royal Doulton Plc
Nordahl, Jens	Managing Director	Habitat UK Limited
Nutbeen, Wayne	Chief Executive	Royal Doulton Plc
O'Reilly, Tony	Chief Executive Officer	Waterford Wedgwood Retail Ltd
Rayner, Julian	Marketing Director	Lakeland Limited
Rayner, Martin	Purchasing Director	Lakeland Limited
Rayner, Sam	Managing Director	Lakeland Limited
Richards, Chris	Operations Director	Royal Doulton Plc
Richards, Tony	Deputy Managing Director	Rosebys Ltd
Rosenblatt, Michael	Chief Executive	Rosebys Ltd
Schwab, Anne-Marie	Group Marketing Manager	Habitat UK Limited
Simons, Carolyn	Managing Director, Rosebys	Rosebys Ltd
Smith, Steve	Finance Director	Cargo Homeshop
Tague, Stephen	Chief Executive	Cargo Homeshop
Timpson, James	Managing Director	Timpson Ltd
Timpson, John	Chairman and Chief Executive Officer	Timpson Ltd
Tragen, Martin	Finance Director	Timpson Ltd
Welby, Michaela	Financial Director	Habitat UK Limited
Williams, Mike	Property Director	Timpson Ltd
Wolstenholme, Bill	Managing Director, Benson Beds	Rosebys Ltd

INTERNET SHOPPING

de Bourcier, Peter	Joint Director	Play.com
Golding, Richard	Joint Director	Play.com
Omidyar, Pierre	Founder and Chairman	eBay UK Ltd
Perree, Simon	Joint Director	Play.com
Whitman, Meg	President and Chief Executive Officer	eBay UK Ltd

JEWELLERY

Adlestone, Mark	Joint Managing Director	Beaverbrooks the Jewellers Ltd
Anderson, Rob	Chief Executive, UK	Signet Group Plc
Boyd, Walker	Group Financial Director	Signet Group Plc
Brown, Andrew	Joint Managing Director	Beaverbrooks the Jewellers Ltd
Brozetti, Gianluca	Retail Director	Asprey & Garrard Ltd
Burman, Terry	Group Chief Executive	Signet Group Plc
Cook, Kevin	Director	HPJ UK Ltd
Coulter, John	Director	Warren James Ltd

Should you be in this directory? See the form at the back for new entries and amendments

Davis, Philip	Marketing Director	Asprey & Garrard Ltd
Dundas, Lord Bruce	Chairman and Chief Executive	Asprey & Garrard Ltd
Evans, Nicholas	Chief Executive	The MW Group Ltd
Harding, Michael	Financial Director	F Hinds Ltd
Hill, Lewis	Managing Director	Fraser Hart Ltd
Hinds, Andrew	Buying Director	F Hinds Ltd
Hinds, David	Managing Director	F Hinds Ltd
Hinds, Neil	Property Director	F Hinds Ltd
Hinds, Roy	Chairman	F Hinds Ltd
Hogg, Sally	Merchandise Director	Asprey & Garrard Ltd
Jones, Ann	Director	Warren James Ltd
Kelly, J	General Manager	Fraser Hart Ltd
McAdam, James	Chairman	Signet Group Plc
McGarvie, Murray	Chief Finance Officer	Fraser Hart Ltd
Nicholson, Brian	Finance Director	Beaverbrooks the Jewellers Ltd
Philpott, Robin	Merchandise and Distribution Director	Goldsmiths Group Plc
Piasecki, Jurek	Chairman and Chief Executive	Goldsmiths Group Plc
Pudney, Bill	Operations Director	Signet Group Plc
Sargent, Steve C	Financial Director	Goldsmiths Group Plc
Shearer, Gwen	Customer Service Manager	HPJ UK Ltd
Taylor, Simon	Property Director	Signet Group Plc
West, Jim E	Sales and Marketing Director	Goldsmiths Group Plc
Williamson, Simon	Managing Director	Asprey & Garrard Ltd
Wordley, Mark	Director	HPJ UK Ltd

MAIL ORDER

Alliance, Sir David	Chairman	N Brown
Andrew, Ian	Company Secretary	Grattan Plc
Basnett, Keith	Customer Services Director	N Brown
Blackwood, Walter	Distribution Director	Grattan Plc *
Blank, Sir Victor	Chairman	GUS
Bolton, Ivan	Director and Company Secretary	Findel Plc
Bullaf, Mike	Merchandise Director	N Brown
Chapman, Keith	Chairman	Findel Plc
Dalby, Simon	Managing Director, Agency	Shop Direct Group Ltd
Daynes, Mark	Managing Director, Littlewoods All-Inclusive	Littlewoods Home Shopping Ltd
Deve, Francoise	Catalogue Director	Redcats UK (Brands) Ltd
Duddy, Terry	Chief Executive, Argos Retail Group	GUS
Evans, Alan	Managing Director, Direct	Littlewoods Home Shopping Ltd
Finnigan, Norman	Human Resources and Customer Services Director	Grattan Plc
Gimpel, Oliver	Marketing Director	Redcats UK (Brands) Ltd
Green, Linda	Managing Director, Direct	Shop Direct Group Ltd
Green, Marianne	Finance Director	Redcats UK (Brands) Ltd
Green, Nigel	Marketing Director	N Brown
Hallett, David	Operations Director	Littlewoods Home Shopping Ltd
Hancox, Mike	Chief Operating Officer	Shop Direct Group Ltd
Hawker, Michael L	Chief Executive	Freemans Plc
Hawker, Michael L	Chief Executive	Grattan Plc
Heavisides, Henry	General Manager, La Redoute UK	Redcats UK (Brands) Ltd *
Hinchliffe, John	Marketing and Strategy Director	N Brown
Imrie, Euan	Finance Director	Littlewoods Home Shopping Ltd
Izard, Olivier	Managing Director	Redcats UK (Brands) Ltd
Johnson, Tony	Chief Executive	Findel Plc
Kowalski, Tim	Finance Director	N Brown
Malcolm, Simon	Head of E-Marketing	Grattan Plc

Should you be in this directory? See the form at the back for new entries and amendments

Malcom, Simon	Head of E-Marketing	Freemans Plc
Martin, Jim	Financial Director	N Brown
McAulay, Janet	Publications Catalogue Director	Grattan Plc
McGeorge, Alistair	Group Chief Executive	Littlewoods Home Shopping Ltd
Otto, Michael	Chairman	Grattan Plc
Padovan, John	Non-Executive Director	Findel Plc
Parker, Andrew	Property Director	Redcats UK (Brands) Ltd
Parkes, Steve	Head of Marketing and E-Commerce, La Redoute UK	Redcats UK (Brands) Ltd *
Peace, John	Chief Executive	GUS
Roe, Andy	Customer Service Director	Littlewoods Home Shopping Ltd
Rudge, Sir Alan	Non-Executive Director	GUS
Skelsey, Jim	Merchandise Director	Grattan Plc
Skelsey, Jim	Merchandise Director	Freemans Plc
Smith, Peter	IT Director	Redcats UK (Brands) Ltd
Stocken, Oliver	Non-Executive Director	GUS
Sutcliffe, Keith	Customer Services Manager	Findel Plc
Tyler, David	Finance Director	GUS
West, Christopher	Finance Director	Grattan Plc
White, Alan	Chief Executive	N Brown
Woodhead, Carol	Distribution Director	Grattan Plc

MIXED RETAILER

Agar-Hutty, S	IT Director	Argos Retail Group *
Allen, Dave	Financial Controller	Wine Cellar Ltd
Allkins, Ian	Commercial Director	Bhs Plc
Ashton, Richard John	Group Finance and Systems Director	Argos Retail Group *
Ashworth, Neil	Supply Chain Director	Woolworths Plc
Barbour, Caroline	Office Manager	Cash Converters UK Ltd
Barr, Gill	Business Development Director	Woolworths Plc
Bentley, Phil	Non-Executive Director	Kingfisher Plc
Bezos, Jeff	Chief Executive	Amazon.co.uk
Bish-Jones, Trevor	Chief Executive	Woolworths Plc
Blank, Sir Victor	Chairman	Argos Retail Group *
Brazil, Eugene	Managing Director, Argos Home Shopping	Argos Retail Group *
Brown, Tony	Retail Director	Bhs Plc
Cheshire, Ian	Chief Executive of International Development	Kingfisher Plc
Coakley, Paul	Finance Director	Bhs Plc
Cogman, Rowland	Company Secretary	Roys (Wroxham) Ltd
Corbett, Gerald	Chairman	Woolworths Plc
Drury, Romney	Marketing Director	Bhs Plc
Gaskell, Paul	Managing Director	Wine Cellar Ltd
Geddes, Paul	Marketing Director	Argos Ltd
Godfrey, Brian	Managing Director	Roys (Wroxham) Ltd
Goodwin, Tony	Commercial and Marketing Manager, Streets Online	Woolworths Plc *
Green, Philip	Owner	Bhs Plc
Hall, Jo	Commercial Director	Woolworths Plc
Harber, Andrew	E-Commerce Director, Streets Online	Woolworths Plc *
Henderson, Dennis	Group Operations Director	Virgin Retail Group Limited
Hepher, Michael	Non-Executive Director	Kingfisher Plc
Idun, B	Stores Director	Argos Ltd
Jones, Helen	Company Secretary	Kingfisher Plc
Kavanagh, Carol	Human Resources Director	Argos Ltd
Kincade, Steve	Commercial Director	Virgin Retail Group Limited

Should you be in this directory? See the form at the back for new entries and amendments

Kramer, Hammut	Non-Executive Director	Kingfisher Plc
Kwakman, Kitty	Head of E-Commerce	Argos Retail Group *
Labroue, Jean Noël	Chief Executive, KESA	Kingfisher Plc
Leath, Warren	Operations Manager	Wine Cellar Ltd
Lee, Kerry	Head of Retail Marketing	Virgin Retail Group Limited
Leighton, Allan	Chairman	Bhs Plc
Lemmon, Mark	Director of Operations, South	Cash Converters UK Ltd
Lewis, Ken	Commercial Director	Woolworths Plc *
Mackay, Francis	Chairman	Kingfisher Plc
Mann, Kirstie	Strategic Development	Woolworths Plc *
Maxwell, Jeremy	Director of Strategy	Kingfisher Plc
Melton, S	Supply Chain Director	Argos Ltd
Morley, Octavia	Marketing Director	Woolworths Plc
Murphy, Gerry M	Chief Executive Officer	Kingfisher Plc
Nelson, John	Deputy Chairman	Kingfisher Plc
Owrid, Tim	Head of Distribution Operations	Woolworths Plc
Pieri, Paolo	Financial Director	Virgin Retail Group Limited
Pilgrim, Richard	Director of Operations, North	Cash Converters UK Ltd
Robinson, Stephen	Finance Director	Argos Ltd
Rogers, Chris	Finance Director	Woolworths Plc
Roy, Edward	Finance Director	Roys (Wroxham) Ltd
Roy, Paul	Merchandising Director	Roys (Wroxham) Ltd
Roy, Peter	Chairman	Roys (Wroxham) Ltd
Salmon, Margaret	Non-Executive Director	Kingfisher Plc
Shane, Denise	Head of Home Business Unit	Woolworths Plc
Spratley, Jim	Finance Director	Cash Converters UK Ltd
Terrell, Robin	UK Managing Director	Amazon.co.uk
Thompson, John	Operations Manager	Wine Cellar Ltd
Thompson, Maria	Commercial Director	Argos Ltd
Urry, Julian	Managing Director	Cash Converters UK Ltd
Walker, David	IT Manager	Wine Cellar Ltd
Wall, R	Argos Direct Director	Argos Retail Group *
Warnes, William	Food Trading Director	Roys (Wroxham) Ltd
Wenham, Alan	Customer Services Director	Woolworths Plc
Whitehead, Martin	Operations Manager	Bhs Plc
Woodhouse, Lorraine	Head of Investor Relations	Kingfisher Plc
Wright, Simon	Chief Executive Officer	Virgin Retail Group Limited

MUSIC AND VIDEO

Barker, Steve	Development Director	Choices Video
Bevin, Bryan	Vice-President International Operations	Blockbuster Entertainment Ltd
Bignall, Sue	Marketing Director	Capital Sound & Vision
Bisset, Alick	Finance Director	Global Video Ltd
Bright, Neil	Group Financial Director	HMV Group Plc
Brown, Roy	Deputy Chairman	HMV Group Plc
Bullock, Jackie	Head of Business Development	HMV Group Plc
Cox, Lesley	Non-Executive Director	HMV Group Plc
Davey, Christ	Managing Director	Disney Consumer Products
Feeney, Amon	Finance Director	Blockbuster Entertainment Ltd
Foulser, Steve	Vice-President	Blockbuster Entertainment Ltd
Gardner, Diane	Managing Director	Choices Video
Giles, Alan James	Chief Executive Officer	HMV Group Plc
Giles, Alan James	Chief Executive Officer	HMV UK Ltd
Goodwin, Tony	Marketing Director, Audiostreet.com	Streets Online
Harper, Andrew	Managing Director, Audiostreet.com	Streets Online
Henderson, Dennis	Group Operations Director	Virgin Megastores Online *

Should you be in this directory? See the form at the back for new entries and amendments

Hill, Peter	Finance Director	HMV Group Plc
Hill, Peter	Finance Director	HMV UK Ltd
Jenkins, Jean	Retail Operations Director	Blockbuster Entertainment Ltd
Kappler, David	Non-Executive Director	HMV Group Plc
Knott, Steve	Managing Director, HMV Europe	HMV Group Plc
Lymath, Mike	Human Resources Director	HMV Group Plc
McCafferty, Mark	Non-Executive Director	HMV Group Plc
McLaughlin, Brian	Chief Operating Officer, HMV Media	HMV Group Plc
Moore, Tessa	Vice-President of Marketing	Disney Consumer Products
Nicoli, Eric	Chairman	HMV Group Plc
Parker, Gary	Managing Director	Capital Sound & Vision
Pieri, Paolo	Financial Director	Virgin Megastores Online *
Rasul, Maqbool H	Managing Director	Global Video Ltd
Rasul, Z	Director	Global Video Ltd
Robinson, Phillip	Managing Director	CD Wow!
Rowe, Stuart	E-Commerce Director	HMV Group Plc
Rowe, Stuart	E-Commerce Director	HMV UK Ltd
Salt, Vernon	Senior Vice-President	Blockbuster Entertainment Ltd
Sealey, John	Finance Director	Choices Video
Skilt, Anthony	Commercial Director	Choices Video
Sparks, Alexander	Managing Director	Blockbuster Entertainment Ltd
Spink, Geoff	Sales Director	Choices Video
Swan, Clive	Chairman	Capital Sound & Vision
Tadler, Steve	Non-Executive Director	HMV Group Plc
Teicher, Ben	Finance Director	Disney Consumer Products
Vandendyck, Pat	Finance Director	Capital Sound & Vision

OFF LICENCE

Alldritt, Nigel	Financial Director	Majestic Wine Warehouses Ltd
Apthorp, John	Chairman	Majestic Wine Warehouses Ltd
Armstrong, David	Purchasing and Marketing Director	Unwins Wine Group Ltd
Benge, Alex	Property Director	Unwins Wine Group Ltd
de Mellow, Steve	Marketing Director	Majestic Wine Warehouses Ltd
Duley, Jacques	Managing Director	Oddbins UK Ltd
Genthialan, Laurent	Finance Director	Oddbins UK Ltd
Gerhrad, Tim	Finance Director	Unwins Wine Group Ltd
Hanns, Dennis	Head of Retail	Oddbins UK Ltd
Harvey, Peter	Director of Commercial Finance	Thresher Group
Headington, Steve	Retail Operations Director	Thresher Group
How, Timothy	Managing Director	Majestic Wine Warehouses Ltd
King, George	Managing Director	G 101 Off Sales Ltd
Lewis, Steve	Retail Director	Majestic Wine Warehouses Ltd
Loring, Philip	Business Planning Director	Thresher Group
Mason, Tony	Trading Director	Majestic Wine Warehouses Ltd
Mayor, Robert	Joint Managing Director	Bargain Booze Limited
McGlenn, Sarah	New Channels Finance Director	Thresher Group
McLernon, Ian	Marketing Director	Unwins Wine Group Ltd
Miekle, Alexander	Finance Director	G 101 Off Sales Ltd
Palmer, Jeremy	E-Commerce Director	Majestic Wine Warehouses Ltd
Styles, Kevin	Managing Director, Marketing	Thresher Group
Turner, Mark	Managing Director of Property	Thresher Group
Waggett, Colin	Finance Director	Thresher Group
Wellesley-Wood, Mark	Chairman	Unwins Wine Group Ltd
Wetz, Phillip	Joint Managing Director	Unwins Wine Group Ltd
Wetz, Simon	Joint Managing Director	Unwins Wine Group Ltd
Whittle, Allan	Joint Managing Director	Bargain Booze Limited

Should you be in this directory? See the form at the back for new entries and amendments

179

Williams, David	Chief Executive	Thresher Group
Wright, Liz	Property Director	Majestic Wine Warehouses Ltd

OFFICE SUPPLIES

Clarkson, Ian	Property Manager	Globus Office World Plc
Etherington, Andy	Chief Executive Officer	Globus Office World Plc
Jenkins, Steven	Customer Service Manager	Globus Office World Plc
Northover, Malcolm	Chief Financial Officer	Globus Office World Plc

PETROL

Ebert, Roger	Executive Vice-President	Chevron Texaco
Goldsmith, Mark	Retail Director	Kuwait Petroleum Ltd
Grimsdale, Simon	Retail Operations Manager	Shell Retail UK
Jacques, David	Chairman	Jack Loggin Ltd
Jacques, Peter	Managing Director	Jack Loggin Ltd
Jones, Malcolm	Managing Director and Chairman	Total UK Ltd
McMahon, Mick	Retail Director	Shell Retail UK
Moody-Stewart, Sir Mark	Chairman	Shell Retail UK
Munro, Gordon	Retail Marketing Director	Esso Petroleum Co. Ltd
O'Reilly, Dave	Chairman and Chief Executive Officer	Chevron Texaco
Richardson, David	Convenience Retail Manager, UK and Ireland	Esso Petroleum Co. Ltd
Ruitinga, Gerrit	Managing Director	Kuwait Petroleum Ltd
Todd, Martin	Retail Director	Esso Petroleum Co. Ltd

PETS

Begley, Michelle	Head of Marketing	Pets at Home Ltd
Davis, Matthew	Finance Director	Pets at Home Ltd
Farrell, John	Development Director	Pets at Home Ltd
Marshall, Catriona	Trading Director	Pets at Home Ltd
Preston, Anthony	Chairman	Pets at Home Ltd

PHOTOGRAPHIC SERVICES

Bowie, Jonathan	Managing Director	Bowie-Castlebank Group Ltd
Doohan, John	Finance Controller	Bowie-Castlebank Group Ltd
Galloway, Mike	Customer Services Manager	Bowie-Castlebank Group Ltd
Kennedy, Sandy	Business Development Director	Bowie-Castlebank Group Ltd

SPORTS

Ashley, Michael	Proprietor	Sports World International Ltd
Atkinson, Peter	Operations Director	John David Group Plc
Beever, David	Non-Executive Director	JJB Sports Plc
Best, Roger	Managing Director	John David Group Plc
Bilton, Howard	Purchase Director	American Golf Discount Centre Ltd
Blackhurst, Malcolm	Financial Director	John David Group Plc
Bradburn, Jeremy	Chief Executive and Financial Director	all:sports Retail Ltd
Bridge, Mark	Marketing Director	American Golf Discount Centre Ltd
Brown, Barry	Chief Executive	John David Group Plc
Cormosh, Phillip	Finance Director	all:sports Retail Ltd
Cornish, Phillip	IT Director	all:sports Retail Ltd
Cronie, Andy	Operations Director	Lillywhites
Crossland, Roy	Group Chief Executive	The Outdoor Group Ltd
Donnelly, Mike	Merchandising Director	all:sports Retail Ltd
Dunn, Barry	Property Director	JJB Sports Plc
Fellows, Johnathan	Finance Director	American Golf Discount Centre Ltd

Should you be in this directory? See the form at the back for new entries and amendments

Forsey, Dave	Managing Director	Lillywhites
Greenwood, David	Finance Director and Company Secretary	JJB Sports Plc
Hall, Andy	Group Finance Director	The Outdoor Group Ltd
Hargreaves, Martin	Chairman	Hargreaves Sports
Hargreaves, Robin	Managing Director	Hargreaves Sports
Heaton, Mark	Merchandising Director	JJB Sports Plc
Helm, Andrew	Marketing Director	John David Group Plc
Higham, Winston	Marketing Director	JJB Sports Plc
Hughes, David E	Chairman	all:sports Retail Ltd
Keen, Nigel	Property Director	John David Group Plc
Knight, Thomas	Chief Executive	JJB Sports Plc
Makin, David	Buying and Merchandising Director	John David Group Plc
McDonald, Chris	Retail Operations Director	American Golf Discount Centre Ltd
Nevitt, Sean	Purchasing Director	Sports World International Ltd
Norton, Tony	Managing Director	American Golf Discount Centre Ltd
Percival, Richard	Director	John David Group Plc
Rome, Ron	Sales Director	all:sports Retail Ltd
Soares Dos Santos, Francisco	Chairman	Lillywhites
Tomlinson, Mark	Distribution Director	all:sports Retail Ltd
Trangmar, Don	Non-Executive Director	The Outdoor Group Ltd
Whelan, David	Executive Chairman	JJB Sports Plc
Wilkinson, Julian	Director	all:sports Retail Ltd

STATIONERY

Bennett, Tony	Financial Director	Confetti.co.uk
Broadbridge, Bob	Managing Director	W H Smith Direct *
Budd, Alastair	Property Controller	Stationery Box Holdings Ltd
Bugler, Mike	Marketing Director	Clinton Cards
Clark, Andrew	Retail Operations Director	Stationery Box Holdings Ltd
Coleman, John	Non-Executive Director	Clinton Cards
Dolman, Steve	Buying Director	Stationery Box Holdings Ltd
Fraser, Craig	Operations Director	The Stationers Ltd
Gaynor, Alan	Chief Executive	Stationery Box Holdings Ltd
Handover, Richard	Chairman	W H Smith Retail Ltd
Hartog, Barry	Finance Director and Company Secretary	Clinton Cards
Hodson, Beverley	Managing Director	W H Smith Retail Ltd
Kilcourse, Mike	Group Marketing Director	The Stationers Ltd
Laidlaw, John	Marketing Director	Staples UK Ltd
Larkin, Simon	Finance Director	The Stationers Ltd
Leahy, Nigel	Marketing Director	W H Smith Retail Ltd
Lethbridge, David	Joint Managing Director	Confetti.co.uk
Lewin, Clinton	Managing Director	Clinton Cards
Lewin, Debbie	Product Development Director	Clinton Cards
Lewin, Donald	Chairman	Clinton Cards
Macritchie, Ian	Chairman	Birthdays Group Ltd
Marinker, Simon	Property Director	W H Smith Retail Ltd
Marsh, Peter	Joint Managing Director	Confetti.co.uk
Mason, Neil	Finance Director	Stationery Box Holdings Ltd
McMenemy, Mark	High Street Finance Director	W H Smith Retail Ltd
Mountford, Cheryl	Operations Manager	Stationery Box Holdings Ltd
Oxley, Karen	Customer Services Manager	The Stationers Ltd
Randall, Andy	Managing Director	Staples UK Ltd
Rivett, Carolyn	Finance Director	W H Smith Direct *
Robinson, John	Operations Director	Clinton Cards
Sargent, Ron	Chief Executive	Staples UK Ltd
Smalley, Richard	Real Estate Controller	Staples UK Ltd

Should you be in this directory? See the form at the back for new entries and amendments

Stirling, Muriel	UK Brand Director	W H Smith Retail Ltd
Street, Richard	Stores Director	W H Smith Retail Ltd
Swann, Kate	Chief Executive Officer	W H Smith Retail Ltd
Tapin, Penny	Customer Service Manager	Staples UK Ltd
Tapp, Chris	Buying and Merchandising Director	Birthdays Group Ltd
Walters, Michael	Financial Director	Staples UK Ltd
Walters, Nick	Finance Director	Birthdays Group Ltd
Warren, John	Group Finance Director	W H Smith Retail Ltd
Wharton, Sue	Trading Director	W H Smith Retail Ltd

TOYS

Burford, Chris	Finance Manager	Hamleys Plc
Carr, Tony	Retail Operations Director	Mothercare Plc
Coogan, Mike	Marketing Director	Toys R Us Limited
Cooper, Julia	Divisional Director, Merchandise	Toys R Us Limited
Davis, Fiona	Brand Marketing Director	Early Learning Centre
Dorkin, Sue	Logistics Director	Early Learning Centre
France, Mike	Managing Director	Early Learning Centre
Glew, Stephen	Finance Director	Mothercare Plc
Goddard, John	Property Director	Early Learning Centre
Gordon, Ben	Chief Executive	Mothercare Plc
Griffiths, David	Finance Director	Early Learning Centre
Martin, Chris	Chief Executive	Mothercare Plc
Muzika, Frank	Finance, Admin and Logistics Director	Toys R Us Limited
Parker, Ian	Finance Director	Hamleys Plc
Peacock, Ian	Chairman	Mothercare Plc
Pomphret, Steve	Strategic Development Director	Mothercare Plc
Revett, Clive	Company Secretary	Mothercare Plc
Rurka, David	Chairman and Managing Director	Toys R Us Limited
Shayer, Phil	Merchandise Director	Toys R Us Limited
Watkinson, John	Chief Executive	Hamleys Plc
Woolford, Adrian	Marketing Director	Hamleys Plc

Should you be in this directory? See the form at the back for new entries and amendments

182

FREE ENTRY/AMENDMENT FORM
Who's Who in Retailing? 2005 Edition

To ensure an accurate entry in the 2005 edition please complete and return this questionnaire or send your full CV to:

Who's Who in Retailing Editor, Verdict, Newlands House, 40 Berners Street, London W1P 4DX
Tel: +44 (0)20 7255 6400 Fax: +44 (0)20 7637 5951 Email: pr@verdict.co.uk

Your company details
(please print in upper case)

Company Name

Company Address

Town

Country   Postcode

Company Tel (main switchboard)   Fax (main switchboard)

Company Website Address

Company Email Address

Your Details

Surname

First Name(s)

Title

Current Position

Department

Direct Tel   Direct Fax

Personal Email address

Date of Birth

Marital Status

Education			
Establishment	From (year)	To (year)	Type of Qualification

Awards

Additional Directorships

Memberships

Leisure Interests

Other Biographical Details

Career history (including current job details)				
Job Title	Main Job Function(s) (Finance, Sales, Personnel, etc.)	Company Name	From (Year)	To (Year)